TRIBAL HISTORY OF CENTRAL INDIA

TRIBAL HISTORY OF CENTRAL INDIA

R.K. SHARMA
S.K. TIWARI

VOLUME - III

TRIBAL COMMUNITIES OF MODERN AGE

ARYAN BOOKS INTERNATIONAL
New Delhi

TRIBAL HISTORY OF CENTRAL INDIA

ISBN-81-7305-227-1 (Vol. III)
ISBN-81-7305-228-X (Set)

First published in **2002** by
ARYAN BOOKS INTERNATIONAL
Pooja Apts., 4B, Ansari Road, New Delhi-110 002
Tel. : 3287589, 3255799; Fax : 91-11-3270385
E-mail : aryanbooks@vsnl.com

Computer Typeset at ABI Prints & Publishing Co., New Delhi
Printed in India at B.B.N. Printers, New Delhi

CONTENTS

LIST OF ILLUSTRATIONS

MAPS

PLATES

LIST OF ABBREVIATIONS

ABIA	:	*Annual Bibliography of Indian Archaeology*, Leiden
ABORI	:	*Annals of the Bhandarkar Oriental Research Institute*, Pune
ACSP	:	*Archaeological Congress and Seminar Proceedings*, Kurukshetra, 1976
AG	:	Garde, M.B., *Archaeology in Gwalior*, 2nd ed., Gwalior, 1934
AI	:	*Ancient India*—The Bulletin of the Archaeological Survey of India, New Delhi
AIHT	:	Porgiter, F.E., *Ancient Indian Historical Traditions*
AIK	:	Majumdar, R. C. (ed.), *The Age of Imperial Kanauj*
AMVT	:	Sircar, D.C., *Ancient Malwa and Vikramadiya Tradition*, Delhi, 1969
AIOC	:	All India Oriental Conference
AR	:	*Asiatic Researches*
ARIE	:	*Annual Report of Indian Epigraphy*
ASIAR	:	Archaeological Survey of India, *Annual Report*
BC	:	Brown, C., *Catalogue of Prehistoric Antiquities in the Indian Museum*, 1917
BDCRI	:	*Bulletin of the Deccan College Research Institute*, Pune
BDG	:	*Bilaspur District Gazetteer* (1910)
Bhandarkar	:	Bhandarkar, D.R., *A List of the Inscriptions of Northern India in Brahmi and its Derivative Scripts from about AD 200. Appendix to Epigraphia Indica*, Vols. XIX-XXIII

BMC, AI	:	*Catalogue of Indian Coins in the British Museum—Ancient India*
BPWM	:	*Bulletin of the Prince of Wales Museum,* Bombay.
BT	:	*Bhilsa Topes*
CAI	:	Cunningham's *Coins of Ancient India*
CASIR	:	Cunningham's *Archaeological Survey of India Reports,* Vols. I-XXIII
CCIMC	:	*Catalogue of Coins, Indian Museum,* Calcutta
CCNP	:	Trivedi, H.V., *Catalogue of Coins of the Naga Kings of Padmavati*
CIGS	:	*Central Indian State Gazetteer Series,* Vols. I, V, pt. A., 1908
CII	:	*Corpus Inscriptionum Indicarum*
CJT	:	Dikshit, R.K., *The Candellas of Jejakabhukti,* New Delhi, 1977
CLAR	:	Cousens' *List of Antiquarian Remains in C.P. and Berar,* Calcutta, 1897
CMI	:	Cunningham's *Coins of Medieval India*
CN	:	*Chalcolithic Navadatoli*
CPMC	:	*Chronology of Punch-Marked Coins,* Varanasi, 1966
CPR	:	Cousens, H., *Progress Report of Archaeological Survey of India*
DD	:	Hiralal, R.B., *Damoh Dipak*
DDG	:	*Durg District Gazetteer,* Bhopal, 1972
DER	:	Chakravarty, K.K., *Dangwada Excavation Report,* Bhopal, 1989
DFGS	:	Garde, M.B., *Directory of Forts in Gwalior State*
DHNI	:	Ray, H.C., *Dynastic History of Northern India,* Vol. I-II
DMDG	:	*Damoh District Gazetteer*
EAK	:	Ansari, Z.A. and Dhavalikar, M.K., *Excavation at Kayatha,* Pune, 1975
EAT	:	Bajpai, K.D. and Pandey, S.K. *Excavation at Tumain*
EI	:	*Epigraphia Indica*

EK	: Sharma, R.K., *Excavation at Kakarahta*, Delhi, 1992
EMN	: Sankalia, H.D. and Subbarao Deo, *The Excavations at Maheshwar and Navdatoli*
GAR	: *Annual Administration Reports*, Archaeology Department, Gwalior State
GC	: Garde, M.P., *Guide to Chanderi*
GDAMI	: Day, N.L., *The Geographical Dictionary of Ancient and Medieval India*, 1927
GDC	: *Gwalior District Gazetteer*, Bhopal, 1965
GGS	: Garde, M.P., *Guide to Survaya*
GOS	: *Gaikwad Oriental Series*, Baroda
GSMD	: Dikshit, S.K., *A Guide to the State Museum*, Dhubela, Nowgong
GSP	: Trivedi, H.V., *Gandhisagar Ka Puratattva*
HC	: *History of Chhattisgarh*, Vol. I (1986)
HI	: Mishra, P.K. and Sullerey, S.K., *Heritage of India—Past and Present* (Prof. R.K. Sharma Fel. Vol.), Delhi, 1994
Hiralal List	: Hiralal, R.B., *Inscriptions in C.P. and Berar*, Nagpur, 1932
HK	: Anand, Mulk Raj, Homage to Khajuraho, *Marg*, X, No. 3, 1957
HMIM	: *Handlist of Monuments*, Indore Museum
HMM	: *Handlist of Monuments*, Mandu
HTM	: Banerji, R.D., *The Haihayas of Tripuri and their Monuments*, Calcutta, 1931
IA	: *Indian Antiquary*
IAL	: *Indian Art and Letters*
IANP	: Sharma, R.K. (ed.), *Indian Archaeology—New Perspectives*
IAR	: *Indian Archaeology—A Review*
IC	: *Indian Culture*
ICPB	: Hiralal, *Inscriptions of C.P. and Berar*, 1932
IHQ	: *Indian Historical Quarterly*
IK	: Kawarlal, *Immortal Khajuraho*, 1965
ILN	: *Illustrated London News*
INC	: *Indian Numismatic Chronicle*

INHAC	:	*Indian Numismatics, History and Culture* (Dr. P.L. Gupta Fel. Vol.), Delhi, 1992
IO	:	Rajguru, S.N., *Inscriptions of Orissa*, Vol. IV
ISPS	:	Shastri, A.M. (ed.), *Inscriptions of the Sarabhapuriyas, Panduvamsis and Somavamsis*, pt. I-II, Delhi, 1995
JA	:	*Journal Asiatique*
JAHRS	:	*Journal of the Andhra Historical Research Society*
JASB	:	*Journal of the Asiatic Society of Bengal*
JBBRAS	:	*Journal of the Bombay Branch of the Royal Asiatic Society*
JBHU	:	*Journal of the Banaras Hindu University*
JBORS	:	*Journal of the Bihar Orissa Research Society*
JESI	:	*Journal of the Epigraphical Society of India*
JIH	:	*Journal of Indian History*
JIM	:	*Journal of Indian Museum*
JKHRS	:	*Journal of the Kalinga Historical Research Society*
JMPIP	:	*Journal of Madhya Pradesh Itihasa Parishad*
JMSUB	:	*Journal of the M.S. University of Baroda*
JNSI	:	*Journal of the Numismatic Society of India*
JOI	:	*Journal of Oriental Institute*, Baroda
JOHRS	:	*Journal of the Orissa Historical Research Society*
JOR	:	*Journal of the Oriental Research*, Madras
JRAS, GB	:	*Journal of the Royal Asatic Society, Great Britain and Ireland*
JUPHS	:	*Journal of the U.P. Historical Society*
JVU	:	*Journal of the Vikram University*, Ujjain
KD	:	Dhama, B.L., *Khajuraho* (Guide-Book), 1953
KDI	:	*Khajuraho Album* by Directorate of Information, M.P. Govt., Bhopal
KDP	:	Awasthi, R.A., *Khajuraho ki Deva Pratimayen*, Agra, 1967
KE	:	*Kalachuri Era*
KKC	:	Chakravarty, K.K., *Khajuraho*
KKD	:	*Khajuraho* (Guide-Book) by Krishna Deva, 1965
KSS	:	Agrawal, Urmila, *Khajuraho Sculptures and their Significance*, Delhi, 1964

KV	:	Sagar, Muni Kanti, *Khandharon Ke Vaibhav*, Kashi, 1953
KVJ	:	*Khajuraho* (Guide Book) by J. Vijaytunga
KVP	:	Vidya Prakash, *Khajuraho*, 1967
KZ	:	Zennas, E. and Auboyer, *Khajuraho*, 1960
MAR	:	*Annual Administration Report, Department of Archaeology*, Madhya Pradesh
MASI	:	*Memoirs of the Archaeological Survey of India*
MB	:	*Madhya Bharati*, Research Journal of Sagar University
MBH	:	*The Mahabharata*
MBI	:	Dwivedi, H.N., *Madhya Bharat Ka Itihas*, Gwalior, 1956
MDG	:	*Mandla District Gazetteer*, 1912
ME	:	*Man and Environment*, Pune
MER	:	Bajpai, K.D. and Pandey, S.K., *Malhar* : 1975-78
MHSP	:	*Mahakoshal Historical Research Society's Papers*, Bilaspur
MP	:	Bajpai, K.D., *Madhya Pradesh Ka Puratattva*, Bhopal, 1970
MPR	:	Dikshit, M.G., *Madhya Pradesh Ke Puratattva Ki Ruprekha*
MPS	:	*Madhya Pradesh Sandesh*, Special No. on Archaeology, June 13, 1970
MPSG	:	Sharma, R.K., *Madhya Pradesh Ke Puratattva Ka Sandharbha Grantha*, Bhopal, 1974
MS	:	Marshall and Foucher, *Monuments of Sanchi*, 3 Vols., Delhi, 1940
MUH	:	Patil, D.R., *Monuments of Udayagiri Hills*
ND	:	*Numismatic Digest*
NDG	:	*Narasimhapur District Gazetteer*, Bhopal, 1971
NIA	:	*New Indian Antiquary*, Bombay
NMAR	:	*Nagpur Museum Acquisition Report*
NMB	:	*Nagpur Museum Bulletin*
NMC	:	*Catalogue of Existing Coins in the Central Museum*, Nagpur, 1908
NNM	:	*Numismatic Notes and Monographs*

NPP	:	*Nagri Pracharini Patrika,* Varanasi
NUJ	:	*Nagpur University Journal*
NS	:	*Numismatic Supplement*
PAI	:	Sharma, R.K. and Tripathi K.K. (eds.), *Recent Perspectives on Prehistoric Art in India and Allied Subjects,* Delhi, 1996
PASB	:	*Proceedings of the Asiatic Society of Bengal.*
PHAI	:	Ray Chaudhury, H.C., *Political Histroy of Ancient India,* 1953
PIHC	:	*Proceedings of Indian History Congress*
PP	:	*Prachya Pratibha*
PPIP	:	Sankalia, H.D., *Prehistory & Proto-history of India and Pakistan,* Pune, 1974
PRASIWC	:	*Progress Report of the Archaeological Survey of India, Western Circle*
PRS	:	Khare, M.D., *Painted Rock Shelters,* Bhopal, 1981
PTS	:	*Pali Text Society*
QJMS	:	*Quarterly Journal of the Mythic Society*
RAHS	:	*Reports of the Administartion of the Holkar State*
RAI	:	Chakraverty, K.K. *et al.* (eds.), *Rock-Art of India*
RDG	:	*Raipur District Gazetteer,* Bhopal, 1973
RGSI	:	*Reports of the Geological Suvery of India*
SAG	:	*Shukla Abhinandan Granth*
SAPI	:	Wakankar and Brooks, *Stone Age Paintings in India,* 1976
SAT. BR.	:	*Satpatha Brahmana*
SC	:	*Science and Culture*
SDG	:	*Sagar District Gazetteer,* Bhopal, 1967
SE	:	Saka Era
SEL. INS.	:	Sircar, D.C., *Select Inscriptions*
SGAMI	:	Sircar, D.C., *Study in the Geography of Ancient and Medieval India*
SI	:	Solomon, R., *Shell Inscriptions,* Calcutta, 1980
SIA	:	de Terra and Paterson, *Studies on the Ice Age in India and Associated Human Cultures,* Washington, 1939

SII	:	*South Indian Inscriptions*
SIS	:	Saraswati, S.K., *Survey of Indian Sculptures*, Calcutta, 1957
SPCPC	:	Seminar of Papers on the Chronology of Punch-Marked Coins, Varanasi
SSS	:	Sharma, R.K. (ed.), *Studies in Shell Script*
TCYB	:	Sharma, R.K., *The Temple of Chaunsatha Yogini at Bheraghat*
TTR	:	*Treasure Trove Reports of M.P.*
UDJ	:	*Ujjain District Gazetteer*, Bhopal, 1982
VE	:	Vikram Era
VRIA	:	Mirashi, V.V., *Vakataka Rajvansh Ka Itihas Tatha Abhilekh*, Nagpur
VS	:	Vikram Samvat
WNDG	:	*West Nimar District Gazetteer*, Bhopal, 1970

VOLUME - III

TRIBAL COMMUNITIES OF MODERN AGE

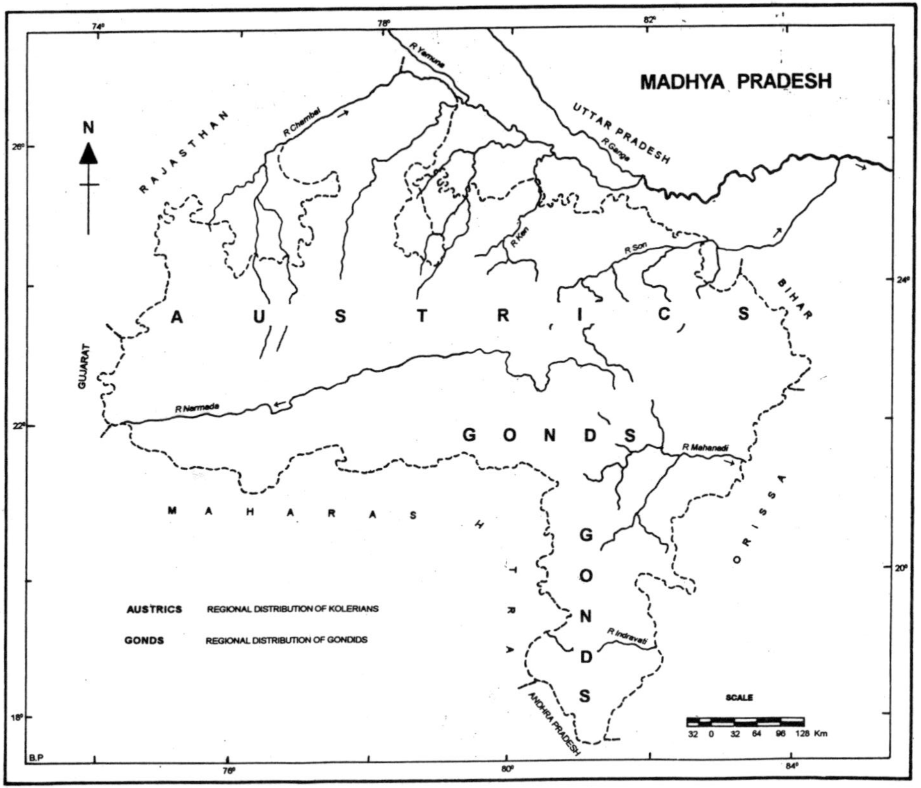

Map 1. Madhya Pradesh: Spacial Distribution of Kolarians and Gonds

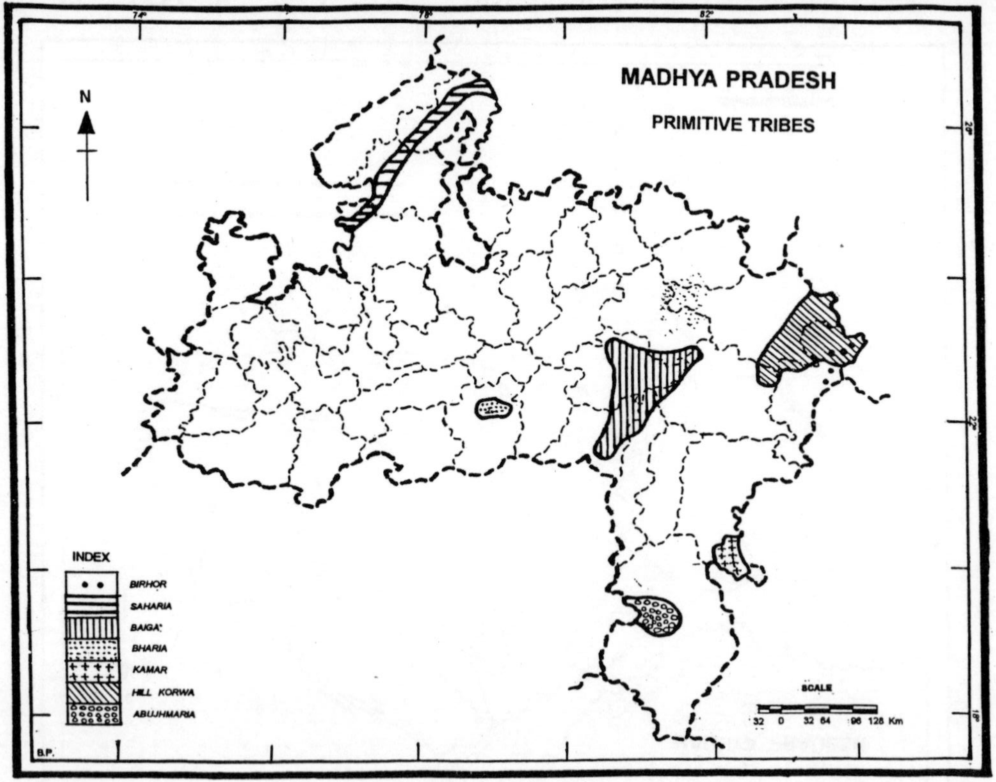

Map 2. Madhya Pradesh: Primitive Tribes

XV

TRIBAL IDENTITY: A NEW CONCEPT

With the advent of British rule in India was formulated the new theory of Tribal Identity. The authors were the British administrators and the Christian missionaries. The crux of the problem was to highlight the difference between the forest-dwelling communities and the surrounding Hindu population. Ghurye termed the former as the 'so-called Aborigines' or 'Backward Hindus'.

It is to be remembered that there were no 'tribes' in Britain or for that matter in Europe which had exceptionally low population of tribals in circumlocular regions which were sparsely populated. The 'tribals' were the original inhabitants of America, Australia and Africa, South of Sahara. In all these continents, tribals had religion, race and language other than the European invaders. Here the tribals constituted a negligible population. The colonising white population nearly decimated the tribal population in all these continents.

In India, things were quite different. Hence the colonisers cleverly advocated a theory that, in India, the tribals are different from the surrounding Hindu population in terms of race, religion and language. Therefore Tribal Identification was a necessity in Indian context. In order to point out the hollowness of this theory we may analyse its contents and discuss briefly the theory of Tribal Identity under the following heads:-

1. Tribe and other related terms in Indian context
2. Dictionary meaning of the term 'Tribe'
3. Literary use of the term 'Tribe'
4. Creation or identification of 'Tribes'
5. Race: The basis of tribal identity
6. Language: The basis of tribal identity

7. Religion: The basis of tribal identity
8. Traditional Indian way of tribal identification
9. Academic Terminology and definitions of the 'Tribe'
10. Alienation
11. Tribes, primitive culture and civilization in other parts of the world

1-3. THE TERM

The term 'Tribal' has not been precisely defined in the Constitution of India which however, refers to such communities as 'Scheduled Tribes'. In Hindi, the synonym used for the 'Scheduled Tribes' is Anusuchit Janajati and the other terms viz. 'Adivasi', 'Vanavasi' or 'Adimjati' are used as synonyms of 'Tribal'. These Hindi terms correspond to three different meanings namely 'Aboriginal', 'Forest-dweller' and the 'Original' or the 'Oldest inhabitant'. These focus merely on the general characteristics of the so-called Indian tribals; the synonyms do not convey either the correct meaning of the term 'tribal' or the social realities of the Indian tribes.

The English term 'Tribe', according to *Reader's Digest Encylopaediac Dictionary* may be used in five different senses, viz.

1. In the first sense, a tribe means a group of primitive or barbarous clans under recognised chiefs.
2. The second meaning is related to Roman history (Clans of Romans were termed as Tribes).
3. In the third sense, the term refers to similar divisions whether natural or political.
4. The fourth meaning relates to a unit of taxonomy (in Biological Sciences).
5. In the fifth sense, the term is used for 'large numbers'.

The term 'Tribe' in literary sense is also used for any group' or 'category' of persons. In newspapers and contemporary books we read about the 'vanishing tribe of truthful people' or 'growing tribe of politicians'. Recently, an article entitled 'Dying of Shame', published in *Reader's Digest*

(August 2001) discusses the role of 'The Tribal Chiefs' which includes some influential persons of twenty-first century Christians and Muslims of Middle East, who are definitely not tribals in the conventional sense.

In India we find many other terms like 'Criminal Tribes' which in due course of time became technical.

4. CREATION OR IDENTIFICATION OF TRIBES

Our contemporary tribal communities, now in hundreds, are the creation of 18th century writings of British officials and missionaries who established in their hundreds and thousands of essays, memoirs and books that forest-dwelling Hindus were not Hindus in real sense and that a large chunk of Hindu society was finally disintegrated. R.V. Russell and Rai Bahadur Hiralal (1916) state: "At each Census the question arises which of them should be classed, and which are animists or worshippers of their own God, and though the classification is necessarily very arbitrary, the process can be clearly observed" (The Tribes and Castes of the Central Provinces of India, p.65). Rai Bahadur Hiralal, although an officer of British administration is remembered with great respect as he was in know of the damage to Indian culture which was being perpetrated by the British policy. Rai Bahadur wrote a number of articles about the cultural realities of the Indian tribes, but Hiralal and similar other scholars had their own limitations in the British system. They were unable to act against the British design which was expressed by Missionary Rev. M.A. Sherring (1872) in the following words:

> In designating many castes, I have frequently employed the word 'tribe' and not word 'caste' and have preferred the use of ethnological terms to a term which is used only very partially in an ethnological sense and is associated with other and different questions'. ('Hindu Tribe and Castes as represented in Benaras'). In designating the tribes, 'Race' 'Language' and 'Religion' have been used as 'Scientific basis.

5. RACE: THE BASIS OF TRIBAL IDENTITY

Europe has no tribes as the Europeans proclaim that they have long left the tribal stage of social organisation and thus the anthropological concept of tribe is eurocentric in nature. The western anthropological literature recognises only two major groups of tribes. In the first group are included those ancient tribes the combined efforts of which gave rise to the western civilization. For the Europeans, ancient tribes of Greece, Rome and Gaul have now only academic value as all the Europeans or more precisely the white race has established itself as one solid race—a 'universal tribe'. Even the African tribals, now citizens of the United States, are no more tribals, for, they are the Americal Blacks. The second group comprises those natives who confronted the white population during the colonial rule. The period started with the times of Columbus, Vasco da Gama, Drake and others. The tribals of this group were different in culture, race and religion than the colonial invaders.

Whereas the tribal population of America, Australia and Africa belonged to the races different from the newly arrived coloniser whites, the situation in India was not similar.

In India, the white colonisers found different strata of social and economic development in population. The Britishers therefore advocated division of the Indian population on the basis of race, language and religion. Thus came into existence the concept of Tribal Communities of India, different from the larger Hindu population.

The task of identification of the so-called Indian Tribal Communities began in the nineteenth century by colonial writers with racial, linguistic and religious bias. There was an attempt to prove that the large segment of forest-dwelling Hindus were animists. In fact, 'tribal' is not a proper term to represent the forest-dwelling communities of India. It is to be remembered that the so-called Indian 'tribals' physically and culturally had been the part of regional variety of the Indian Hindus. Thus, the tribals of Kerala, Karnataka, Andhra or Madhya Pradesh had been no different in their general appearance and belief than their neighbouring rural and urban Hindu communities. Since the tribals lived in forests and lead the simplest way of living, minor physical variations were noted in them. In the religious belief also, they followed the simpler version of religion, which formed basic fibre of Hinduism.

By 'discovering' many more tribal communities, the Britishers named these forest living people variously. In most cases, such names were never accepted by the communities. For instance, our largest tribe never accepted the name 'Gond', as they called themselves 'Koitur'. In the nineteenth century it had been a forcible attempt to give new names to the forest-living people. The communities were divided and subdivided arbitrarily. In the process, old names were lost. Gradually it became immaterial what these communities called themselves or how they have been named.

Human Race and the Tribals

In the history of life forms, two incidents were of utmost importance. The first was the appearance of life as such, and, the second, the emergence of consciousness. Although man has evolved from animal kingdom, he is unique in it. Man is represented by a single species 'Sapiens' of the monotypical genus 'Homo'. Since all the men belong to the same species, all of them on earth are, to a large extent, biologically similar. The normal set of chromosomes in every person is 46 (23 pairs). Unlike many animal sub-species or races, different human population do not show any taxonomic variations in chromosomal structure.

It has to be remembered that, since mankind has come into existence, as Homo sapiens (a process which took 40,000 years), man has not undergone any appreciable evolutionary changes in terms of genetics. The consciousness, referred to above, characteristic only of man, makes an unbridgable gap between him and other life forms. It is due to this that his structure needed no change in such a long period of time.

The modern problem of race arose with the beginning of modern scientific nomenclature. Linnaeus (1707-78) thought the mankind to be a single species; he recognised four sub-species. His contemporary, Blumen made a division of mankind into five races.

Then came the concept of racial superiority. The

Europeans, who had begun to conquer the world, thought their race to be the most superior. Then came the concept of 'Aryan race'. In the four volumes of his 'Essay on Inequality of Human Races' (1853-55), Gobineau explained how Aryans were the biological master race.

Chamberlain (1895-1927) and Gatton (1822-1911), the founder of eugencies, held that Nordics were a superior race. Lapouge (1864-1936) advocated methods to replace Africans, Asians, 'inferior' whites by whites of the 'Superior race'. The cult of Aryanism led the atrocities of genocide.

Our own Indian anthropologists were competing with each other to prove a section of Indian population belonging to one or the other superior sub-sections of white race.

In this academic background of anthropology, colonial administrators, missionaries and ethnographers of the nineteenth century intruded upon the discourses between tribe and civilization in the Indian context.

The Indians were arbitrarily divided into tribal and non-tribal population, supposed to be on 'Scientific basis'. The science of 'Anthropology', in yet its infancy, was used by the Britishers as tool to 'divide' the country in as many groups as possible. The divisions were 'authenticated' with each Census Report and each Census Report was final verdict on the anthropological status of any human population.

Arbitrary Use of the Word Race

The Britishers had their own concept of race in the context of Indian tribals. The following extracts give a glimpse of racial views of some Britishers.

Brodley Birt in 'Chotanagpur' (p.23) thinks that the Kols are 'The oldest most Characteristic race of the land'.

Varrier Elwin in 'Loss of Nerve' (p.35) suggests that all aboriginal tribes (excluding those of Assam) should be classed in the Census as Hindus, but he wanted 'Separate returns of their numbers by race'.

Shoobert in 'Census of India, C.P. and Berar Report' (p.396-97) points out that when the aboriginals themselves claim to be included into Hindu fold, their idea is to enhance their social status. 'To the more simple among them, the term Hindu does not convey any connection with religion, but merely indicates a race".

During the British period the 'Scientific Classification' of human races mostly appeared in the Census Reports.

The most accepted classification of British period was that of Guha (1935), who listed six main races, with nine sub-types of Indian population, viz.:

1. Negrito
2. The proto-Australoid
3. The Mongolid
   - i) Placeo-Mongoloids
     - a) long-headed
     - b) broad-headed
   - (ii) Tibeto-Mongoloids
4. The Mediterranean
   - (i) Palaeo-Mediterranean
   - (ii) Mediterranean
   - (iii) Oriental type
5. The western Brachycephals
   - (i) Alpinoid
   - (ii) Dinaric
   - (iii) Armenoid
6. The Nordic

Guha summed up his conclusions specifically as regards the racial composition of tribal India (1952) as follows:

1. The Kadars, the Irulas, and the Paniyans of South India, with frizzly hair, have an undoubted Negrito stain.
2. The tribes of middle India belong to the proto-Australoid stock.
3. The brachycephatic Mongoloids of northeastern India have typical features of the face and the eye.
4. A slightly different Mongoloid type with medium stature, high head and medium nose lives in the Brahmaputra valley.

According to him (Guha, 1935), tribal people of India can be grouped into three major categories.

(a) *The proto-Australoids:-* This group is characterized by dark skin colour, sunken nose and lower forehead, (e.g.) the Munda, the Oraon, the Ho, the Gond, the Khond, etc.

(b) *The Mongoloids:-* Tribal people of the Himalayan region specially of North Himalaya, come under this category.

(c) *The Negrito:-* The Kadars of Kerala and the Andamanis of the Andaman Island come under this stock.

One more classification is based on the ethnic roots of the tribes. The more predominant are:

(1) *The Mongoloid Origin:-* The Nagas, Mizo, Sema, Jausari, Apa-Tanis, Tharu, etc.

(2) *proto-Austroloid:-* This group usually speaks the so-called Kherwarian or Kaularian languages and includes the Munda, Ho, Bhils, Pahadia, Korku, Korwa, Baiga, Gonds, etc.

(3) *The Negrito:-* Whom we usually recognise as being of Dravidian origin and include Toda, Kota, etc.

Modern Concepts of Human Races

Considering that mankind is a species consisting of Mendelian population engaged in gene exchanged race, typology presents quite a problem. Dynamic genetic interaction is taking place between all population. Hence the difficulty of subdividing into races, the whole diversity of mankind.

The antigen investigations reveal that human heredity carries evidence of both isolation and mixture. The present intensive mixture is clearly tending to fuse all human races into a single, but greatly variable population.

Population diversity can be expressed quantitatively in terms of varied concentrations. The distribution of antigens in human population indicates that they are radically different from animal races and sub-species.

Human population variations may derive from genetic

drift and population mixtures that are historical and social in origin. Under such circumstances, natural selection plays a secondary role. Each human population is a diversified manifestation of what constitutes a single whole. The differences between them relate to minor features, and are negligibly small compared to the common genetic endowment that is the biological basis of every man on earth who belongs to Homo sapiens.

However, several classifications have been proposed, in which the genetics of blood antigens are combined with other anthropological features. Some of them are as follows:

Boyd (1953)

1. European (Caucasoid): high frequencies of Ph cde and CDe, moderate frequencies of the other blood-group genes; M usually slightly above 50% and N below 50%.
2. African (Negroid): very high frequency of Ph cDe, moderate frequencies of the other blood-group genes.
3. Asian (Mongoloid): high frequency of B, few, if any, cde.
4. American Indian: mostly homozygous O, but sometimes high frequencies of A; absence of B, few, if any, cde, high M.
5. *Australoid: moderate to high A, few or no B or cde, high N.*

Garn (1961)

1. Amerindian: the pre-Columbian population of the Americas.
2. Polynesian: islands of the Eastern Pacific, from New Zealand to Hawaii and Easter Island.
3. Micronesian: islands of the western Pacific, from Guam to Marshall and Gilbert Islands.
4. Melanesian-Papuan islands of the western Pacific, from New Guinea to New Caledonia and Fiji.
5. Australian: Australian aboriginal population.

6. Asian: from Indonesia and southeast Asia to Tibet, China, Japan, Mongolia, plus the native tribes of Siberia.
7. Indian: population of the subcontinent of India.
8. European: population of Europe, the Middle East, and Africa, North of the Sahara.
9. African population of Africa, South of the Sahara.

Coon, Garn, Birdsell (1950) and Dobzhansky (1962)

1. Northwest European: Scandinavia, northern Germany, northern France, United kingdom, Ireland.
2. Northeast European: Poland, European part of the Soviet Union, most of the present population of Siberia.
3. Alpine: from Central France, South Germany, Switzerland, northern Italy eastward to the shores of the Black Sea.
4. Mediterranean: people on both sides of the Mediterranean, from Tangiers to the Dardanelles, Arabia, Turkey, Iran.
5. Hindu: India, Pakistan.
6. Turkic: Turkestan, western China
7. Tibetan: Tibet
8. North Chinese: northern and Central China and Manchuria.
9. Classic Mognoloid: Siberia, Mongolia, Korea, Japan.
10. Eskimo: Arctic America.
11. southeast Asian: South China to Thailand, Burma, Malaya and Indonesia.
12. Ainu: aboriginal population of northern Japan.
13. Lapp: Arctic Scandinavia and Finland.
14. North American Indian: indigenous population of Canada and the United States.
15. Central American Indian: from southwestern United States, through Central America, to Bolivia.
16. South American Indian: primarily the agriculture peoples of Peru, Bolivia, and Chile.

17. Fuegian: non-agricultural inhabitants of southern South America.
18. East African: East Africa, Ethipoia, part of Sudan.
19. Sudandese: most of Sudan.
20. Forest Negro: West Africa and much of the Congo.
21. Bantu: South Africa and part of East Africa.
22. Bushman and Hottentot: the aboriginal inhabitants of South Africa.
23. African Pygmy: a small-statured population living in the rain forests of Equatorial Africa.
24. Dravidian: aboriginal population of southern India and Ceylon.
25. Negrito: small-statured and frizzly-aired population scattered from the Philippines to the Andamans, Malaya and New Guinea.
26. Melanesian Papuan: New Guinea to Fiji.
27. Murrayian: aboriginal population of southeastern Australia.
28. Carpentarian: aboriginal population of northern and Central Australia.
29. Micronesian: islands of the western Pacific.
30. Polynesian: islands of the Central and Eastern Pacific.
31. Neo-Hawaiian: an emerging population of Hawaii.
32. Ladino: an emerging population of Central South America.
33. North American Coloured: Negro population of North America.
34. South African Coloured: the analogues population of South Africa.

Dravidian and Kolarian Groups

Central Indian tribes have been divided into two racial groups, but how these two groups differ racially remains obscure and unexplained because anthropological studies do not find any significant difference between the two groups. Russell and Hiralal (1916) write: "Though the physical characteristics of the two sets of tribes display no marked points of difference, it has been generally held by ethnologists who know them that they represent two distinct waves of immigration, and the absence of connection between their languages bears out this view" (p.504).

It is very clear that there is hardly any scientific reason to believe that one or the other tribe belongs to Munda or Dravidian groups of tribes, because the language is an acquired trait. It becomes more difficult when we say that a particular tribe has forgotten its language and has adopted a new one. The Dravidian languages, whether tribal or non tribal Gondi, Kurku, Khond belong to the family to which Tamil, Telugu, Malayalam and Canarese belong, and their home is South India. The existence of the small Brahui tribe in Baluchistan, who speak of Dravidian language but have no physical resemblance to other Dravidian races has never been satisfactorily explained.

6. LANGUAGE: THE BASIS OF TRIBAL IDENTITY

According to another usage, tribes from South India like the Gonds, Kolam, Toda, Koya, etc. are called Dravidian in origin though they are considered a part of the Australoid group. Herbert Rislay has also mentioned Indo-Aryan, Aryo-Dravidian, Mongoloid-Dravidian, Sitho-Dravidian and Turki-Iranain as mixed ethnic roots.

Among the numerically most important tribes in India are the Gonds of Madhya Pradesh, Maharashtra and Andhra Pradesh and include the Koiturs, Koyas, Madias, Murias, Raj-Gonds, Pardhans, Dhurves, Khatuwars, Parajas.

The second largest group of tribal communities described as Kaularian tribes and include the Santhals, Munda and Ho spread over in Bihar, Orissa and West Bengal as well as the Bhils and Korwas from Rajasthan, Gujarat and the Korkus in Madhya Pradesh and Maharashtra. This group speaks the "so-called" Kherwarian or the Kaularian group of languages which include the Munda group of dialects, and are supposed to be of pre-Dravidian origin.

Linguistic Classification

G.A. Grierson in his *Linguistic Survey of India*, Vol. IV (Munda and Dravidian Languages) (First Reprint 1967), gives references hinting at links between the Munda and Dravidian group of languages (pp. 167-82). Hodgson classed the languages under the head of Tamilian. Ho, Santhali, Bhumji, Kurakh and Mundari (all from Munda family) were considered as dialects of Kol languages. Loan also followed Hodgson and called them as North Dravidian. Grierson quotes Max Muller stating".... I can see many coincidences between Uraon, Rajmahali and Gondi on the one side and Sinbhum, Santhal, Bhamji and Mundala words on the other.... Both are two different races... came in contact in these regions... with ethnic name 'Munda'. This analysis helps us in understanding that there were cultural contacts amongst the tribal groups which are dispersed in different parts and are assigned different ethnic origins and dialects. The similarities in many cultural traits found in distant tribal groups in India can be interpreted on this basis.

Looking at the linguistic map of India and the languages found among the tribals, we note that the Dravidian languages family is in use in the Dravidian region in South India and a few pockets in middle India in Chotanagpur and northwestern border near Baluchistan. Another language family, 'Austro-Asiatic' is found in certain pockets in the northeastern Himalayan region in Meghalaya, in Nicobar Islands and extensively in middle India and adjoining western India. The third language which is traced on the map and is prevalent all along the Himalayan region is Tibeto-Chinese. The Indo-European language is found in the remaining major part of India.

All these suggest a linguistic drift from northwestern to South Indian and then in the pockets of middle India in the case of Dravidian languages. There is much controversy over the origin of the Austro-Asiatic language. W. Schnidt named the Munda languages as Austro-Asiatic. In 1928 Heine Geldern suggested that the Mongoloid people entered India from the northeastern side and brought with them the Munda languages which later spread in middle India. But Hutton opines that the Austro-Asiatic language was brought by the Kolarians through the West-end of the Himalayas and by the Mon-Khmer-speaking people from the East of the Himalayas. The Tibeto-Burmese language entered our country from the North and spread all along the Himalayas.

With this background we come to classify the tribals linguistically. They speak different languages in different regions and groups, and can be broadly classified into four main linguistic families. viz.:

I. AUSTRO-ASIATIC FAMILY

- (a) Mon-Khmer Branch: Khasi and Nicobari
- (b) Munda Branch: Santhali, Kharwari, Ho, Mundari, Gondi, Kharia, Savara, Khond, Gadaba, etc.

II. TIBETO-CHINESE FAMILY

1. Siamese: Chinese Sub-family
2. Tai group: Khampti, Phakial, etc.
    - (i) Tibeto-Himalayan Branch: Bhotia of Darjeeling.
    - (ii) western sub-group of Pronominalized Himalayan Group—Chamba, Lahauli, Swangli, Kanauri, etc.
    - (iii) Non-Pronominalized Himalayan Group—Rong or Lepcha, Toto, etc.
    - (iv) Arunachal Branch—Aka or Hrusso, Abor, Miri, Dafla, Mishmi, etc.
    - (v) Assam-Burmese Branch
        - (a) Bara or Bodo group-plain Kachari, Dimasa or (Hill) Kachari, Garo, Tripura, etc.
        - (b) Naga Group
            - (i) Naga-sub-group,Angami, Ao, Sema, Rengma, etc.
            - (ii) Naga-Bodo sub-group—Kachcha Naga, Kabui Naga, etc.
        - (c) Kachin Group—Singpho
        - (d) Kuki-Chin Group—Manipuri, Thado, Sokte, Ralte, Lushai, etc.

III. Dravidian Family

Dravidian group—Korawa, Yerukala, Yarava, Badaga, Todo, Kota, Kurukh or Oraon, Malto or Maler, Kui Kandhi or Khon Gondi, etc.

IV. Indo-European Family

Hajong, Bhili, etc.

Max Muller, who popularized the philology or the so-called science of languages denied the existence of Aryan race.

Suniti Kumar Chatterjee, who was a scholar in the western tradition of Orientalism has thrown light on the fusion of the tribal and non-tribal cultures of India. He is the best known linguist, hence his views on the relationship of tribal and non-tribal are important.

According to late Professor Chatterjee, the Austric Nishadas (Kols or Mundas), Dramidas or Dravidians, the Aryans and Kiratas or Mongoloids lived together in different geographical areas of India, some three or four thousand years ago. Then began a racial fusion and cultural and linguistic misgeneration among them.

What we loosely call Sanskrit, as the vehicle of Hindu culture, can, with greater accuracy, be described as 'spoken Aryan', as it evolved roughly between 500 B.C. and A.D. 500. It included not only classical Sanskrit as it evolved from Vedic Sanskrit under the impact of Dravidian and Kol (tribal) speeches, but also contemporary Prakrit or Vernacular Aryan dialects and all other speeches within the Aryan orbit as used from 500 B.C. onwards, as well as the vital matters of syntax and vocabulary, both classical Sanskrit and various and Austric (tribal) languages. 'In evolution of the Aryan speech, the Dravidians and Austrics had almost an equal hand as original speakers of old Indo-Aryans'. He further writes: 'Sanskrit looms large behind all Indian languages, Aryan and non-Aryans'.

Language as a Parameter of Tribal Identity

Almost all the tribes of Central India have been termed as

Kolarian or Dravidian, as all the known tribal groups of Central India are said to speak the original language of either of the two major groups.

The Kolarians speak a language which is spoken by the tribals living in northern peninsular zone of India, but this group of languages is also spoken by the tribes of Malayan peninsula as well tribals of some islands of Indian Ocean including Madagascar. The term Dravidian is restricted to peninsular India, but a pocket of Dravidian-speaking persons (the language is Brahui) also exists in Afghanistan.

Then there are certain Kolarian tribes who have switched over to Dravidian and Aryan languages whereas Bhils have switched over to Aryan languages. Baigas and Bharias have forgotten their Kolarian language and now speak a Dravidian language.

As discussed earlier, these two groups even if evolved separately were influenced by Sanskrit and the languages which evolved from it. These languages were thus the mixture of languages since thousands of years.

7. RELIGION: THE BASIS OF TRIBAL IDENTITY

During the British regime, forest-living Hindus were enumerated separately also on the ground of religion as they were thought to have been the followers of different religions. For this, the following parameters were used:

1. The forest-dwelling Hindus did not belong to one of the Hindu 'castes'.
2. They did not employ Brahmin priests on social occasions and rituals.
3. They did not have their temples similar to Hindus.
4. They are animists, worshipping many gods, ghosts, etc. They have their own gods.
5. They eat beef.

Just as their differentiation with rest of the Hindu population on the basis of 'race' and 'language' was unscientific, so was the basis of religion.

The tribals and the Hindus both believe in many gods

and thus both are 'animists', and do not belong to any particular 'caste' even if the caste is a dominant feature of Hinduism. Not employing a Brahmin or not having a temple is the result of culture and not of the religion. There are many religious similarities which have been overlooked in formulating the theory of tribal identity.

The British writers had different views on this point. Some of them, even conflicting are cited below.

Forsyth, writing about the similarities of the Gonds and the Hindus writes: 'I believe that, were the Gonds not associated with hills and forests into which Hindus have penetrated very far, they would long since have come to be looked on merely as another caste in the vast social fabric of Hinduism'.

Mr. C.U. Wills observes: 'The Paikara Kanwars... in all the seven northern zamindaris (of Bilaspur), are an instance of what Hinduism can do to teach primitive people social decency and self-respect, carrying with it lessons of thrift, industry and self-restraint'.

Dr. Hutton however, thinks differently: 'The tragedy is that the object of the tribalist in claiming caste, or in allowing his tribal membership to be treated as membership of a caste, is to obtain social uplift but the more general degradation'.

Verrier Elwin reviewing the impact of 'Hinduism' on tribals in many of his works found that tribals should be 'saved' from the ill effects of 'acculturation'. For this he propagated 'National Park Policy' for tribals.

It is needless to say that whereas most of the British authors could see one or the other defect in 'Hindu influence', they established that the 'Christian influence' was the need of the hour!

8. TRADITIONAL INDIAN WAY OF TRIBAL IDENTIFICATION

The Indian history as discussed in earlier chapters of this work recognises the following types of tribes:

1. Aryan tribes or civilized tribes
2. Aranyak or forest-dwelling tribes

For our purpose of study, forest-dwelling tribes were classed with foreigners and all those who were either cursed to live in forests or who for any other reason lived outside the fold of caste system.

Caste system might have been established during the period of Lord Rama of Kosala or earlier. Before him there were many forest-dwelling totemic tribes like the Vanaras, the Riksas, the Nagas, the Suparnas, etc. Some of these totemic tribes continued to live afterwards.

During the period of Lord Krishna, the caste system strengthened more and now all those living outside the system were termed as 'Mlechcha'.

वर्णाना निगमोनास्ति योनीनां च विशेषत:
आश्रमाणां जनानां च सर्वम्लेच्छा: कलौयुगे

—*Devi Bhagwat*

गो मांस भक्षको यस्तु लोक बाह्यं च भाषते
सर्वाचार विहानौऽतौ म्लेच्छ इत्याभिधीयते

—*Amarkosh*

In the above extract, forest-dwelling tribes have been dealt with the communities which were outside the pale of Varnasrama. The general life pattern of these communities was not in conformation with the Aryans or civilized tribes. Thus, the Mlechhas had following categories

Mlechhas

1. Foreigners (irrespective of colour, cultural level and material richness)	2. Sudras (not all, but some of the lowest)	3. Outcastes (who were forced to live in forests)	4. Forest-dwellers (uncivilized)

THE FOREST-DWELLERS

In ancient times, the following people inhabited the forests:

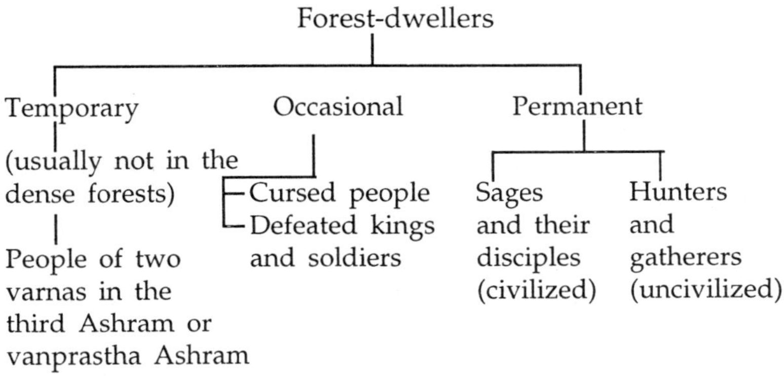

Hunters and Gatherers

All the hunters and gatherers were counted as Mlechhas.

> पुलिन्दाः नाहला निष्ट्या शबरा बखरा भराः ।
> माला भिल्लाः किरातश्च सर्वेऽपि म्लेच्छजातयः ।।
>
> —*Abhidhana Chintamani*

Absorption in Castes

It seems that when a section of such communities by its behaviour attained the 'civilised state', it was admitted in one of the higher castes, e.g. from 'Sudra' to 'Ksatriya'. The justification for this exists in the form of an ancient tale preserved in the Puranic literature. It is stated that once some of the Pulindas attained the status of 'Ksatriyahood'. They were said to be the old Ksatriyas from which status they are said to have been degenerated as forest-dwelling tribals on account of a curse. In the *Mahabharata,* they are thus called 'Vrisala' or mixed-Ksatriyas.

Then, we find many totemic and non-totemic tribes like Kharaparika, Sanakanika, Kaka, Andhraka, Guha, Chuchuka Madraka and many more mentioned in ancient Indian literature and inscriptions.

During the Mughal period, major groups of tribes of Central India identified were Kol, Nishad, Gond and Bhil.

9. TERMINOLOGY

Different terms have been popularized by different authors for meaning these groups. Aborigines or Aboriginals are the terms which connote that they were the first or original inhabitants of the land, having original habitat, native to the soil or indigenous.

While Risley, Greison, Elwin, A.V. Thakkar prefer this term, Dr. Ghurye calls them "so-called" Aborigines or Backward Hindus. The Hindi term 'Advasi' is having the same connotation as Aborigines. Hutton called them "Primitive Tribes". Some scholars, however, dislike the term 'Aborigines' or 'Advasi' and prefer the term 'Vanavasi' (forest-dwellers) or 'Girijan' (mountain-dwellers) which indicates the nature of their present habitat or that in the immediate past. The term 'primitive' has also been used by different authors with different meanings. While some use it just to indicate tribal groups, others use it to indicate a lower level of acculturation amongst tribal groups. Thus a primitive tribal group should mean a relatively more backward tribal group which is still nearer to its original cultural level.

The Government of India has recognised some tribal groups as being 'primitive' and special plans as well as grants are sanctioned for their development. In Maharashtra, three tribal groups are recognised as 'primitive' namely, Madia-Gonds from Gadchiroli district, Kolams from Yavatmal district and Kinwat and Katkaris from Thane district.

Since long, solution to the problem of definition of a tribe has been eluding the administration. Anthropologists and sociologists have attempted different definitions.

W.J. Perry defines tribe as a group speaking a common dialect and inhabiting a common territory.

Bogardus defines tribe as a tribal group based on the need for protection, on ties of blood-relationships and on the strength of a common religion.

Gillin and Gillin consider any collection of pre-literate local group which occupies a common general territory, speaks a common language and practises a common culture, as a tribe.

D.N. Majumdar defines a tribe as a collection of families or groups of families bearing a common name, members of which occupy the same territory, speak the same language and observe certain taboos regarding marriage, profession or occupation and have developed a well-assessed system of reciprocity and mutuality of obligations.

Dr. Revers defines a tribe as a social group of a simple kind, the members of which speak a common dialect and act together for such common purposes as welfare.

The Imperial Gazetteer of India has defined a tribe a collection of families bearing a common name, speaking a common dialect, occupying or professing to occupy a common territory and which is not usually endogamous, though originally it might have been.

Kamaladevi Chattopadhyaya defines a tribe as a social group usually with a definite area, dialect, cultural homogeneity, and unifying social organisation. It can include several sub-groups.

The Dictionary of Anthropology (E.B. Tylor) defines a tribe as a social group usually with a social area, dialect, cultural homogeneity and unifying social organization. It may include sub-groups such as Sibe. The tribe ordinarily has a leader and may have a common ancestor, as well as a patron deity. The families or small communities making up the tribe are linked through economic, social, religious, family or blood ties.

Funk and Wagnalls Standard Dictionary (Comprehensive International Edition) defines tribe as "a division, class or group of people, varying ethnologically according to circumstances from which their separation or distinction is supposed to originate", or "a group or aggregate of persons among primitive peoples, usually consanguineous and endogamous, under one chief characterised by its own culture and having a name".

10. ALIENATION

In India, within a period of 200 years or so, the European academicians have established that the forest-dwelling population of India was not only different from the surrounding

Hindu population, but such population were original inhabitants of India. The later population or the Hindus were their exploiters, right from the beginning of the history.

It was established without any historical or archaeological evidence that the first to settle in India were the Kolarians and then came the Dravidians. However, even some British writers were sceptical about this theory.

Mr. Shoobert, who considers the Baigas to be the original inhabitants of the province, is not sure about other tribes, as he remarks: "How far the ancestors of these people were the earliest inhabitants of the province can only be a matter of conjuncture until further investigations have been made".

But the conjunctural hypothesis was deep-rooted in Indian academics. The Anglo-European writers in the second half of the century at first blamed caste Hindus, and then even the policies of Government of India. To get rid of the evils of alienation, Varrier Elwin suggested the 'National Park Theory' and Haimendorf went a step further and appreciated the tribal terrorism or the Naxalite movement of the Andhra.

Our contemporary anthropologists and sociologists talked much on 'Alienation', 'Sanskritization' and 'Hinduization' of tribes. These theories were found to be 'secular' and 'democratic' by a section of our social scientists. The problems due 'Christianization' and the rise of 'separatist movement' in tribal states now turned as Christian states were overlooked and they were looked upon as fundamentalist and narrow Hinduistic. The contemporary thought is to look conversion to Christianity as a synonym of 'progressiveness' of the tribals.

Now, in some of the tribal pockets, history begins after the baptisation of the tribal leader. Tribal history is being written afresh in India.

In Central India, as per this new history, all the development works like construction of dam, creation of National Parks and sanctuaries and the establishment of new industrial plants are now looked down as the works of 'Alien people' and probably the 'Alien Government'. In a democratic country like India, where tribal M.P.s, MLAs and sarpanchs are being elected as per democratic norms and where the forest-dwelling communities get the benefits of development, plans do not yet have a systematic and true history of Indian tribals.

11. TRIBES, PRIMITIVE CULTURES AND CIVILIZATION IN OTHER PARTS OF THE WORLD

According to sociologists, civilization is postulated as a historic form of social life that has evolved along a measured line of savagery, barbarism and civilization. The contemporary human groups in a state of, or carrying traces of the original conditions of life are the survival of the lower grades of culture, namely, savagery and barbarism. They are branded as 'primitive', characterised as: a complete world; a mental universe; with its own special caste or character; autonomous; isolated, remaining always within a small territory; a single biological type; in a state of homogeneity and uncritical mind; with norms and behaviour conventionally patterned; strongly ethnocentric, etc. But, as anthropologists realised that few real societies could correspond to the ideal type 'primitive', they began using an alternative term 'tribe'. Tribe refers to a constellation of somewhat reformed aspects of primitive life, generally constituting a homogeneous unit, speaking a common language, claiming a common ancestry, living in a particular geographical area, lacking in scientific knowledge and modern technology, and having a social structure based on kinship. The subtlety of the definition is that tribe in relation to modern society is a separate humanity.

Sociologists and anthropologists do not normally differentiate between the 'aboriginals' and 'tribals'. For the Americans in their own country, Red Indians (or simply Indians in American use) are the tribals. The American Negros or the Blacks though they are far backward than their native lands in Africa, are recognised as 'civilized' people in the U.S.A. for the simple reason that they are Americans.

In spite of the above-mentioned limitations, the ghost of the theory of Tribal Identity continues to haunt us till today, as the national policy regarding the tribal population of India is entirely based on nothing but the erroneous foundations laid by the British administrators and the missionaries. Sooner we come out of it, the better.

NOTES AND REFERENCES

1. Boyd, W.C. (1953): "The Contribution of Genetics to Anthropology", in A. Kroeber (ed.), *Anthropology Today*, University of Chicago Press, pp. 488-506.
2. Chatterjee, Suniti Kumar (1960): *Indo-Aryan and Hindi*, Firma KLM, Calcutta, p.136.
3. Coon, C.S., Garn, S.M., and Birdsell, J.B. (1950): *Races: A Study of Problems of Race Formation in Man*, Springfield, Illinois, U.S.
4. Dobzhansky, Th. (1962): *Mankind Evolving*, New Haven-London: Yale University Press.
5. Elwin,V. (1952): *The Loss of Nerves: A Comprehensive Study of the Contact of People in the Aboriginal Areas of Bastar State, Central Provinces of India.*
6. Forsyth, J. (1889): *The Highlands of Central India*, Reprinted, Asian Publication Services, New Delhi.
7. Garn, S. (1961): *Human Races*, Springfield, Illinois, U.S.
8. Grierson, G.A. (1905): *Linguistic Survey of India*, Calcutta.
9. Guha, B.S. (1944): *Racial Elements in Indian Population*, Oxford, Pamphlets on Indian Affairs, No.22.
10. Guha, B.S. (1935): The Racial Affinities of People of India, *Census of India*, 1931, Vol 1, Part III B.
11. Guha, B.S. (1951): *The Tribes of India*, 2 Vols, Bhartiya Adimjati Sevak Sangh, New Delhi.
12. Hollister, J.N. (1979): *The Shias of India*, Reprint, Munshiram Manoharlal, Delhi, p.333.
13. Hutton, J.H. (1931): *Census Of India*, Vol 1. Govt of India Press, Part III, Ethnographic Notes, Simla, India.
14. Russell and Hira Lal (1916): *The Tribes and Castes of the Central Provinces of India*, McMillan, London, Reprinted, 1997, Delhi.
15. Sally, Armstrong (2001): Dying of Shame, *Reader's Digest*, Aug, 2001, p.123.
16. Sherring, M.A. (1872): *Hindu Tribes and Castes as represented in Benaras.*
17. Tiwari, S.K. (1991): *Encyclopaedia of Indian Tribals*, New Delhi.

XVI

TRIBAL COMMUNITIES OF MODERN INDIA

India's tribal population has grown from 54 million in 1981 to 67.7 million in 1991. The distribution of tribal population is uneven not only in the country as a whole but on the state level also. The seven eastern states are predominantly tribal. Then there are states where the tribal population is either negligible or absent, such as Delhi, Haryana and the Punjab. Most of the tribals live in small villages usually situated in forests. Out of the total Scheduled Tribe population of India in 1991 which was 67,757,380, 62,751,026 was rural and the remaining 5,006,354 was urban. In terms of percentages, the rural was 92.16 while the urban was only 7.39 of the total Scheduled tribe population.

There is, however, little decadal variation in the percentage of tribal population in the whole population of the country.

Out of the total population of India, the Scheduled Tribes constituted 7.95 per cent in 1991 compared to 7.83 per cent as per 1981 Census.

TRIBAL POPULATION OF INDIA

A perusal of the various Census Reports of India since 1891, reveals that the Indian tribal population has been described variously from census to census. The tribals have been enumerated under different names and heads in different Census Reports, such as people having a tribal form or religion (1891), animists (1901), tribal animists or tribal (1911), hill and forest tribes (1921), primitive tribes (1931), tribe (1941) and Scheduled Tribes (1951, 1961, 1971, 1981 and 1991).

In 1891, the tribal population was estimated by Baine to be nearly 1.60 crore. Of these, about 93 lakh were re-termed under their tribal form of religion. Sir Marten, in his Census Report of 1921 estimated the total number of those tribals who had been considered inhabitants of the hills and jungle including such tribes as Gonds, the Santhals and the Oraons, to be roughly over 1.6 crore. Of these, 97.5 lakh were listed as followers of tribal religion. Hutton, finding Marten's estimate defective, made a fresh enumeration in 1931. He put the number of people (primitive tribes) of India and Burma at a little over 2.46 crore. In 1941, the computation of their number gave the figure of 2,47,12,000.

TABLE-16.1

Population through Years—General as well as Tribal with their Percentage Increase

Census Years	*Total Population (crore)*	*% of Increase*	*Scheduled Tribes Population (crore)*	*% of Increase*	*Scheduled Tribes % of Totala Population*
1951	36.12	-	2.25*	-	6.25
1961	43.91	21.58	2.99	32:73	6.87
1971	54.79	24.80	3.80	27.23	6.94
1981	68.52	25.06	5.38**	41.58	7.85
1991***	83.86	23.79	6.78	25.67	8.08

* Considered the Modification Order, 1956

** Includes projected estimates of Assam.

*** Excludes Jammu & Kashmir.

Table 16.1 shows that the percentage increase of tribal population has been much faster (41.58%) than that of the general population (25.06%) during the decade 1971-81. The same trend may be seen in the previous Census decades of 1951-61 and 1961-71 also. The rate of increase of tribal population in these decades also was much more (32.73%) and (27.23%) respectively than that in respect of the general population of India, which increased at the rate of 21.58% rate of 21.58% and 24.80%. 'The population (as is evident form

TABLE-16.2

Statewise Growth of Tribal Population in India, 1951-71

Sl. No.	*State/U.T.*	*1951*	*1961*	*%age of Growth 1951-61*	*1971*	*% age of Growth 1961-71*
1.	Andhra Pradesh	1149919	1324368	15.17	1657657	25.17
2.	Assam	1554801	2065816	32.80	1606648	-22.19
3.	Bihar	3880097	4204784	8.37	4932767	17.31
4.	Gujarat	2092556	2754446	31.63	3734422	35.58
5.	Himachal Pradesh	27925	108194	287.40	141610	30.89
6.	Karnataka	80402	192096	138.92	231268	20.39
7.	Kerala	132767	212762	57.89	269346	26.60
8.	Madhya Pradesh	4844128	6678410	37.87	8387403	25.59
9.	Maha-rashtra	1650852	2397169	45.21	2954249	23.27
10.	Manipur	194239	249049	28.22	334466	34.30
11.	Meghalaya	NA	NA	-	814230	-
12.	Nagaland	2633	343697	66.33	457602	33.14
13.	Orissa	3009580	4223757	40.34	5071937	20.08
14.	Rajasthan	1774278	2351470	30.16	3125506	32.92
15.	Sikkim	NA	NA	-	52056	-
16.	Tamil-Nadu	136376	251991	84.78	311515	23.62
17.	Tripura	192293	360070	87.25	450544	25.13
18.	Uttar Pradesh	NA	NA	-	198565	-
19.	West-Bengal	1566868	2054081	31.00	2532969	23.31
20.	Andaman & Nicobar	NA	14122	-	18102	-
21.	Arunachal Pradesh	NA	NA	-	369408	-

Sl. No.	State/U.T.	1951	1961	%age of Growth 1951-61	1971	% age of Growth 1961-71
22.	Dadar & Nagar Haveli	NA	41269	-	64445	25.70
23.	Goa, Daman & Diu	NA	NA	-	7654	-
24.	Laksha-dweep, etc.	13486	23391	73.45	29540	26.29
25.	Mizoram	NA	NA	-	313299	-
	India	2511854	30172221	32.23	38067218	26.17

Sources: (i) A Statistical Hand Book of Tribal Welfare and Development;
(ii) Tribal Sub-Plan Area.

the Table) of Scheduled Tribes after remaining static at (about) 6.9% of the total population in 1961-71 decade, rose to (about) 7.9% in the 1971-81 decade. It, however, needs to be recalled that the population of Scheduled Tribes went up on account of the removal of area restriction for scheduled communities in 1976'.

TABLE-16.3

Percentage distribution of India's Total and Scheduled Tribes Population among States/Union Territories, 1981-91.

S. No.	States/UTs	Total Population		STs Population	
		1981	1991	1981	1991
1.	Andhra Pradesh	8.12	8.15	6.15	6.47
2.	Arunachal Pradesh	0.10	0.11	0.85	0.85
3.	Bihar	10.60	10.58	11.26	10.20
4.	Goa	0.15	0.14	**	**
5.	Gujarat	5.17	5.06	9.39	9.50
6.	Himachal Pradesh	0.65	0.63	0.38	0.34

S. No.	States/UTs	Total Population 1981	Total Population 1991	STs Population 1981	STs Population 1991
7.	Karnataka	5.63	5.51	3.54	2.95
8.	Kerala	3.86	3.57	0.51	0.49
9.	Madhya Pradesh	7.91	8.11	23.22	23.73
10.	Maharashtra	9.52	9.67	11.18	11.28
11.	Manipur	0.22	0.23	0.75	0.912.
12.	Meghalaya	0.20	0.22	2.09	2.34
13.	Mizoram	0.07	0.08	0.89	1.01
14.	Nagaland	0.12	0.15	1.26	1.64
15.	Orissa	4.00	3.88	11.46	10.84
16.	Rajasthan	5.20	5.39	8.10	8.44
17.	Sikkim	0.05	0.14	0.05	0.14
18.	Tamil Nadu	7.34	6.84	1.01	0.88
19.	Tripura	0.31	0.34	1.13	1.32
20.	Uttar Pradesh	16.82	17.04	0.45	0.44
21.	West Bengal	8.28	8.34	5.95	5.87
	Union Territories				
1.	Andaman & Nicobar Island	0.03	0.03	0.04	0.04
2.	Dadra & Nagar Haveli	0.02	0.02	0.16	0.17
3.	Daman & Diu	0.01	0.01	0.02	0.02
4.	Lakshadweep	0.01	0.01	0.07	0.07
	All India Population (million)	659.30 (7.83%)	816.17	51.63	64.88 (7.95%)

* Excluding Assam and Jammu & Kashmir where Census could not be held during 1981 and 1991 respectively

** In Goa, as per 1991 Census, ST population was only 376 (90) households which is negligible as compared to population of India.

Source: *Census of India*, 1991, Series 1, Paper 2 of 1991: p.40.

As is evident from Table 16.1, during 1981-91 also the percentage increase of tribal population has been faster (25.67%) than that of general population (23.79%). In proportionate terms, it constituted 8.08% of the total population

(1991) as compared to 7.85% (1981). Thus, there has been a constant increase in tribal population in the country ever since 1951, both in absolute terms as well as their percentage share in the entire population of India.

It is worth noting that the tribal population in India is not evenly distributed, whether statewise or districtwise. When we consider the geographical distribution of the tribes on a district basis, there are only five districts, viz. Ranchi, Singhbhum, Santhal Pargana, Koraput and Bastar (Census 1971) with more than a million tribals. On the basis of the Census 1971 the districts can be classified according to the tribals concentration therein. Nearly half of the total districts in the country have more than one per cent of tribal population. There are 17 districts having 70 per cent or more tribal population: Lakshadweep and Mizoram have more than 90 per cent, 13 districts 50-69 per cent, 18 districts 30-49 per cent, 46 districts 10-29 per cent.

TRIBAL COMMUNITIES OF INDIA

In 1950, the number of tribal communities, thus, scheduled was 212. This number increased in 1956 with the revised list of 1956, when the Scheduled Tribes List (Modification) Order, was issued. The Anthropological Survey of India, in 1967, estimated the number of tribal communities at being 314, considering number of tribes to be the constituents of group of tribes designated by a common name such as Gonds and Bhils, etc.

As per census 1991, in all the States/Union Territories inhabiting tribals, the aggregation of Scheduled Tribes or group of tribes notified together comes to 573.

Major tribes with the strength of more than 10 lakh each are six, viz. the Bhils, the Gonds (both are groups of tribes designated with generic names), the Santhals, the Minas, the Mundas and the Oraons. The Hos, the Khonds and the Kols follow them with a population of more than 5 lakhs. Again there are other 42 tribes, i.e. about 10 per cent of the total, which have a population of between 1 and 5 lakhs. These are: the Adis, the Baigas, the Bathudis, the Bhottadas, the Bhuiyas, the Bhumias, the Bhumijs, the Boro-Kacharis, the Chandhris,

TABLE-16.4

Number of Scheduled Tribes or Groups of Tribes notified together among States and Union Territories 1991.

S.No.	*India/States/Union Territories*	*No. of Scheduled Tribes*
	India States	**573**
1.	Andhra Pradesh	33
2.	Arunachal Pradesh	12
3.	Assam	14
4.	Bihar	30
5.	Goa	5
6.	Gujarat	29
7.	Himachal Pradesh	8
8.	Jammu & Kashmir	8
9.	Karnataka	49
10.	Kerala	35
11.	Madhya Pradesh	46
12.	Maharashtra	47
13.	Manipur	29
14.	Meghalaya	17
15.	Mizoram	17
16.	Nagaland	5
17.	Orissa	67
18.	Rajasthan	12
19.	Sikkim	2
20.	Tamil Nadu	36
21.	Tripura	19
22.	Uttar Pradesh	5
23.	West Bengal	38
	Union Territories	
1.	Andaman & Nicobar	6
2.	Dadra & Nagar Haveli	7
3.	Daman & Diu	5
4.	Lakshadweep	*

* Inhabitants of Lakshadweep who, and both of whose parents were born in this territory, have been treated as Scheduled Tribes.

Source: *Census of India* 1991. Series 1, Paper 2 of 1992, p. 38

the Dhankas, the Dhondias, the Dublas, the Gamits, the Garos, the Halbas, the Kacharis, the Kathodis, the Kawars, the Kharias, the Kharwars, the Khasis, the Kisans, the Coknas, the Kolhas, the Koli Mahadeos, the Konds Dhoras, the Korkus, the Koyas, the Lodhas, the Malayalis, the Mikis, the Mizos, the Nakdas, the Porjas, the Rabhas, the Rathwas, the Saoras, the Thakurs, the Tripuris, the Warlis, the Yenadis and the Yerukulas.

Among the Scheduled Tribes, numerically the most important are the Gonds of Madhya Pradesh, Maharashtra and Andhra Pradesh, the Bhils of Rajasthan, Gujarat, Maharashtra and Madhya Pradesh and the Santhals of Bihar, Orissa, and West Bengal. The first two of these communities have the numerical strength of about 40 lakh each, the third also has numerical strength of more than 30 lakhs. The smallest tribal community is the Andamanese, with the numerical strength of only 18 (1971 Census).

There are a number of ways in which the tribals may be classified viz.: (i) by region, (ii) by language, (iii) by race, (iv) by their level of integration with rural folks to which they are connected, (v) by their economy, (vi) by their cultural pattern as a whole, and (vii) by their level of education.

To some extent we have already discussed the racial integration of the tribals. Their economy and development have been discussed in one of the later chapters. The present chapter proposes to discuss the distribution of the tribal communities of India on the basis of regions only. To achieve this objective, a brief survey of the researches conducted in each region, based on the work of Vidyarthi and Rai (1985) has been given. In fact, Vidyarthi and Rai (1976) have appreciably covered a wide range of tribal literature in their book 'Tribal Culture of India'. Works in 1980's of many other social scientists are noteworthy but even a brief survey of these works is not possible in the present context in view of limitations. However, works of K.S. Singh, like 'Tribal Situation in India' (edited, 1972), 'Tribal Movement in India', (1982) and 'Tribal Society in India' (1982) to 'The Scheduled Castes' (1999) are noteworthy for their diverse aspects of discussion.

In fact, after 1980, many aspects of tribal life have been studied with a fresh viewpoint. The tribals thought to be 'without history' before Independence, has drawn attention of the historians. The roots of Indian tribes and their relationship with the ancient Indian tribes are being traced now. In this respect, a clear change in the attitude of Indian intelligentsia is visible. Sarat Chandra Roy gave a new insight to understand the tribal culture of India. G.P. Singh (1990) extensively elaborated the culture of one of the ancient Indian tribes viz. the Kiratas in his 'The Kiratas in Ancient India'. Dr. Hiralal Shukla (1980-99) in his works has tried to establish relationship of the Gonds with known dynasties of Central India. Many such works are on anvil and the present one is also an attempt in the same direction.

Guha (1951, 1955) proposed threefold regional distribution of Indian tribes, Dube (1960) has given four geographical regions, but Rouburman (1971) puts Indian tribes in five territorial groups. Vidyarthi and Vinay Kumar Rai (1976) also divide India into five but the schemes of Roy Burman and Vidyarthi are not identical, as Roy Burman does not identify islands as an independent unit. Vidyarthi *et al.* (1976) combine Andhra Pradesh in 'South Indian Region' but Roy Burman includes it within 'Central and East India'.

TRIBAL REGIONS AND ASSOCIATED TRIBAL COMMUNITIES

Both geography of India and tribal demography permit a regional grouping and a zonal classification of the tribal people. Three tribal zones were demarcated by Guha (1951, 1955) which include (i) the northern and northeastern area in the mountain valleys and eastern frontiers of India, (ii) the central belt which occupies the older hills and plateaus along the dividing line between peninsular India and the Indo-Gangetic Plains. This zone also includes the hills and the converging lines of the western Ghats, (iii) this falls in the peninsular India, i.e. below 16^0 N latitude. Majumdar and Madan (1956: 253) also refer to these zones and present a somewhat similar distribution. They have called them northern and northeastern Zone, the Central or Middle Zone, and the southern Zone.

The northern and northeastern Zone would be approximately between 31°7′ N and 35° N at its western and 23°30′ N and 28° N on its eastern end; between 77°33′ E and 97° E, having for its outposts Simla in the West and the Lushai Hills and the Mishmi Tract in the East. The region broadens at its ends and narrows down in the middle. The areas of eastern Jammu and Kashmir, Himachal Pradesh, the Tarai of Uttar Pradesh and northeastern region fall in this tribal zone.

The Central or Middle Zone would lie approximately between latitudes 20° N and 25° N and longitudes 73° E and 90° E. It includes West Bengal, Bihar, southern Uttar Pradesh, Madhya Pradesh, Orissa, Rajasthan, Gujarat and Maharashtra. In area and a number of States it is the largest of the three tribal zones.

The third zone, i.e. the southern Zone, lies approximately between latitudes 80 N and 20° N and longitudes 75° E and 85° E. Andhra Pradesh, Karnataka, Kerala and Tamil Nadu fall within this zone. There are also tribal communities in the Nicobar and Andaman Islands which are a constituent of this zone.

Dube (1960) has given four geographical regions of the tribals, viz. the North and northeastern Zone, the Middle Zone, the South Zone and the West Zone. The first three are similar to those of Guha. The fourth has been carved out of the Middle Zone comprising Rajasthan and the area of the Sahyadri group of tribals in Gujarat and Maharashtra. Atal (1965: 13) has again given a fourfold geographical classification of the tribes, viz. North and northeastern, West and northwestern, Middle and South Zones.

The tribal communities living in different regions have been divided by Roy Burman (1971:2) into the following five territorial groups, taking into consideration their historical, ethnic and socio-cultural relations.

(a) northeast India comprising Assam, Meghalaya, Nagaland, Manipur, Arunachal Pradesh, Mizoram, and Tripura.

(b) Sub-Himalayan region of North and northwest India comprising the northern submontane districts of Uttar Pradesh and Himachal Pradesh.
(c) Central and Eastern India comprising West Bengal, Bihar, Orissa, Madhya Pradesh, and Andhra Pradesh.
(d) South India comprising Tamil Nadu, Kerala and Karnataka.
(e) western India comprising Rajasthan, Gujarat and Maharashtra.

Taking into account the above-mentioned classification as well as geographical, ecological, social, economic, administrative, ethnic and racial factors we propose a four fold distribution of geographical regions along with one district sub-region of the islands. These are:

(I) Himalayan Region

It has three sub-regions, viz. (1) northeastern Himalayan region, (2) Central Himalayan region, and (3) northwestern Himalayan region. Assam, Meghalaya, the mountainous region of West Bengal, i.e. Darjeeling, Arunachal Pradesh, Nagaland, Manipur, Mizoram, and Tripura fall in the northeastern Himalayan region whereas the Tarai areas of Uttar Pradesh and Bihar come in the Central Himalayan region. Himachal Pradesh and Jammu and Kashmir constitute the northwestern Himalayan region. More than one-third of the region's population is made of tribals which is one-eighth of the tribals in India.

(II) Middle India Region

It comprises Bihar, West Bengal, Orissa, and Madhya Pradesh with more than 2 crore of tribal people, i.e., 55 per cent of the total tribals in the country.

(III) Western India Region

It includes Rajasthan, Gujarat, Maharashtra, Goa, and Dadra and Nagar Haveli with about 1 crore tribal population.

(IV) SOUTH INDIA REGION

It comprises Andhra Pradesh, Tamil Nadu, Karnataka, and Kerala with a meagre tribal population (1.66 per cent of the region), constituting one-sixteenth of the tribals of the country.

(V) THE ISLAND REGION

The islands of Andaman and Nicobar in the Bay of Bengal and Lakshadweep in the Arabian Sea with 54.3 per cent tribal population constitute a distinct sub-region.

TABLE-16.5

Regional Distribution of Tribal Population (After Vidyarthi and Rai, 1985)

Region	*Tribal Population in States/Union Territories*	*Per cent w.r.t. Total Population of the State/Union Territory*	*Per cent w.r.t. Tribal India*
Himalayan Region			
(i) Northeastern Himalayan Region			
1. Assam	16,06,648	10.99	
2. Meghalaya	8,14,230	80.48	
3. Arunachal Pradesh	3,69,408	65.09	
4. Nagaland	4,57,602	88.61	
5. Manipur	3,34,466	31.18	
6. Mizoram	3,13,299	94.26	
7. Tripura	4,50,544	28.94	
(ii) Central Himalayan Region			
8. Uttar Pradesh	1,98,565	0.22	
(iii) Northwestern Himalayan Region			
9. Himachal Pradesh	1,41,610	4.09	
Total	46,86,372	44.87	12.33

Region	*Tribal Population in States/Union Territories*	*Per cent w.r.t. Total Population of the State/Union Territory*	*Per cent w.r.t. Tribal India*
Middle India Region			
10. Bihar	49,32,767	8.75	
11. West Bengal	25,32,969	5.72	
12. Orissa	50,71,937	23.11	
13. Madhya Pradesh	83,87,403	20.14	
Total	2,09,25,076	14.43	55.04
Western India Region			
14. Rajasthan	31,25,506	12.13	
15. Maharashtra	29,54,249	5.86	
16. Gujarat	37,34,422	13.98	
17. Goa	7,654	0.89	
18. Dadra & Nagar Haveli	64,445	86.89	
Total	98,86,276	26.91	26.01
South India Region			
19. Karnataka	2,31,268	0.79	
20. Andhra Pradesh	16,57,657	3.81	
21. Tamil Nadu	3,11,515	0.76	
22. Kerala	2,69,356	1.26	
Total	24,69,796	1.66	6.49
Island Region			
23. Andaman & Nicobar	18,102	15.72	
24. Lakshadweep	29,540	92.90	
Total	47,642	54.31	0.13
All India Grand Total	3,80,15,162		100.00

The remaining States of Jammur & Kashmir, Punjab, Haryana and the Union Territories of Chandigarh, Delhi and Pondicherry did not show any Scheduled Tribe.

We may discuss the tribal communities of each of these regions in somewhat greater details as follows:

Western India Region

In western India, the early British administrators took up the study of some of the major tribes, like the Bhils. The Census organisation, however, continued its usual operations to record some details about the tribal communities of this region. In absence of any full-fledged Department of Anthropology in any of the universities, the task of tribal studies fell on the sociologists, who by and large were interested in the non-tribal societies. Some of the societies like the Anthropological Society, established by P.G. Shah, and the Indian Branch of the Anthropos Institute also shared the responsibility with a few Departments of Sociology of some universities like Bombay, Baroda and Udaipur. After Independence, however, Tribal Research Institutes have been started in Maharashtra at Poona, in Gujarat at Ahmedabad and in Rajasthan at Udaipur. Of late, these Institutes have brought out a few publications in the shape of a monographs and books about the tribes of the respective States. The Human Factor Study Division of the Central Arid Zone Research Institute with a small team of researchers has conducted researches in the tribal and non-tribal desert villages, and have, to their credit, several publications.

Rajasthan

From the point of view of tribal studies, we do not find the early British administrators directly interested in western India including Rajasthan. The early interests date back to 1867, with the appearance of John Shortt's (1867-69) paper on the habits and manners of the "Marvar tribe" of India. The other works worth mentioning are by Hendly (1875) on the Mewar Bhils, Baden-Powell (1899) on Lunar and Solar Aryan tribes and Barnes (1907) on the Bhils of Western India.

Along with these foreign scholars, mention may be made of Kavi Raj Shyamal Das (1886) who wrote a paper on the Mina tribe of Jaipur in Mewar and Sarat Chandra Roy (1924) who wrote a long paper on the customs of the Black Bhils of the Jaisamand hills in Rajputana. In addition to these papers, L.P. Tessitori (1914, 1916, 1917, 1919, 1920) wrote a series of papers in the *Journal Asiatic Society of Bengal* during 1924-26 on the bardic and historic communities of Rajputana.

The Rajputana Gazetteers prepared during 1879-80, as well as various Census Reports from 1901 to the present time, also contain rich material on the land and people of Rajputana. Among such generalized Reports, special mention may be made of the *Annals and Antiquities of Rajasthan* written in two volumes by James Tod (1920, 1950).

The works on the Bhils of different areas in Rajasthan by William F. Pledger (1944) and G.M. Carstairs (1952, 1953-54, 1957) who was born and brought up in Rajasthan in a family of Missionaries are commendable.

The Tribal Research Institute, Udaipur, also published a monograph on the Bhils of Rajasthan in Hindi in 1965. Braj Raj Chauhan (1966) has developed the concept of 'tribalization' while studying the Bhils and the Minas. N.N. Vyas (1969) has observed that the Bhils of the international border of the country with Pakistan have social relations with their counterparts across the border and are also dependent on the Muslims and Rajputs of the area. Keeping the geographical view in mind, he lays emphasis on improving their lot.

P.C. Dave (1960) has written a monograph on the Grasias.

Scheduled Tribes of Rajasthan

Rajasthan has the following Scheduled Tribes:

1. Bhils, Bhils Garasia, Dholi Bhil, Dungri Bhil, Dungi Garasia, Mewasi Bhil, Rawal Bhil, Tadvi Bhil, Bhagalia, Bhilala, Pawra, Vasava, Vasave.
2. Bhils Mina
3. Damor, Damaria
4. Dhanka, Tadvi, Tetaria, Valvi

5. Garasia (excluding Rajput Garasia)
6. Kathodi, Katkari, Dhor Kathodi, Dhor Katkari, Son, Kathodi, Son Katkari
7. Kokna, Kokni, Kukna
8. Koli Dhor, Tokre Koli, Kolcha, Kolgha
9. Mina
10. Naikda, Nayaka, Cholivala Nayaka, Kapadia Nayaka, Mota Nayaka, Nana Nayaka
11. Patelia
12. Seharia, Sehria, Sahariya

The nomadic Godulia Lohars of Rajasthan, who have their mobile house-cum-workshop in a bullock-cart, have been studied by Satyapal Ruhelia (1967).

Another nomadic tribe the Banjaras has been studied by N.N. Vyas (1967.

Another nomadic tribe of Rajasthan and neighbouring areas is Kathodis which is also called Katkaris, meaning a wood-cutter or a person engaged in occupations like bamboo-cutting, felling of trees, etc. Several speculations have been made regarding the origin of the Kathodis. Fuchs calls them a sub-section of the Bhils (Fuch, S., 1957), Haddon and Keny call them Dravidian while J.V. Ferriera (1962) thinks the tribe has a considerable intermixture of several ancient tribes. The Tribal Research Institute of Rajasthan made a study of the Kathodis of Rajasthan in 1967 with the help of a number of investigators.

Thus, it may be seen that there are a few monographs on Rajasthan tribes. At the same time, the historical-political and geographical nature of the research is important as the State is situated on the international border.

Gujarat

Scheduled Tribes of Gujarat

Gujarat has the following Scheduled Tribes:

1. Baroda
2. Bavacha, Bamcha
3. Bharwad (in the forests of Alech, Barada and Gir)

4. Bhil, Bhil Garasia, Dholi Bhil, Dungri Bhil, Dungri Garasia, Mewasi Bhil, Rawal Bhil, Tadvi Bhil, Bhagalia, Bhilala, Pawra, Vasava, Vasave
5. Charan (in the forests of Alech, Barada and Gir)
6. Chaudhri (in Surat and Valsad districts)
7. Chodhara
8. Dhanka, Tadvi, Tetaria Valvi
9. Dhodia
10. Dubla, Talavia, Halpati
11. Gamitm Gamta, Gavit, Mavchi, Padvi
12. Gond, Rajgond
13. Kathodi, Katkari, Dhor Kathodi, Dhor Katkari, Son Kathodi, Son Katkari
14. Kokna, Kokni, Kukna
15. Koli (in Kutch district)
16. Koli Dhor, Tokre Koli, Kolcha, Kolgha
17. Kunbi (in the Dangas district)
18. Naikda, Nayaka, Cholivala Nayaka, Kapadia Nayaka, Mota Gayaka, Nana Nayaka.
19. Padhar
20. Paradhi (in Kutch district)
21. Pardhi, Advichincher, Phanse Pardhi (excluding Amreli, Bhavnagar, Jamnagar, Junagadh, Kutch, Rajkot and Surendranagar districts)
22. Patelia
23. Pomla
24. Rabari (in the forests of Alech, Barada and Gir)
25. Rathawa
26. Siddi (in Amreli, Bhavnagar, Jamnagar, Junagadh, Rajkot and Surendranagar districts)
27. Vaghri (in Kutch district)
28. Varli
29. Vitola Kotwalia, Barodia

The Tribal Research Institute of Gujarat located in the Gujarat Vidyapith, Ahmedabad, and founded by Mahatma Gandhi has also undertaken field researches on the tribes of Gujarat and is deeply engaged in the study of revitalization movement among the tribes of Gujarat.

Taken together, the research tradition in Gujarat, especially from the diagnostic point of view, has been quite strong.

Under the guidance of D.N. Majumdar who initiated him to fieldwork in 1943 (Naik, T.B. 1957) Y.V.S. Nath (1960) also made an intensive study of the Bhils in 1956, and brought out the interrelatedness of the economic, social and religious systems operating among the Bhils.

I.P. Desai actively engaged himself with his small team of researchers in the studies of the tribes of South Gujarat.

Maharashtra

Scheduled Tribes of Maharashtra

Maharashtra has the following Scheduled Tribes:

1. Andh
2. Baiga
3. Barda
4. Bavacha, Bamcha
5. Bhaina
6. Bharia Bhumia, Bhuinhar Bhumia, Pando
7. Bhattra
8. Bhil, Bhil Garasia, Dholi Bhil, Dungri Bhil, Dungi Garasia, Mewasi Bhil, Rawal Bhil, Tadvi Bhil, Bhagalia, Bhilala, Pawra, Vassava, Vasave.
9. Bhunjia
10. Binjhwar
11. Birhul, Birhor
12. Chodhara (excluding Akola, Amravati, Bhandara, Buldana, Chandrapur, Nagpurm Wardha, Yavatmal, Aurangabad, Bhir, Nanded, Osmanabad and Parbhani districts)
13. Dhanka, Tadvi, Tetaria, Valvi
14. Dhanwar
15. Dhondia
16. Dubḷa, Talavia, Halpati
17. Gamit, Gamta, Gavit, Mavchi, Padvi
18. Gond Rajgond, Arakh, Arrakh, Agarai, Asur, Badi, Maria, Bada Maria, Bhatola, Bhimma, Bhuta,

Koilabhuta, Koilabhuti, Bhar Bison-horn Maria, Chota Maria, Dandami Maria, Dhuru, Dhurwa, Dhoba, Dhulia, Dorla, Gaiki-Gatta, Gatti, Gaita, Gond, Gowari, Hill Maria, Kandra, Kalanga, Khatola, Koitar, Koya Khirwar, Khirwara, Kucha Maria, Kuchaki Maria, Madia, Maria, Mana, Mannewar, Moghya Mogia, Monghya, Mudia, Muria, Nagarchi, Naikpod, Nagawanshi, Ojha, Raj, Sonjhari Jhareka, Thatia, Thotya, Wade Maria, Vade Maria.

19. Halba, Halbi
20. Kamar
21. Kathodi, Katkari, Dhor, Kathodi, Dhori Kathkari, Son Kathodi, Son Katkari
22. Kawar, Kanwar, Kaur, Cherwa, Rathai, Tanwar, Chattri
23. Khairwar
24. Kharia
25. Kokna, Kokni, Kukna
26. Kol
27. Kolam, Mannervarlu
28. Koli, Dhoir, Tokre Koli, Kolcha, Kolgha
29. Koli Mahadev, Dongar Koli
30. Koli, Malhar
31. Kondh, Khond, Kandh
32. Korku, Bopchi, Mouasi, Nihal, Nahl, Bondhi, Bondeya
33. Koya, Bhine Koya, Rajkoya
34. Nagesia, Nagasia
35. Naikda, Nayaka, Cholivala Nayaka, Kapadia Nayaka Mota Nayaka, Nana Nayaka
36. Oraon, Dhangad
37. Pardhan, Pathari, Saroti
38. Pardhi; Advichincher, Phans Pardhi, Phanse Pardhi, Langoli Pardhi Bahelia, Bohellia, Chita Pradhi, Shikari, Takankar, Takia
39. Parja
40. Patelia
41. Polma

42. Rathawa
43. Sawar, Sawara
44. Thakur, Thakar, Ka Thakur, Ka Thakar, Ma Thakur, Ma Thakar
45. Thoti (in Aurangabad, Bhir, Nanded, Osmanbad and Parbhani districts and Rajura tehsil of Chandrapur district)
46. Varli
47. Vitolia, Kotwalia, Barodia

Dadra and Nagar Haveli

Scheduled Tribes of Dadra and Nagar Haveli

These consist of the following:

1. Dhosa
2. Dubla including Halpati
3. Kathodi
4. Kokna
5. Koli Dhor including Kolgha
6. Naikdaor Nayaka
7. Valri

Goa, Daman and Diu

Scheduled Tribes of Goa, Daman and Diu

These consist of the following:

1. Dhodia
2. Dubla (including Halpati and Talavia)
3. Naikda (including Nayaka)
4. Siddi
5. Varli

MIDDLE INDIA REGION

The tribals of Middle India have been exposed to anthropological researchers since 1774 with the establishment by Sir William Jones of the Asiatic Society of Bengal to study "Nature and Man" in India. The first set of researches was undertaken by some scholarly-oriented administrators who took pains to collect the facts, and put them in the shape of notes, handbooks, district gazetteers and learned papers. These administrators followed by missionaries, travellers, social workers and the like wrote about their customs and manner, their language and folklore, and their physical types. During the formative period of writing notes and handbooks, the contributions of scholars like Dalton (1872), Risley (1891, 1905), O Malley (1906-25, 1932, 1934), Russell and Hiralal (1916), Bainbridge (1907) and others continued for sometime. Again during the same formative period, the decennial Census of 1881, 1891, 1901, 1921 as part of an all-India scheme also provided rich data on the tribes of Middle India. The tempo of researches in tribal studies received a fillip when a Department of Anthropology was established in Calcutta University in 1921 to prepare students for advanced anthropological researches in India. With the recognition of anthropology as a section in the Indian Science Congress in 1912 and the publication of the *Journals of Bihar and Orissa Research Society* and *Man in India* from Ranchi (1921), the climate for anthropological researches became more congenial, and a new tempo was created in the whole of Middle India.

The development of tribal studies in Middle India can be systematically reviewed by taking into consideration the present territorial divisions of West Bengal, Bihar, Orissa, and Madhya Pradesh as follows.

Madhya Pradesh

It was only in 1916 that a handbook on the Tribes and Castes of the then Central Provinces was published by Russell and Hiralal. This was followed by a monograph with an appraisal of cultural changes in the Maria Gonds (Bison-horn and the Bhils) of Bastar by W.G. Griegson (1938).

Verrier Elwin started his career as an ethnographer in Madhya Pradesh and brought a turning point in the history of tribal studies in the State. He wrote a series of monographs on the Baigas (1939), the iron-smelting Agarias (1942), the Marias (1943, 1950), and the Murias (1947) and brought to light the rich heritage of the tribal culture of Madhya Pradesh. In his first book he developed the concept of "Park Land theory", which evoked controversial issues regarding the approach to tribal problems.

He also advocated the policy of planned acculturation and suggested that if a genuine protection is given and real life is restored, there will be a happy future for those tribal men who are suffering from the loss the nerve (1952). Elwin also made a very valuable contribution to the study of myths of Middle India (1947) and Tribal Art (1951).

The contribution of foreign missionary anthropologists in studying some of the tribes of Madhya Pradesh also deserves special mention. Griffiths (1946) brought out the impact of the neighbouring Hindus on the Kols. Stephen Fuchs conducted researches in a comparative style among the Gonds and the Bhumiyas of Eastern Mandla between 1945 and 1947 (Fuchs, S., 1960). The Rev. T.S. Wilkinson examined the functional significance of the Ghotul nomenclature and Matthias Hermanns (1952) wrote about the magic and religion among the Bhils.

Among Indian anthropologists, mention may be made of S.C. Dube and T.B. Naik who were initiated in the fieldwork by D.N. Majumdar to work among the tribes of Madhya Pradesh. Dube (1951) published a commendable monograph on the Kamars, Naik worked with his team from the Tribal Research Institute, Chhindwara and published his results in the shape of monograph. Among their works special mention may be made of the study of the socio-economic life of the Abujh Marias (Nailk, 1963).

A study of tribal economy and market has been made by Naik with Bouraskar (1964). Naik also edited a book on Changing Tribes (Naik, 1967). Recently he has published a monograph on the Binjhwars of Bilaspur and Raipur.

A Handbook on the Tribes of Madhya Pradesh (Dube, N.K. and Bahadur, F., 1967) as well as a book on Tribal Demography of the State (Ali, 1973) present a general picture of the tribals of the area.

The Department of Anthropology in Saugar University

(started in 1957) has also trained a number of scholars who have taken up researches in tribal areas in different capacities. The Department of Anthropology in the Bastar area was opened by Ravishankar University at Raipur in 1964. The students under the direction of T.B. Naik (former Director of the Tribal Research Institute, Chhindwara) have undertaken field researches on the problems of tribals of Raipur, Durg and Bastar districts.

Coming to non-anthropologist specialists we find D.S. Nag and R. Saksena, two economists, who have taken initiative to study tribal economics. They have studied tribal economy of the Baigas in the context of modern economic theories. R. Saksena (1964) has studied the tribal economy of the western hills is Madhya Pradesh extending from the Vindhyas to the Satpuras.

In recent years, the Department of Tribal Studies, Rani Durgawati University, Jabalpur (established in 1990) has published books on Central Indian tribes dealing with social, cultural and development aspects. Doctoral thesis on individual tribes, like Kondar, Pao, Manjhi and Son have also been submitted, and are in the process of publication. Research projects studying the historical and environmental problems related to tribes have been completed. *Encyclopaedia of Indian Tribals* (1994) was published by the Department.

In Madhya Pradesh, Bhopal-based cultural centres have published valuable works on Central Indian tribes. The Tribal Research Institute of Chhindwara has now been shifted to Bhopal. Field researches on tribal health are being conducted by RMRC (ICMR) Headquarters, situated at Jabalpur.

Tiwari (1993) has initiated researches on tribal history. 'The Raj Gonds' describes the rise and fall of Gond kingdom. 'Baigas of Central India' documents the edible plant material which Baigas use as food and medicine. In 'Riddles of Indian rock-shelter paintings', an attempt to trace the link between prehistoric and contemporary tribal cultures has been made. 'Antiquity of Indian Tribes' narrates the contribution of tribals in the mainstream Indian culture of byegone eras. Madhya Pradesh Hindi Granth Academy, Bhopal, published *Madhya*

Pradesh Ke Adivasi (1984), *Madhya Pradesh Ki Janjatiyan* 1994) and *Madhya Pradesh Ki Janjatiya Sanskriti* (1999), all written by S.K.Tiwari, to promote the knowledge about tribal cultures in the Hindi heartland of the country.

TABLE-16.6

Scheduled Tribes of Madhya Pradesh

S.No.	*Name of the Tribe*	*Population Figures* (1981)
1.	Agaria	55,757
2.	Andh	153
3.	Baiga	2,48,948
4.	Bhaina	39,135
5.	Bharia, Bhumia or Bhuinhar-Bhumia including Pando, Bhumia, including Bhumia and Paliha	1,95,480
6.	Bhatra	1,17,297
7.	Bhil, Bhil Mina, Bhilala, Bhil and Bhilala including Barela, Patelia and other subtribes	25,00,530
8.	Bhil Mina	5,358
9.	Bhunjia	9,524
10.	Biar, Biyar	7,369
11.	Binjhwar	92,080
12.	Dhanwar	34,386
13.	Gadaba, Gadba	3,255
14.	Gond, Gond including Arakh, Agaria, Asur, Badi Maria or Bada Muria, Bhatola, Bhumia, Bhuta, Koilabhuta or Kailabhuti, Bhar, Bisonhorn Muria, Chota Muria, Dandami Maria, Ahuruar Dhurwa, Dhurwa, Dhulia, Dorla, Gaiki, Gatta or Gatti, Gaita, Gond Gowari, Hill Maria, Kandra, Kalonga, Khatola, Koitwar, Koya, Khirwar or Khirwara, Kutcha Maria, Kachaki Maria, Madia (Mana)	53,49,883

S.No.	*Name of the Tribe*	*Population Figures* (1981)
	mana, Murnewar, Moghya, or Manghya, Mudia, Nagwanshi, Ojha, Raj Songhari, Jarekha, Thaita or Thotya wade Muria or Vade Maria, Gond or Darai, Gond including Pathari.	
15.	Halbà Halbi	2,36,376
16.	Kamar	17,516
17.	Korku	470
18.	Kawar, Kanwar, Kaurcherwa Rathia Thanwar or Chottria	5,62,199
19.	Keer	9,893
20.	Khairwar, Khairwar including Kondur	14,37521
21.	Kharia	6,892
22.	Kol Kol (Dahait)	1,23,810
23.	Kalan	299
24.	Kondha or Kandh	1,670
25.	Korku, Korku including Bopchi, Mouridi Nihil or Hanur	66,781
26.	Korwa including Kodaku	15,341
27.	Manjhi	11.074
28.	Manjhwar	6,509
29.	Mawasi	11,011
30.	Mina	382
31.	Mogia	
32.	Munda	1,579
33.	Nagesia or Nagasia	14,473
34.	Oraon including Dhurwa and Dhangad	88,817
35.	Panika	52,980
36.	Pao	7,222
37.	Pardhan, Pathari and Saroti	18,234
38.	Pardhi, Pardhi including Bahelia or Bahellia Chita Pardhi, Largali Pardhi, Phano Pardhi Sekari, Takam and Takia	1,830
39.	Bahatra	8,065
40.	Parja	1,400

S.No.	Name of the Tribe	Population Figures (1981)
41.	Sahariya, Sasia or Sor, Sahariya Seharia or Sahariya	2,61,816
42.	Sanota or Saunta	3,173
43.	Saur	68,034
44.	Sawar or Sawara	63,774
45.	Sonr	48,658
46.	Karku (Correct name is Korku)	-

The tribal situation in Madhya Pradesh has much in common with the tribal situation in Bihar. The scope of tribal researches in Madhya Pradesh is therefore at par with that in tribal Bihar, and it is not necessary to repeat the investigations here excepting some references to certain specific projects like full-length studies on the tribes selected on a typological basis.

Bihar

Earlier Reports on Tribes and Castes in Bihar had been prepared by the British administrations like Dalton (1872), Risley (1891, 1905), O'malley (1906-25), F.B. Bradley-Birt (1903) and Bainbridge (1907). The history of tribal studies in Bihar was given a turning point by the zealous interest in the subject by the late Rai Bahadur S.C. Roy who undertook detailed monographic studies of some of the tribes of Chotanagpur. His first monograph entitled *The Mundas and their Country*, published in 1912, marked the beginning of a full-length study of a tribe in Chotanagpur by an Indian national. This book was followed by a series of four monographs on the Oraon (1915), the Birhor (1925), Oraon Religion and Customs (1928), and the Kharia (1937 with R.C. Roy) of Chotangapur. These works of Roy have been acknowledged in international field as component studies, and Hutton honoured by calling him the "Father of Indian Ethnology" in 1938.

In these monographs, Roy presented an exhaustive picture of the life, cultural changes and history of the respective tribes. Roy also attempted to examine the antiquity of the tribes in terms of certain archaeological and literary evidences, and modern Asuras were taken up as a case (Roy, S.C., 1915, 1916, 1920).

The tribal studies in Bihar received further encouragement with the establishment of the Department of Anthropology in Calcutta University in 1921. Several anthropologists like T.C. Das (1931, 1932), S.S. Sarkar (1938), G.S. Roy and their students made frequent visits to the tribal areas of Bihar and published a series of papers and books.

As early as 1924, D.N. Majumdar was initiated by S.C. Roy to undertake field researches among the Hos. Majumdar initially spent about three years among the Hos of Kolhan and published his first book on the Ho tribe in 1937, and made a review after 12 years (in 1947-49) in the light of the latest impacts of mines, factories and of war.

The Tribal Welfare Research Institute has undertaken some welfare oriented research projects, and in addition to several bulletins it has published a few books like the *Land and People of Tribal Bihar* edited by N. Prasad (1964), *Life and Times of Birsa Bhagwan* highlighting the tribal rebellions (Sinha, S.P. 1964), and a Report on Land Alienation (Sinha S.P., 1968), etc.

A few administrators and Census Superintendents have also brought out some publications, e.g. *The Study of the Asuras* by K.K. Leuva (1963), *Dust-storm and Hanging Mist: A Study of Birasa Munda and His Movement* by Suresh Singh (1966), and four village monographs by Census Superintendent S.D. Prasad (1961, 1963) and his associates.

To conclude, tribal Bihar ranks as one of the most extensively studied areas in India from the point of view of basic ethnography.

Scheduled Tribes of Bihar

The Scheduled Tribes of Bihar may be enumerated as follows:

1. Asur
2. Baiga
3. Bajnara

4. Bathudi
5. Bedia
6. Bhumji (in North Chotangapur and South Chotanagpur division and Santal Parganas districts)
7. Binjhia
8. Birhor
9. Birjia
10. Chero
11. Chik Baraik
12. Gond
13. Goarit
14. Ho
15. Karmali
16. Kharia
17. Kharwar
18. Khond
19. Kisan
20. Kora
21. Korwa
22. Lohara, Lohra
23. Mahli
24. Mal Paharia
25. Munda
26. Oraon
27. Parhaiya
28. Santal
29. Sauria Pahar
30. Savar

Orissa

During the formative period, tribal studies in Orissa started as part of an all-India project and the first two authoritative works were done by Dalton (1872) and Hunder (1872-73). Some British administrators like Samurl (1956), Frye (Frye, J.P.: 1860) and May (May, J.A.: 1873) wrote first-hand ethnographic notes on the Juangs, the Khonds, the Bondos of different parts of Orissa. The first full-length monograph on a tribe of Orissa was published by S. C.Roy on the Hill

Bhuiya (1935). Roy also encouraged Bose (1928, 1929), Mukherjee (1939) to study the Juangs and the Santhals.

The Orissan ethnography witnessed a turning point when Verrier Elwin, in the course of ten years, published papers and books on the Juangs (1948), Bondos (1950), and the Savaras (1955). These present a vivid and intimate picture of the style of life of the respective tribes. His study of the Savaras especially deals with the religious aspects of a primitive tribe which leads him to develop the concept of spiritism. He also collected their myths and legends which were rightly observed by him as "tribal Puranas", as they provided charters for their behaviour patterns (1951).

Orissa also attracted a few foreign anthropologists like Herman Neiggermeyer from Germany (1964), Izskowitz from Sweden (1953) and Bailey (1955, 1955, 1958, 1960) from England who worked on the Kuttia Khonds, the Godabas and on the tribe-caste continuum process respectively.

Among the anthropologists from Orissa, mention may be made of L.K. Mahapatra of the Department of Anthropology of Utkal University (the Department was established in 1959), N. Das and S.P. Rout of the Tribal Research Bureau (established in 1955), N. Pattanayak and a few others. Mahapatra did field researches in a Bhuiya village as early as 1954. He also studied the shifting cultivation and social changes among the Pauri Bhuiyas (1956) and the little-known tribe of Charengas. Rout (1966-69) has depicted the Juang and Pauri Bhuiya life whereas Das (1967-68) has studied the interaction of the Saoras and the Paros. They are also working on problem-oriented researches on Orissan tribes.

C.P. K. Mahapatra (1970) has tried to give a monographic account of the Koyas and Samantarary (1971) describes the Kondhs.

Scheduled Tribes of Orissa

The following is the list of the Scheduled Tribes of Orissa:

1. Bagata
2. Baiga
3. Banjara, Banjari

4. Bathudi
5. Bhottada, Dhotada
6. Dhotoda
7. Bhuiya, Bhuyan
8. Bhumji
9. Bhunjia
10. Binjhal
11. Binjhia, Binjhoa
12. Birhor
13. Bondo Poraja
14. Chenchu
15. Dal
16. Desua Bhumji
17. Dharua
18. Didayi
19. Gadaba
20. Gandia
21. Ghara
22. Gond, Gondo
23. Ho
24. Holva
25. Jatapu
26. Juang
27. Kandha Gauda
28. Kawar
29. Kharia, Kharian
30. Kharwar
31. Khond, Kond, Kandha, Nanguli Kandha, Sitha Kandha
32. Kisan
33. Kol
34. Kolah Loharas, Kol Loharas
35. Kolha
36. Koli, Malhar
37. Kondadora
38. Kora
39. Korua
40. Kotia

41. Koya
42. Kulis
43. Lodha
44. Madia
45. Mahali
46. Mankidi
47. Mankirdia
48. Matya
49. Mirdhas
50. Munda, Mudda Lohara, Munda Mahalis
51. Mundari
52. Omanatya
53. Oraon
54. Parenga
55. Paroja
56. Pentia
57. Rajuar
58. Santal
59. Saora, Savar, Saura, Sahara
60. Shabar, Lodha
61. Sounti
62. Tharua

West Bengal

Calcutta (West Bengal) has been the primary centre of anthropological research from the very inception of such researches in the country. The early phases of anthropological researches were conducted in the Asiatic Society of Bengal located in Calcutta. In course of time, the Indian Science Congress Association, the Department of Anthropology, Calcutta University, and after India's Independence, the Anthropological Survey of India continued to play their respective roles as the foci of transmission for anthropological researches in various parts of India

In addition to the studies of tribes undertaken by the British administrators and missionaries during the formative period of Indian anthropology, the first ethnographic work of a monographic nature was published by M.N. Basu in 1935.

T.C. Das (1943) studied the modern trends of primitive culture on the borders of Bengal, Culshaw (1947), Dutta-Majumdar (1956), B. Mukherjee (1960) studied the Santhals of West Bengal and presented monographic materials on community in terms of total study, change and interdependence with the Hindus.

The Bhumji-Hindu interactions have been the subject-matter of a detailed study of Surajit Sinha (1957, 1957, 1958, 1959, 1961, 1962, 1965) who examines the tribal-caste interactions in the series of his papers, and proposes several useful concepts like "tribal-caste" and "tribal-peasant continuum", Bhumji-Kshatria as well as tribal-Rajput continuum.

Scheduled Tribes of West Bengal

The Scheduled Tribes of West Bengal may be listed as follows:

1. Asur
2. Baiga
3. Bedia, Bediya
4. Bhumji
5. Bhutia, Sherpa, Toto, Dukpa, Kagatay, Tibertan, Yolmo
6. Birhor
7. Bijjia
8. Chakma
9. Chero
10. Chik Baraik
11. Garo
12. Gond
13. Gorait
14. Hajang
15. Ho
16. Karmali
17. Kharwar
18. Khond
19. Kisan
20. Kora
21. Korwa

22. Lepcha
23. Lodha, Kheria, Kharia
24. Lohara, Lohra
25. Magh
26. Mahali
27. Mahli
28. Mal Pahariya
29. Mech
30. Mru
31. Munda
32. Nagesia
33. Oraon
34. Parhaiya
35. Rabha
36. Santal
37. Sauria Paharia
38. Savar

Recent researches among the Mahalis of Midnapur district (Sengupta, S.K. 1969) and of the Bauris also confirm the patterns of tribal-caste interactions in West Bengal (Shasmal, K.C. 1967).

Action-oriented research in Bengal by a few scholars of the University Department of Anthropology as well as of the Cultural Research Institute are also worth mentioning. P.K. Bhowmick (1963) undertook an extensive field survey of 21 Lodha villages in Midnapur district.

The Cultural Research Institute, in addition to preparing a series of monographs on the tribes of Bengal, has completed problem-oriented researches on the tribal workers in the tea gardens, factories and collieries with the active participation of A.K. Das and his associates (1962, 1962, 1963, 1964, 1964, 1966, 1968 and 1969).

HIMALAYAN REGION

The review of Himalayan anthropology can be undertaken under three geographical regions: (i) northwestern Himalayan region, (ii) central Himalayan region, and (iii) northeastern Himalayan region.

I & II) Northwestern and Central Himalayan region

During the formative period, the ethnographic work in the northwestern Himalayan area was undertaken by a few travellers and the Census officers. It was in 1871 only when Harcourt travelled extensively and wrote an eye-witness account of the land and people of the Himalayan districts of "Koolo", "Lahaul" and "Spiti" (Harcourt, A.F.P., 1871). Mention about Koolo, Lahaul and Spiti appeared in 1883-84 in the Gazetteer on Kangra district (Gazetteer, 1883-84). There is also a special volume of the Gazetteer published in 1918 which includes details about Koolo and Saraj, Lahaul and Spiti (Gazetteer, 1918).

The early efforts of the Census operations to record some sketches and ethnographic accounts about the tribes and castes of this region are embodied in the Census volume on Kashmir edited by Gulam Ahmed Khan (Census Report, 1901 and 1902) and H.A. Roses (1914), Glossary of Tribes and Castes of the then Punjab and northwest Frontier Provinces (1914) and above all in D. Ibbetson's three volumes on the Tribes and Castes of the Punjab (1916, 1919).

After a long gap, village study in this area was undertaken by the Census Operation 1961 when a few villages in Jammu and Kashmir and Himachal Pradesh were selected under the Village Survey Monograph Scheme.

Uttar Pradesh

The Scheduled Tribes of Uttar Pradesh

These are as follows:

1. Bhotia
2. Buksa
3. Jaunsari
4. Raji
5. Tharu

Himachal Pradesh

The Scheduled Tribes of Himachal Pradesh

These are the following:

1. Bhot, Bodh
2. Gaddi (excluding the territories specified sunder sub-section 91 of Section 5 of the Punjab Reorganisation Act, 1966 [31 of 1966], other than the Lahaul and Spiti districts).
3. Gujjar (excluding the territories specified in sub-section [1] of section 5 of the Punjab Reorganisation Act, 1966 [31 of 1966])
4. Jad, Lamba, Khampa
5. Kanaura, Kinnara
6. Lahaula
7. Pangwala
8. Swangla.

Sikkim

The Scheduled Tribes of Sikkim

These include the following:

1. Bhutia (including Chumbipa, Dopthapa, Dupka, Kagatey, Sherpa, Tibetan, Tromopa, Yolmo).
2. Lepcha.

III) NORTHEASTERN HIMALAYAN REGION

Northeast India is mosaic of seven sisters and these are the States of Assam, Meghalaya, Nagaland, Manipur and Tripura and the old Union Territories of Arunachal Pradesh and Mizoram. Each one of them, excepting Assam, Manipur and Tripura, has got overwhelming tribal population. Since they practically remained isolated from the mainstream of Indian events, they are not very often referred to in the historical writings of India. But Pragjyotishpur, that is modern Assam, and Manipur, have found their place in the epic of *Mahabharata*.

The Raksasa princess Hidimba and her son Ghatotkacha by the second Pandava brother Bhima are characters in the *Mahabharata*. It is believed that Hidimba was a Kachari princess, and the Kachari kings had their seat in Dimapur in present Nagaland. Thus, we can say that Nagaland has been referred to in the *Mahabharata*, though indirectly. If we accept this proposition, that is, Hidimba was a Kachari princess of Dimapur, we should say that the history of Dimapur area of Nagaland goes back to the time of the *Mahabharata* war in which fell Ghatotkacha, the son of Hidimba by Bhima. It is also believed that the Princess Ulupi whom the third Pandava brother Arjuna married and begot a son named Prabira was a princess of Zeliang area which lies in the southeast of the present Nagaland.

The northeastern region of India is full of problems and these are basically anthropological and linguistic. Almost the entire region, excepting the valleys of Brahmaputra and Barak, are inhabited by people of Mongoloid origin and they are divided in many tribes speaking different languages. These divisions and subdivisions in the character of the local population have made the problem complicated and possibly it will take sometime to solve the political problems of the region to the satisfaction of all concerned.

In view of the immense significance of the northeast Himalayan region from the point of view of tribal administration, the colonial scholars and anthropologists were greatly attracted to study the land and the people of this area. During the formative period a number of British administrators, foreign missionaries, military officers and officers of the Census operations wrote about the life and culture of the tribes of this region. Among the early scholars to write about the tribes of Assam in the form of handbooks, ethnographic glossaries and district gazetteers, mention may be made of Robinson (1841), Hodgson (1848), Butler (1855-75), Dalton (1872), Risley (1891, 1905), Cole (1912), Nevlie and Bardolai (1923), J.H. Hutton (1931) and others. In addition to publishing notes and papers on the tribes of India, the Government of the then Assam in the year 1904 took a decision to bring together all the scattered and fragmentary information in order to publish it as monographs. Under this scheme of Sir Gamplyld Puller, the then Chief Commissioner of Assam in 1902, Colonel P.R.T. Gurdon was appointed Editor of the monograph services as well as Superintendent of Ethnography in Assam.

In order to set a model, Gurdon brought out (1906, 1914) an ethnographic monograph on the Khasis.

In the present context it is not necessary to refer to all the sixteen monograph writers and authors, who wrote on the tribes of hill regions of Meghalaya, Nagaland and Manipur, written under a well-organized scheme which was executed by the Directorate of Ethnography, during the period 1906-37. However, a passing reference may be made to R. Playfair (1909), S. Engle (1911), J. Shakespeare (1912), E.A. Gait (1926) and N. E. Perry (1932) who have written classical works on individual tribes of the region.

A systematic ethnographic study of this area, however, was undertaken by Verrier Elwin and his team of anthropologists posted by administration at the headquarters of each district of Arunachal Pradesh. The monographs to appear in this series were on the Dafla (Shukla, B.K., 1959), the Tangsas (Dutta, M.P., 1959), the Idu Mismis (Barua, T.K.M., 1960), the Sherdukpens (Sharma, R.R.P., 1961), the Gallong (Srivastava, L.R.N., 1962), the Akas (Sinha, R., 1963) and an analytical monograph on Padam Miniyong (Roy, Sachin, 1960). These monographs, more or less based on the same model, examine the physical and historical settings, domestic and economic life, village pattern, household pattern and ornaments, music and dance, social life including the details of family, the life-cycle of an individual and the divisions of a tribe, political life including warfare, legal systems and customary laws, religious beliefs and practices, and lastly, general impression of the author regarding the tribe, summarized in the conclusion.

Apart from the Census organization, the Anthropological Survey of India has finalized a number of projects to study the current problems of the northeastern Himalayan region. Their major projects contemplate, (1) the study of the tribal solidarity movement in Assam and Meghalaya especially among the Khasis and the Garos, (2) understanding Arunachal as a cultural area, and (3) study of acculturation. Taken together, the Anthropological Survey of India aims at making an intensive study of the tribes of the Arunachal region from different angles. The Survey has also undertaken the study of the urbanization process in the Khasi hills and total study of the Mizos.

Areawise lists of the Scheduled Tribes of northeastern Himalayan region are as follows:

Assam

In the Autonomous Districts

1. Chakma
2. Dimasa, Kachari
3. Garo
4. Hajong
5. Hmar
6. Khasi, Jaintia, Synteng, Pnar, War, Bhoi, Lyngngam
7. Any Kuki Tribe, including:
   - i) Biate, Biete
   - ii) Changsan
   - iii) Chongloi
   - iv) Doungel
   - v) Gamalhou
   - vi) Gangte
   - vii) Guite
   - viii) Hanneng
   - ix) Hao Kip, Hanpit
   - x) Haolia
   - xi) Hengna
   - xii) Hongsungh
   - xiii) Hrangkhwal, Raogkhol
   - xiv) Jongbe
   - xv) Khawchung
   - xvi) Khawathlang, Khothalong
   - xvii) Khelma
   - xviii) Kholhou
   - xix) Kipgen
   - xx) Kuki
   - xxi) Lengthang
   - xxii) Lhangum

xxiii) Lhouhem
xxiv) Lhouvun
xxv) Lupheng
xxvi) Mangjel
xxvii) Misao
xxviii) Riang
xxix) Sairthem
xxx) Selnam
xxxi) Singosn
xxxii) Sitlhou
xxxiii) Sukto
xxxiv) Thado
xxxv) Thangngeu
xxxvi) Uibuh
xxxvii) Vaiphei

8. Lakher
9. Man (Tai speaking)
10. Any Mizo (Lusnai) tribe
11. Mikir
12. Any Naga tribe
13. Pawi
14. Syntheng

In the State of Assam excluding the Autonomous Districts:

1. Barmans in Cachar
2. Baro, Borokachari
3. Deori
4. Hojai
5. Kachari, Sonwal
6. Lalung
7. Mech
8. Miri
9. Rabha

In the midst of warm, rain, drenched forests of Tripura-Manipur, Nagaland, Mizo district and NEFA, there live a number of tribal communities who depend principally upon a rather simple form of cultivation.

Manipur

1. Aimol
2. Anal
3. Angami
4. Chiru
5. Chote
6. Gangte
7. Hmar
8. Kabui
9. Kacha Naga
10. Koirao
11. Koireng
12. Kom
13. Lamgand
14. Mao
15. Maram
16. Maring
17. Many Mizo (Lushai) tribes
18. Monsang
19. Moyon
20. Paite
21. Purum
22. Ralte
23. Sema
24. Simte
25. Suhte
26. Tangkhul
27. Thadou
28. Vaiphui
29. Zou

In 1931, T.C. Das with his students visited four Purum villages in Manipur hills and published his excellent monograph on the Purums in 1945 and presented an integrated and complete picture of theirs, covering the physical, linguistic, demographic and ethnographic dimensions of anthropological enquiry (Das, T.C., 1945).

K.P. Chattopadhyay (1941, 1949) of Calcutta University trained under W.H.R. Rivers was attracted to the study of the

Khasi kinship, social organization and inheritance.

J.K. Bose concentrated on the study of the Garo tribe and wrote a number of papers on the Garo law of inheritance, their religious ceremonies and so on (Bose, J.K., 1934, 1935, 1934, 1935, 1938, 1941).

The Department of Anthropology started in Gauhati University in 1952 and in Dibrugarh University in 1967 gave an impetus to the scientific and analytical building up of an excellent ethnographic literature.

The interests of the Anthropological Survey of India in the study of the tribes in the northeast region are reflected in the establishment of its station in Shillong in as early as 1953. Anthropologists from the Anthropological Survey of India have done field researches in northeast India on the physical, linguistic, prehistoric and social aspects of the tribes of the region and a large number of papers have been published on different tribes like the Abors, the Nokte Nagas, the Garos, the Riangs, the Lushais, the Pnars, the Khasis, etc.

Among recent researches in the northeastern tribal area, mention may be made of Burling's work (1963) on a Garo village. It is a study of the kinship and social structure of the Garos.

Meghalaya

1. Chakma
2. Dimasa, Kachari
3. Garo
4. Hajong
5. Hmar
6. Khasi, Jaintia, Synteng, Pnar, War, Bhoi, Lyngngam
7. Many Kuki Tribes, including:
   - i) Biate, Biete
   - ii) Changsan
   - iii) Chongloi
   - iv) Doungel
   - v) Gamalhou
   - vi) Gangte
   - vii) Guite

viii) Hanneng
ix) Hao Kip, Hanpit
x) Haolia
xi) Hengna
xii) Hongsungh
xiii) Hrangkhwal, Raogkhol
xiv) Jongbe
xv) Khawchung
xvi) Khawathlang, Khothalong
xvii) Khelma
xviii) Kholhou
xix) Kipgen
xx) Kuki
xxi) Lengthang
xxii) Lhangum
xxiii) Lhouhem
xxiv) Lhouvun
xxv) Lupheng
xxvi) Mangjel
xxvii) Misao
xxviii) Riang
xxix) Sairthem
xxx) Selnam
xxxi) Singosn
xxxii) Sitlhou
xxxiii) Sukto
xxxiv) Thado
xxxv) Thangngeu
xxxvi) Uibuh
xxxvii) Vaiphei

8. Lakher
9. Man (Tai speaking)
10. Many Mizo (Lusai) tribes
11. Mikir
12. Many Naga tribes
13. Pawi
14. Syntheng

Tripura

1. Bhil
2. Bhutia
3. Chaimal
4. Chakma
5. Garoo
6. Halam
7. Jamatia
8. Khasia
9. Kuki, including the following sub-tribes:
    - i) Balte
    - ii) Belalhut
    - iii) Chhalya
    - iv) Fun
    - v) Hajango
    - vi) Jangtei
    - vii) Khareng
    - viii) Khepong
    - ix) Kuntei
    - x) Laifang
    - xi) Lentei
    - xii) Mizel
    - xiii) Namte
    - xiv) Paitu, Paite
    - xv) Rangchan
    - xvi) Rangkhole
    - xvii) Thangluya
10. Lepcha
11. Lushai
12. Mag
13. Munda, Kaur
14. Noatia
15. Orang

16. Riang
17. Santal
18. Tripura, Tripuri, Tippera
19. Uchai

Nagas comprise about 27 major tribes, living in and outside the State of Nagaland. Each tribe has its own language and some villages have their own dialect. As may happen in a hill country, due to bad communications, the Naga tribes have tended to become cut off from each other. But they do have a common culture with minor difference.

Their most common appellation has been "head-hunters", though, of course, the term is widely misused. Warlike nature, valour and love of hunting being mainly attractions, fighting with the neighbouring tribes was frequent. It was then that heads were taken. The heads collected were kept as examples of village or individual prowess. Nevertheless, there was an elaborate code of war. There were tribal tribunals, respected by all and sundry. Failure to respect them or abide by their decisions meant punishment.

The early history of mankind shows that head-hunting was practised by many primitive peoples of the world, though in different forms. In Madhya pradesh, head-hunting scenes have been painted in the rock-paintings of Pachmarhi which are datable to prehistoric times. As late as (1965), some good people surprised me by their adverse feelings against the Nagas in believing that they are a cruel, ferocious and merciless people. Such an attitude has naturally resulted in wounding the feelings of the Nagas who are in revolt now.

The Nagas, like all emerging people of the world, are highly sensitive. As a race, they are a self-respecting people—with proud stories of the valour of their forefathers handed down to them in the form of oral traditions, songs and dances. They live in a beautiful country which yields its wealth to them. Elwin (1960) also wrote a book on Nagaland to trace its emergence as an independent State.

Nagaland

1. Naga
2. Kuki
3. Kachari
4. Mikir
5. Garo

The Naga tribes are believed to have migrated from Far Eastern countries. They migrated in different waves, in groups, and later each individual group was divided into different tribes according to extent of isolation. It is difficult really to precisely assess their migration since the Nagas do not have recorded history for ages. However, their folk stories give some idea about their migration. It is said that the two tribes Yimchunger and Khumnungans migrated together as one tribe through Upper Burma. They believe that they emerged at a village Mari somewhere on Burma border. Later they migrated to village Moru from where the two tribes separated themselves to settle in the respective areas of their present settlement.

Nagaland is inhabited by sixteen recognised tribes. Of their settlement Tuensang district is having a peculiar inhabitance sincea number of tribes are settled there. These tribes, according to population, may be termed as minor tribes and they are subject to dominance of other major tribes. Hence they are considered as backward financially among the backwards. However, one of the main reasons for which these tribes fail to avail of the facilities is the topography of the region of their settlement.

The isolated and wild terrain of Arunachal Pradesh (the then NEFA) was unexplored till Haimendorf was invited as a Special Officer in the years 1944-45 to conduct an exploratory survey of the area. In course of his explorations conducted between 1944 and 1962, he made contacts with the three tribes viz. the Dafla, the Meres and the Apa Tanis and published a book (Furer-Haimendorf, C.Von., 1947, 1955, 1962).

In addition to his supervision of a number of monographs, Elwin wrote a few books based on his personal field and library work in Arunachal Pradesh (1958, 1959). The most widely read and appreciated of these is his *Philosophy for NEFA* (Elwin, V., 1960). This book summarizes the material on the life and culture of the tribes of Arunachal Pradesh and makes out a case for the people of the area to develop on the lines of their own "choice and genius". The five-fold principles for the development of the tribals outlined by the then Prime Minister Nehru in his foreword of this book, are well-known.

In course of about ten years, Elwin brought the colourful Arunachal culture into the limelight. What the scholarly oriented administrators did for Nagaland and other hill regions of Assam between 1906 and 1937, Elwin and his team did for Arunachal Pradesh in the comparatively shorter period from 1957 to 1965.

Arunachal Pradesh

All tribes of the Union Territory of Arunachal Pradesh include the following:

1. Abor
2. Aka
3. Apatani
4. Dafla
5. Galong
6. Khampti
7. Khowa
8. Mishmi
9. Momba
10. Many Naga tribes
11. Sherdukpen
12. Singpho

SOUTH INDIA REGION

The first information about South Indian tribes was brought to light in the descriptive notes on the tribes and castes published by the British administrators and Census officers stationed in different parts of South India. Some early missionaries like Samuel Mati also made periodical publications on the tribes of South India. Among the earlier administrators the name of Thurston figures prominently. He published the Ethnographic Notes on South India in 1906 and wrote, in seven volumes, *The Tribes and Castes in South India* (Thurston, E., 1906, 1909).

Thurston, a pioneer in tribal studies of South India, has provided a brief account of all the tribes and castes of that area, arranged alphabetically. The notes on some of the important tribes like the Toda, the Kota, the Badaga, the Kurumba, the Paniya, the Kadar, the Irual, the Urali, and the Muthuvan are based on his personal observations. He initiated his field researches as early as 1896, 1897 and also took help from L. Anantakrishna Iyer.

Andhra Pradesh

Though Andhra Pradesh has a considerable proportion of tribal population in the South India region, the anthropological researches in this State are almost at the stage of infancy. When Hyderabad was a separate Nizam State (present Telegana area of Andhra), a few anthropologists, especially Haimendorf, were invited to study the tribal problems of Hyderabad. First of all Haimendorf described the primitive economy of the Chenchus and related it with their seasonal nomadism (Furer-Haimendorf, Von C., 1941) and then wrote on the fortunes of the primitive tribes, the Chenchu (Furer-Hainmendorf, Von C., 1942-43). His monograph on the Chenchus appeared in 1943. His next monograph (in two volumes) on the Reddis of the Bison hills, was written in collaboration with his wife Elizabeth (Furer-Haimendorf, Von C., 1945).

Haimendorf continued to do fieldwork among other tribes in Hyderabad. As a result of his and his wife's fieldwork, he presented the first full-length account of the present culture of a plain tribe, the Raj Gonds (Furer-Haimendorf, Von C., 1948). Later he wrote on the Pradhans, the bards of the Gonds (1950-51). He also encouraged several scholars to undertake researches among the tribes. Mention among them may be made of Gulam Ahmad Khan who wrote a long paper on the Chenchus (Khan, G.A., 1942) and Sayed Khwaja Mahboob Hussain who wrote a descriptive note on the Chenchus (Hussain, S.K.M., 1950, 1951).

The teaching of anthropology in Andhra University was started at Waltair in 1964 and now senior scholars and lecturers are doing comprehensive ethnographic studies on half-a-dozen tribes. R.P. Rao (1952-53) of the Tribal Research Institute of Andhra has studied the nomadic, trading and stock-breeding Lambadas. P.C. Reddy (1940) has concentrated on the study of the Yanadis.

The following is the List of Scheduled Tribes in Andhra Pradesh:

1. Andh
2. Bagata
3. Bhil
4. Chenchu, Chenchwar
5. Gadabas
6. Gond, Naikpod, Rajgond
7. Goudu, (in the Agnecy tracts)
8. Hill Reddis
9. Jatapu
10. Kammara
11. Kattunayakan
12. Kolam, Mannervarlu
13. Konda Dhoras
14. Konda Kapus
15. Kondareddis
16. Kondhs, Kodi, Kodhu, Desaya Kondhs, Dongria Kondhs, Kuttiya Kondhs, Tikiria Kondhs, Yenity Kondhs
17. Kotia, Bentho Oriya Bartika, Dhulia, Dulia, Holva, Paiko, Putiya, Sanrona, Sidhopaiko
18. Koya, Gond, Rajah, Rasha Koya, Lingadhari Koya (ordinary), Kottu Koya, Bhine Koya, Rajkoya
19. Kulia
20. Malis (excluding Adilabad, Hyderabad, Karimnagar, Khammam, Mahbubnagar, Medak, Nalgonda, Nizamabad, and Warangal districts)
21. Manna Dhora
22. Mukha Dhora, Nooka Dhora

23. Nayaks (in the Agency tracts)
24. Pardhan
25. Porja, Parangiperja
26. Reddi Dhoras
27. Rona
28. Savaras, Kapu Savaras, Maliya Savaras, Khutto Savaras
29. Sugalis, Lambadis
30. Thoti (in Adilabad, Hyderabad, Karimnagar, Khamman, Mahbubnagar, Medak, Nalgonda, Nizamabad and Warangal districts)
31. Valmiki (in the Agency tracts)
32. Yenadis
33. Yerukulas.

Karnataka

The study of tribal cultures in Karnataka is at the stage of infancy. The ethnographic study of the Karnataka tribes has been prepared in four volumes by L.K. Anantakrishna Iyer entitled "The Mysore Tribes and Castes" (1928, 1930, 1931, 1935).

In continuation of the tradition of writing handbooks, L.A. Krishna Iyer wrote another authoritative volume on the Coorg tribes and castes, published in 1948. Along with these two scholars, C.H. Rao wrote a long paper on the Mysore castes and tribes in 1922-23 and compiled the Karnataka Gazetteer in 1927.

The study of Karnataka in modern times has attracted a number of Indian and foreign scholars. At the institutional level, the teaching of social anthropology in Mysore was started in Dharwar in 1959. The South India station of the Anthropological Survey of India is situated in Karnataka. It is hoped that the Department of Anthropology of Karnataka University in collaboration with the South Indian headquarter of the Survey will draw up an integrated scheme for publication of monographs on the tribes of Mysore, in the first instance, and for studying their interactions with the non-tribal societies, later.

The Scheduled Tribes of Karnataka are as follows:

1. Adiyan
2. Barda
3. Bavacha, Bamcha
4. Bhil, Bhil Garasia, Dholi Bhil, Dungri Bhil, Dungri Garasia, Mewasi Bhil, Rawal Bhil, Tadvi Bhil, Bhagalia, Bhilla, Pawra, Vaava, Vasave.
5. Chenchu, Chenchwar
6. Chodhara
7. Dul, a Talavia, Halpati
8. Gamit, Gamta, Gavit, Mavchi, Padvi, Valvi
9. Gond, Naikpod, Rajgond
10. Gowdalu
11. Hakkipikki
12. Hasalaru
13. Irular
14. Iruliga
15. Jenu Kuruba
16. Kadu Kuruba
17. Kammara (in South Kanara district and Kollegal taluk Mysore district)
18. Kaniyan, Kanyan (in Kollegal taluk of Mysore district)
19. Kathodi, Katkari, Dhor Kathodi, Dhor Katkari, Son Kathodi, Son Katkari
20. Kattunayakan
21. Kokna, Kokni, Kukna
22. Koli Dhor, Tokre Koli, Kolcha, Kolgha
23. Konda Kapus
24. Koraga
25. Kota
26. Koya, Bhine Koya, Rajkoya
27. Kudiya, Melakudi
28. Kuruba (in Coorg district)
29. Kurumans
30. Maha Malasar
31. Malaikudi
32. Malasar
33. Malayekandi
34. Maleru

35. Maratha (in Coorg district)
36. Marati (in South Kanara district)
37. Meda
38. Naikda, Nayaka, Cholivala Nayaka, Kapadia Nayaka, Mota Nayaka, Nana Nayaka
39. Palliyan
40. Paniyan
41. Pardhi, Advichincher, Phanse Pardhi
42. Patelia
43. Rathawa
44. Sholaga
45. Soligaru
46. Toda
47. Varli
48. Vitolia, Kotwalia, Barodia
49. Yerava

Some of the most primitive tribes of the world are found in Southern India. Among the tribes considered extremely backwards in anthropological literature, the Vaddahs of Ceylon are the nearest to us, but some of the South Indian tribes such as Aranadans even now do not know the elements of the most primitive methods of agriculture; they depend for subsistence on roots, tubers and small games.

With the increasing penetration of people from the plains into the jungle areas, a good number of the Aranadans find employment as farm and forest labourers. As late as the last century, these miserable tribesmen did not know how to make a hut and were living in rock-shelters. They are less than 200 in a number and so low and despised and neglected that it is not possible to think of a more depressed little group in any part of the world. There are half-a-dozen other tribes in the same taluk who are only slightly better off than the Aranadans. The jungle provides them with food though the quest for tubers is time consuming and not easy, particularly in the rainy season. Contact with the plainsmen has increased their wants. More cloth, tobacco, tea and beedi are now in demand and the craving for rice is also on the increase.

Kerala

Kerala has the following Scheduled Tribes:

1. Adiyan
2. Aranadan
3. Eravallan
4. Hill Pulaya
5. Irular, Irulan
6. Kadar
7. Kammara [in the areas comprising the Malabar district as specified by sub-section (2) of Section 5 of the States Reorganisation Act, 1956 (37of 1956)]
8. Kanikaranh, Kanikkar
9. Kattunaytakan
10. Kochu Velan
11. Konda Kapus
12. Kondareddis
13. Koraga
14. Kota
15. Kudiya, Melakudi
16. Kurichchan
17. Kurumans
18. Kurumbas
19. Maha Malasar
20. Malai Arayan
21. Malai Pandaram
22. Malai Vedan
23. Malakkuravan
24. Malasar
25. Malayan [excluding the areas comprising the Malabar district as specified by sub-section (2) of Section 5 of the State Reorganisation Act, 1956 (36 of 1956)]
26. Malayarayar
27. Manna
28. Marati (in Hosdrug and Kasaragod taluks of Cannanore district)
29. Muthuvan, Mudugar, Muduvan
30. Palleyan
31. Palliyan

32. Palliyar
33. Paniyan
34. Ulladan
35. Uraly

Tamil Nadu

The List of Scheduled Tribes inTamil Nadu is as follows

1. Adiyan
2. Aranadan
3. Eravallan
4. Irular
5. Kadar
6. Kammara (excluding Kanyakumari district and Shenkottah taluk of Tirunelveli district)
7. Kanikaran, Kanikar (in Kanyakumari district and Shenkottan taluk of Tirunelveli district)
8. Kaniyan, Kanya
9. Kattunayakan
10. Kocu Velan
11. Konda Kapus
12. Kondareddis
13. Koraga
14. Kota (excluding Kanyakumari district and Shenkottah taluk of Tirunelveli district)
15. Kudiya, Melakudi
16. Kurichchan
17. Kurumbas (in the Nilgiri district)
18. Kurumans
19. Maha Malasar
20. Malai Arayan
21. Malai Pandaram
22. Malai Vedan
23. Malakkuravan
24. Malasar
25. Malayali (in Dharmapuri, North Arcot, Pudukottai, Salem, South Arcot and Tiruchirapalli districts)
26. Malayekandi
27. Mannan

28. Mudugar, Muduvan
29. Muthuvan
30. Palleyas
31. Palliyan
32. Palliyar
33. Paniyan
34. Sholaga
35. Toda (excluding Kanyakumari district and Shenkottah taluk of Tirunelveli district)
36. Uraly

ISLAND REGION

The tribals living in the islands of Andaman and Nicobar in the Bay of Bengal and the Lakshadweep in the Arabian Sea have not been lost sight of. The British administrators of the Andamans and anthropologists have studied these people during the last two centuries. However, the Lakshwadeep inhabitants have attracted the attention of scholars very late.

Archibald Blair (1788) was the first administrator deputed to prepare a Survey Report on the Andamans. He considered that the Andamanese were Negroes, the sons of slave Negroes brought by the Portuguese in the fifteenth century A.D. But this was not acceptable. The Andamanese, the Onges, the Jarwas, and the Sentinelese belong to the Negrito stock and this has been accepted by modern anthropologists. Among the earlier works on the Andamans, mention may be made of the Voyage Reports of Duquesne (1696), Captain Dampier (1729), W.H.Leigh (1839), and F.J.Mouate (1862). M.V. Portman (1899) presented a historical account. E.H. Man wrote a number of papers in the *Journal of the Royal Anthropological Institute of Great Britain and Ireland* during 1878-94, and gave a detailed information about the aboriginal inhabitants of Andaman and Nicobar Islands. For the first time in 1922, a social study was made of the islanders by A.R. Brown (1922).

The Census Reports of Temple (1901), Lowie (1911, 1921), and Bonnigton (1931) are also informative. Apart from giving ethnographic details, they contain several articles as Appendices by authorities like Man, Dampier Park, Whitehead,

Mart, Stevenson, etc. Temple (1901) considers the Nicobarese to be the descendants of the Indo-Chinese race but does not explain the strong Malay influence which is prominent among the Shompen. Kloss (1903) also attempted to trace the racial history and believes that the Shompens are a remnant of the Malay race.

In modern times, the islanders have been accounted for in the Census Reports of 1951 and 1961. Cipriani (1951) tells about the origin of the Andamanese. Chengapa (1951), Chatterjee (1953) and Kumar (1954), have described the Onges, and their papers have appeared in *Vanyajati.*

Lakshadweep

Original inhabitants of the Laccadive, Minicoy and Amindivi islands have now been included in the List of Scheduled Tribes.

Andaman Islands

The aboriginal population of the Islands belongs to Negrito stock. They are the purest Negrito group in the world and as such the study of the aborigines of the Andaman is very interesting. Some scholars have attributed the origin of these aborigines to slaves who had survived by coming to these islands after a shipwreck. However, this is totally untenable. There are sufficient grounds to believe that these aboriginals came down from the lower region of Burma. On arrival they moved to the different parts of the islands and have developed different social and economic traits and the ways of earning their livelihood as per their immediate environment. A broad twofold division of the aboriginal population may be made, viz.:

Aborigines of the Great Andaman Groups

These comprise all the aborigines of the Great Andamans with the exception of the Jarawas, living in the southwestern part of the islands.

Aborigines of the Little Andaman Groups

They are the Onges of the Little Andaman, the Jarawas of the South Andaman and the Sentinelese of the North Sentinel island.

As to how these two groups came into existence and what was their and their area of distribution, various theories have been put forward. Eickstedt had been of opinion that the aborigines entered the Great Andamans in two groups—the earlier group comprise the Onges, Jarawas and Sentinelese while the later group belonged to the ancestors of the Great Andaman group.

The aboriginal population of the Andamans is fast declining in a number. The causes of decay may be summed up as follows:

1. Disease
2. Murder of the aborigines by later settlers
3. Little productive capacity of the aboriginal women

The aboriginal inhabitants of the Andaman Islands depend upon themselves entirely for their livelihood. They have no trade relations with others. Individual groups are so much isolated from each other that the Onge of Little Andaman do not understand the language of the Jarawas of the Great Andaman or of the inhabitants of the North Sentinel island, all of which are situated close by. All of these groups meet their entire needs themselves with the help of local resources and exercise considerable ingenuity in maintaining themselves, although technologically they are very poorly equipped.

The Andamanes fish very little with nets. They use bows, arrows and spears for the purpose. There are coral reefs round some of the islands where the water is shallow and crystal clear. It is easy to spot fishes and turtles from their canoes in shallow water, while turtle eggs can be collected easily from the beaches. Shell-fishes of various kinds and crabs are also collected for food. But it is interesting to note that so far as the Onges are concerned, they do not shoot birds for meat, although the bird population of the Islands is small. It has been suggested that they do not do so for fear of losing their arrows in the thick vegetation which cover the island.

The food which the Andamanese eat by simple boiling is never enriched by salt. If meat cooked with salt is offered to them, they reject it forthwith. Honey is one of their favourite foods and from January to March they spend long time in gathering honey from hives. There is some kind of leaf called tongee the juice of which is mixed with saliva and besmeared over body. This prevents the bees from stinging men who come to loot their hives.

Andaman and Nicobar Islands have the following tribes:

1. Andamanese, Chariar, Chari, Kora, Bo, Tabo, Yere, Kede, Bea, Balawa, Bojigiyab, Juwai, Kol
2. Jarawas
3. Nicobarese
4. Onges
5. Sentinelese
6. Shom Pens

NOTES AND REFERENCES

1. Aiyappan, A., 1973: "Social and Physical Anthropology of the Nayadis of Malabar", *Bulletin of the Madras Government Museum,* General Section,Vol. 2, No. 4.
2. Ali, S.A., 1973: *Tribal Demography in Madhya Pradesh,* Bhopal, Jai Bharat Publishing House.
3. *Anthropological Survey of India,* Calcutta, Anthropological Suvery of India.
4. Atal, Yogesh; 1965: *Adivasi Bharat,* Delhi, Rajkamal Prakashan.
5. Bainbridge, R.B., 1907: "The Soarias of the Rajmahal Hills", *Memoirs of the Asiatic Society of Bengal,* Vol. 2, No. 4.
6. Baine, Sir A., 1891: *Census of India,* 1891, Report.
7. Basu, M.N., 1939: "Bunas of Bengal", *Journal of the Department of Letters,* University of Calcutta, Vol. 32.
8. Bhowmick, P.K., 1963: *The Lodhas of West Bengal: A Socio-Economic Study,* Calcutta, Punthi Pustak.
9. Blair, A., 1978: *A Report on a Survey of Andaman.*
10. Bose, J.K., 1934: "Social Organisation of the Aimol Kukis", *Man*

in India, Vol. 14.
11. Bose, J.K., 1935: "Gana Mokma Ceremony of the Garos of Assam", *Man in India,* Vol. 15.
12. Bose, J.K.,1938:"Dangla Festivals of the Garos", *Man in India* Vol.18.
13. Bose, J.K., 1941: *Garo Laws of Inheritance,* Anthropological Papers No. 6, University of Calcutta.
14. Bose, N.K., 1928: "Marriage and Kinship among the Juangs", *Man in India,* Vol. 8.
15. Bose, N.K.,1929: " Juang Association", *Man in India,* Vol. 9.
16. Bose, N.K.,1941: "Hindu Method of Tribal Absorption", *Proceedings of the Indian Science Congress,* reprinted in Cultural Anthropology, Calcutta (first published in 1928).
17. Brown, A.R., 1922: *Andaman Islands, A Social Study,* London.
18. Butter, John; 1855: *Travels and Adventure in the Province of Assam during a Residence of Fourteen Years,* London, Smith Elder & Co. S.T. Comhill.
19. Butter, John; 1875: "Rough Notes on the Angami Nagas and the Language", *Journal of the Asiatic Society of Bengal,* Vol. 44, Part I.
20. Campbell, J.M., 1856: "Ethnography of India", *Journal of Asiatic Society of Bengal,* Vol. 35.
21. Carstiars, G.M., 1952: "Bhil Villages of western Udaipur: A Study in Resistance to Social Change", *Economic Weekly,* Vol. 4.
22. Carstiars, G.M., 1953-54: "The Bhils of Koitra Bhomat", *Eastern Anthropologist,* Vol. 7.
23. Carstiars, G.M.,1957: *The Twice-Born: A Study of Community of High Caste Hindu,* London, The Hogenth Press.
24. *Census of India,* 1961: Delhi, The Manager of Publications.
25. *Census of India;* 1971: Delhi, The Manager of Publications.
26. Chattopadhyay, K.P., 1922: "Some Malavalam Kinship Terms", *Man in India,* Vol. II, No. 2.
27. Chattopadhyay, K.P.,1941: "Khasi Kinship and Social Organisation", *Anthropological Paper* No. 6, University of Calcutta.
28. Chattopadhyay, K.P., 1949: "Khasi Land Ownership and Scale", *Eastern Anthropologist,* Vol. 2.
29. Chauhan, B.R., 1966: "Tribalization", *Tribe* (a quarterly of the Tribal Research Institute, Udaipur), Vol. 2, No. 1-2.
30. Chengapa, B.S.,1951: "On the Shompen of Great Nicobar", *Appendix to Census Report,* 1951.
31. Cipriani, Lidio; 1951: "On the origin of the Andamanese", *Appendix to Census Report,* 1951, Delhi.
32. Cole, W.H.G., 1912: "Ethnographical Notes: The Lushais", *Census of India 1911,* Vol. III, Assam Part, Shillong, Government Secretariat Press.

33. Dalton, E.T., 1872: *Descriptive Ethnology of Bengal,* Calcutta, Superintendent, Government Printing Press.
34. Das, A.K., Raha, M.K.& Roychoudhary, B.K., 1966A: *The Malpaharias of West Bengal,* Calcutta, Cultural Research Institute, Government of West Bengal.
35. Das, A.K., Raha, M.K.& Roychoudhary, B.K., 1966 B: *Handbook on Scheduled Castes and Tribes of West Bengal,* Calcutta, Cultural Research Institute, Government of West Bengal.
36. Das, K.R.S., 1886: "The Mina Tribes of Jaipur in Meywar", *Journal of Asiatic Society of Bengal,* Vol. 55, Part I.
37. Das, N., 1967-68: "Tribal Interaction of the Saoras and Paros of Ganjam Agency", *Adivasi.*
38. Das, N., 1943: "The Modern Trend of Primitive Culture on the Borders of Bengal", *Calcutta Review,* Vol 139.
39. Das, N., 1945: "The Purums L: An Old Kuki Tribe of Manipur", *Anthropological Papers* No. 7, University of Calcutta.
40. Dave, P.C., 1960: *The Grasias,* Delhi, Bhartiya Adimjati Sevak Sangh, kingsway.
41. Dube, B.K. & Bahadur, F., 1967: *A Study of the Tribal People and Tribal Areas of Madhya Pradesh,* Indore, Government Regional Press.
42. Dube, B.K. & Bahadur, F., 1956: "The Urgent Task of Anthropology in India", *Proceedings of the 4th International Congress of Anthropology and Ethnological Congress held in Vienna in 1952.*
43. Dube, B.K. & Bahadur, F., 1960: *Manav Aur Sanskriti,* Delhi, Rajkamal Prakashan (2nd ed, 1969).
44. Dube, B.K. & Bahadur, F., 1962: "Social Anthropology in India", *Indian Anthropology: Essays in Memory of D.N. Majumdar,* ed. by T.N. Madan & Gopala Sarana, Bombay, Asia Publishing House.
45. Duquesne, S.A., 1996: *New Voyage to the East Indies in 1990-91—Full Description of Isle of Cucos,* Andaman, London.
46. Dutta, Majumdar N., 1956: *The Santal: A Study in Culture Change,* Delhi, Manager of Publication, Government of India Press.
47. Ellis, R.H., 1924: *A Short Account of the Laccadive and Minicoy,* Madras.
48. Elwin, Verrier., 1939: *The Baiga,* London, John Murray.
49. Elwin, Verrier., 1942: *The Agaria,* Oxford University Press.
50. Elwin, Verrier., 1942: 1943: *Maria Murder and Suicide,* Bombay, Oxford University Press, Ist ed. 1943 and 2nd ed. 1950.
51. Elwin, Verrier., 1943A: *The Aboriginals,* Bombay, Oxford University Press.
52. Elwin, Verrier., 1947: *The Muriya and Their Ghotul,* Geoffery Cambridge, Oxford University Press.

53. Elwin, Verrier., 1947: *Myths of Middle India*, Geoffery Cambridge, Oxford University Press.
54. Elwin, Verrier., 1948: "Notes on the Juang", *Man in India*, Vol. 28.
55. Elwin, Verrier., 1950: *Bodo Highlanders*, Bombay, Oxford University Press.
56. Elwin, Verrier., 1951: *The Tribal Art of Middle India*, Bombay, Oxford University Press.
57. Elwin, Verrier., 1952: *The Loss of the Nerves: A comparative study of the contact of people in the aboriginal areas of Bastar State, Central Province of India.*
58. Elwin, Verrier., 1954: *The Tribal Myths of Orissa*, Bombay, Oxford University Press.
59. Elwin, Verrier., 1955: *The Religion of an Indian Tribe*, Geoffery Cambridge, Oxford University Press.
60. Elwin, Verrier., 1960 A: *A Philosophy of NEFA*, Shillong, The Adviser to Governor of Assam.
67. Elwin, Verrier., 1960 B: *Nagaland*, Shillong, Research Department, Adviser's Secretariat.
68. Ferriera, J.V., 1962: "Katkaris and an Evaluation of Available Material", *Journal of Social Research*, Vol. 5, No. 2.
69. Ferriera, J.V., 1965: *Totemism in India*, Oxford University Press.
70. Frye, J.P., 1860: "On the Uriya and Khond Population of Orissa", *Journal of the Royal Asiatic Society of Great Britain and Ireland*, Vol. 17.
71. Fuchs, Stephen., 1957: *Social Origins*, Bombay.
72. Fuchs, Stephen., 1960: *The Gond and Bhunia of Eastern Mandala*, Bombay, Asia Publishing House.
73. Furer Haimendorf., 1941: "Seasonal Nomadism and Economics of the Chenchus of Hyderabad", *Journal of Royal Asiatic Society of Bengal*, Vol. 7, Letters.
74. Furer Haimendorf., 1947: *Exploration in the Eastern Himalayas: Tour Diaries of the Special Officer, Subansari Area 1944-45*, Shillong, Assam Government Press.
75. Furer Haimendorf., 1950-51: "The Pradhans: The Bards of Raj Gond", *Eastern Anthropologist*, Vol.4.
76. Furer Haimendorf., 1955: *Himalayan Barbary*, London, John Murray, Albemark St. W.
77. Furer Haimendorf., 1962: *The Apa Tanis and Their Neighbours: A Primitive Civilization of the Eastern Himalayas*, New York, Routledge and Kegan Paul.
78. Ghurye, G. S., 1936-37: "A Note on the Cross-Cousin Marriage and Dual Organisation in Kathiawar", *Journal of the University of Bombay*, Vol. 5. No. 1.

79. Griffith, W.G., 1946: *The Kol Tribe of Central India*, Calcutta, Royal Asiatic Society of Bengal.
80. Greigson, W.G., 1931: *Census of India* 1931, C.P. and Berar.
81. Greigson, W.G., 1938: *The Maria Gonds of Bastar*, London, Oxford University Press.
82. Guha, B.S., 1935: "The Racial Affinities of People of India", *Census of India 1931*, Vol. I, Part IIIB, pp.1,xxi+116, Simla.
83. Guha, B.S., 1944: *Racial Elements in Indian Population, Oxford paper on Indian Affairs, No. 22*, Bombay, Oxford University Press.
84. Guha, B.S., 1951: *The Tribes of India*, 2 vols. (ed.), New Delhi, Bharatiya Admijati Sevak Sangh.
85. Guha, B.S., 1955: "Indian Aborigines and who they are", Delhi Publication Division (Revised 1960).
86. Gunthorpe, E.J., 1886-89: "Notes on the Bhonde Koomars", *Journal of the Anthropological Society of Bombay*, Vol. 1.
87. Hendley, T.H., 1875: "An Account of Meywar Bhils", *Journal of Asiatic Society of Bengal*, Vol. 44.
88. Hodgson, B.H., 1848: "The Aborigines of the Eastern Frontier", *Journal of the Royal Asiatic Society of Bengal*, Vol. 18, Part II.
89. Hutton, J.H., 1921: *The Angami Nagas, with some notes on the neighbouring tribes*, London, Macmillan and Co.
90. Hutton, J.H., 1921: *The Seam Naga*, London, Macmillan and Co.
91. Hutton, J.H., 1923: "The connection of Different Nagas and other Tribes in Assam", *Census of India 1921*, Vol. III, Assam, Shillong.
92. Hutton, J.H., 1931: Ethnographic Notes by various Hands, *Census of India* 1931, Vol. 1, India, Part III B, Simla, Government of India Press.
93. Ibbetson, D., 1916: *Punjab Castes*, Lahore, Superintendent, Government Press, Punjab.
94. Ibbetson, D., 1919: *A. Glossary of the Tribes and Castes of Punjab and Northwest Frontier Province* (3 vols.), Lahore, Superintendent, Government Press, Punjab.
95. Iyer, L.K. Ananta., 1908: *Cochin Tribes and Castes*, Vol. I, Government of Cochin, London, Higginbotham and Co.
96. Iyer, L.K. Ananta., 1912: *The Cochin Tribes and Castes, Vol.2*, London, Higginbotham and Co.
97. Iyer, L.K. Ananta., 1928: *The Mysore Tribes and Castes*, Vol.2, Mysore, Mysore University.
98. Iyer, L.K. Ananta., 1930: *The Mysore Tribes and Castes*, Vol.3, Mysore, Mysore University.
99. Iyer, L.K. Ananta., 1931: *The Mysore Tribes and Castes*, Vol.4, Mysore, Mysore University.
100. Iyer, L.K. Ananta., 1935: *The Mysore Tribes and Castes*, Vol.1, Mysore, Mysore University.

101. Izskowitz, K.G., 1953: *The Goir Ceremony of Baro Gadaba.*
102. Karve, Irawati., 1957: "Social Education of Scheduled Tribes", *Vanyajati,* Vol.5, No. 4.
103. Karve, Irawati., 1958: "Bhils of western Khandesh", *Journal of Anthropological Society of Bombay.*
104. Karve, Irawati., 1969: "The Tribals of Maharashtra", *Urgent Researches in Social Anthropology,* Simla, Indian Institute of Advanced Study.
105. Khan, G.A., 1901, 1902: "Kashmir", *Census of India,* Vol. XXIII, Civil and Military Gazette Press, Lahore, 2 Vols.
106. Khan, G.A., 1942: "The Chenchus", *Essays in Anthropology, presented to Rai Bahadur S.C. Roy,* ed., by J.P. Mills and others, Lucknow Maxwell and Co.
107. Kloss, B.C., 1903: *In the Andaman and Nicobar—The Narative of a Cruise in the Schooner,* London.
108. Leuva, K.K., 1964: *The Asur, A. Study of Primitive Iron Smelters,* New Delhi, Bharatiya Adimjati Sevak Sangh.
109. Luiz, A.A.D., 1962: *Tribes of Kerala,* New Delhi, Bharatiya Adimjati Sevak Sangh (1st ed.).
110. Mahapatra, C.P.K., 1970: "Handbook on Koya", *Adivasi,*Vol.II, No. 4.
111. Majumdar, D.N., 1950: "Anthropology under Glass", *Journal of Anthropological Society of Bombay.*
112. Majumdar, D.N., 1950: *The Affairs of a Tribe: A Study in Tribal Dynamics,* Lucknow, Universal Publishers Ltd.
113. Majumdar, D.N., 1956: "Special Report on the Teaching of Social Anthropology", *The Teaching of Social Sciences in India,* UNESCO Publication.
114. Majumdar, D.N., 1961: *Races and Culture of India,* Bombay, Asia Publishing House (rev. ed.).
115. Majumdar, D.N., 1963: *Himalayan Polyandry,* Bombay, Asia Publishing House.
116. Majumdar, D.N., 1963: *Fortunes of the Primitive Tribe,* Lucknow, The Universal Publishers Ltd.
117. Majumdar, D.N., *Matrix of Indian Culture,* Lucknow, the Universal Publishers Ltd.
118. Majumdar, D.N.(Jr.); 1969: "A Study of Sanskritisation among the Bodo-speaking tribes of Garo hills", Paper read in the Seminar on Tribal Situation in India, Indian Institute of Advanced Study, Simla.
119. May, J.A., 1873: "Notes on the Bondos of Jaypur", *Indian Antiquary,* Vol. 2.
120. Nag, D.S., 1958: *Tribal Economy (An Economic Study of the Baiga),* Delhi, Bharatiya Adimjati Sevak Sangh.

121. Naik, T.B., 1956: *The Bhil: A Study*, Delhi, Bharatiya Admijati Sevak Sangh.
122. Naik T.B., 1963: *The Abujh Marias* (ed.), Chhindwara, Tribal Research Institute.
123. Naik T.B., 1969: *Urgent Researches in Social Anthropology* (with reference to Madhya Pradesh), ed. B.L. Abbi and S. Saberwal, Simla, Indian Institute of Advanced Study.
124. Naik, T.B., and Bhouraskar, K.M., 1961: *Changing Tribes*, Chhindwara, Tribal Research Institute.
125. Nath, Y.V.S., 1960: *Bhils of Ratanmal* (An Analysis of the *Social Structure of western Indian Community*), Baroda, M.S. University of Baroda.
126. Neigggemeyer, H., 1964: *Khuttia Khond*.
127. O'Malley, I.S., 1906-25: *Bengal District Gazetteers*, Calcutta, Bengal Secretriat Book Depot, 38 Vol.
128. O' Malley, L.S., 1932: *Indian Caste Customs*, Cambridge, Cambridge University Press.
129. Playfair, A., 1909: *The Garoas*, London, David and Nutt.
130. Pledger, W.F., 1944: "The Bhils: A Brief Anthropological Study", Ph.D. dissertation submitted to Hartford Seminary Foundation, Kennedy School of Mission.
131. Portman, M.V., 1899: *A History of Our Relation with the Andamanese* (2 vols.), London.
132. Rao, R.Prakash; 1952-53: "Ethnographic Study with Special Preference to Social Organisation, Myths and Ritual and Culture change".
133. Reddy, P.C., 1940: "The Yanadis of Madras Presidency", Ph.D. Thesis, Lucknow University.
134. Risley, H.H., 1891: "The Tribes and Castes of Bengal" (Official edition, circulated for criticism), *Ethnographic Glossary* in 2 Vols., Calcutta, Bengal Secretariat Press.
135. Risley, H.H., 1901: *Census of India*, India Report.
136. Risley H.H., 1905: *The People of India*, Calcutta, Secretariat Press.
137. Rivers, W.H.R., 1906: *The Todas*, London, Macmillan & Co. Ltd.
138. Rout, S.P., 1960: "Socio-Economic Implications of Put Puni Rituals of the Hill Juang of Keonjhar, *Adivasi*.
139. Rout, S.P., 1966-67: "The Juang and Culture Change", *Adivasi*, Vol. VIII, No.1
140. Rout S.P., 1967-68: "Social Organisation of the Bhuiyans of Kalahandi", *Adivasi*, Vol. IX, No.1.
141. Roy Burman, B.K., 1961: "Warmoung, An Ao-Naga Village", Monograph Series, Part VI, *Census of India, 1961*, New Delhi, Office of the Registrar-General, India, Ministry of Home Affairs.

142. Roy Burman, B.K., 1969: "Tribal Demography in India-A Preliminary Appraisal", Paper read in a seminar on Tribal Situation in India, Indian Institute of Advanced Study, Simla.
143. Roy Burman, B.K., 1970: "Demographic and Socio-Economic Profiles of the Hill Areas of North East India", New Delhi, Office of the Registrar-General, India, Ministry of Home Affairs.
144. Roy Burman, B.K. with Harit, H.L., 1971: *A Preliminary Appraisal of the Scheduled Tribes of India*, New Delhi, Office of the Registrar-General, India.
145. Roy, Sacin, 1960: Aspects of Padam-Minyong Cultures, Shillong, Adviser's Secretariat.
146. Roy, S.C., 1928: *Oraon Religion and Customs*, Ranchi, *Man in India Office.*
147. Ruhelia, Satyapal., 1967: *Godulia Lohars*, Bombay.
148. Russel and Hiralal, 1916: *Tribes and Castes of Central Provinces of India* (4 vols.), London, Macmillan and Co.
149. Sachchidananda; 1964: *Culture Change in Tribal Bihar*, Calcutta, Bookland Pvt. Ltd.
150. Saksena, R., 1964: *Tribal Economy in Central India*, Calcutta, K.K. Mukhopadhyaya,
151. Saletore, R.N., 1938: "The Bhils of Maharashtra", *New Indian Antiquary*, Vol. 1.
152. Samantaray, D.K., 1971: "The Khonds of Nayagarh", *Adivasi*, Vol. 12. No. 1-4.
153. Samuell, E.A., 1856: "Notes on a Forest Race called Putto or Juang", *Journal of the Asiatic Society of Bengal*, Vol. 25.
154. Sandhwar, A.N.: 1973: "The Korwa of Palamau: A Study of their Society and Economy" (Ph.D. Thesis, Ranchi University).
155. Sengupta, S.K., 1969: The Portrait of Mahali Economy in Midnapur. The Earning Putters of Tribal Basket-makers, Calcutta, Edition Indian.
156. Shakespeare, J., 1912: *The Lushai Kuku Clans*, Parts I and II, London, Macmillan and Co.
157. Shortt, John, 1967-69: "Habits and Manners of the Marvar Tribes of India", *Memoir of the Anthropology Society of London*, Vol. 3.
158. Sinha, R., 1963: *The Akas*, Shillong, Adviser's Secretariat.
159. Sinha, Surajit; 1957: "Tribal Culture of peninsular India: Dimension of Little Tradition in Study of Indian Civilization", *Man in India*, Vol. 37.
160. Sinha, Surajit; 1965: "Tribe-Caste and Tribe-Peasant Continuum in Central India", *Man in India*, Vol. 45, No.1.
161. Sinha, S.P., 1964: *Life and Times of Birsa Bhagwan*, B Ranchi, Bihar Tribal Welfare Research Institute.
162. Tessitori, L.P., 1914: *Native life in the Andaman Island* cont, Illustrated.

163. Tessitori, L.P., 1917: Progress Report on the work done during the year 1916 in connection with the proposed "Scheme for the Bardic Historical Survey of Rajputana".
164. Thakkar Bapa; 1941: "Hamare Adivasi Bhai" in *Thakakr Bapa* by Viyogi Hari, New Delhi, Prakashan Vibhag.
165. Thurston, E., 1896: "Anthropology of the Todas and Kotas of the Nilgiri Hills; and of Brahmans, Kammalans, Pallis and Paraihs of Madras City", *Bulletin of Madras Government Museum,* Vol. 1, No. 4.
166. Thurston, E., 1897: "Badagas and Irulas of Nilgiris: Paniyans of Malabar: A Chinese Tamil cross; acheruman skull; kuruba or Kurumba; Summary of Results".
167. Thurston, E., *Castes and Tribes of southern India,* Vol. 1-7 (assisted by K. Rangachari), Madras Government Press.
168. Tod, James, 1950: *Annals and Antiquities of Rajasthan or the Central and the western Rajput States in India,* 2 Vols., London, Routledge and Kegan Paul (First printed in 1920).
169. Vidyarthi, L.P., 1963: *The Maler: A Study in Nature Man-Spirit Complex of a Hill Tribe,* Calcutta, Book and Private Ltd.
170. Vidyarthi, L.P., 1966 B: "Social Anthropological Researches in India: Some Preliminary Observation", *Journal of Social Research,* Vol. IX No.1.
171. Vidyarthi, L.P., 1968: "Cultural Change in the Tribes of Modern India", Presidential address to the Anthropology and Archaeology Section of the 55th Session of the Indian Science Congress. Also published in *Journal of Social Research,* Vol. XI, No. 1.
172. Vidyarthi, L.P., 1972: "Tribal Ethnography in India", A Survey of Research in Social Anthropology and Sociology, New Delhi, I.C.S.S.R..
173. Vyas, S.N., 1967: *India in the Ramayana Age,* Delhi, Atma Ram and Sons.
174. Wilkinson, T.S., 1953: "The Functional Significance of Ghotul Nomenclature Anthropology on the March, ed. by Balaratnam, *Social Science Association,* Madras.

XVII

KOL TRIBES OF CENTRAL INDIA

Munda or Kol group tribes still have their own language called 'Mundari' or simply 'Munda'. This is one of the archaic languages of India. Those who speak are also termed as Austrics, although there are some Austrics who have altogether forgotten their language. For the worshippers or the believers of Bonga, 'Bonga' is a sort of power or spirit omnipresent in all the objects of the world. It is very near to the Vedic Brahma. The manifestations of 'Bonga' are numerous and they are from Odaks Bongas (House Bongas) to Abge Bongas (Clan Bongas).

In fact, the Austrics all over their distribution believe mainly in All Father God or Sin-Bonga and Maran Buru. The Gonds, who, as per some scholars, came from the southern peninsular India believed in mother goddesses and sacrifices. They worship the Almighty female deity as well as local deities. Totemism amongst both the tribal groups is present.

Chanda (1969) strongly advocates that the 'Munda' was spoken language of the Kolarians. He also opines that some of Kolarians who were in contact with the Aryans and the Dravidians used Indo-Aryan and Dravidian dialects.

Although 'Niṡada' represented the generic term for the non-Aryan tribes of India, it is likely that a majority might have been Kolarians. It is interesting to note that even in India today many of the primitive occupations are still being traditionally carried out by the Kolarians. Rudradhyaya of Yajurveda mentions the Kolarians associated with many non-agrarian occupations. These are listed in the Table 17.1.

It is likely that the taming of elephants might have been one of the occupations of Kolarians, which continued up to Middle Ages. Shihab-i-Hakims, *Maasir-i-Mahmud-Shahi* (Persian), ed. N.H. Ansari, (Delhi 1968) has presented vivid description of Sarguja, its enormous elephants and the tribal method of trapping the elephants.

TABLE-17.1

Non-Agrarian Occupation of Kolarians (Nisadas) as mentioned in Yajurveda

S. No.	*Occupation*	*Meaning*
1.	Vratya	Nomads
2.	Taksan	Carpenters
3.	Rathakara	Chariot-making
4.	Kulala	Potters
5.	Karmara	Blacksmiths
6.	Punjistha	Fowlers
7.	Svanin	Dog-keepers
8.	Mrigayu	Hunters

Kolarians have their own language. The term Akol is probably the Santhali har, hara, no and korci all of which means 'man'. In Chotanagpur, Kols began to be called 'Munda', which actually meant 'Head' or 'Head-man'. Their group of languages is spoken by the primitive tribes of not only a large section of northern peninsular tribes of India but also by the tribes of Indo-Pacific islands and Malay peninsula.

According to Grierson, "The Mundas, the Monkhemer and other tribes of the Malay peninsula and Nicobarese, all use forms of speech which can be traced back to a common source though they mutually differ widely from each other".

Munda languages in India are spoken in West Bengal, Bihar, Madhya Pradesh, Orissa and Tamil Nadu. These are spoken in tribal belts of the states concerned.

Classification of Munda languages

Korku Kharia Juang Savar Godba Kherwari

Kherwari has ten districts. These are:

1. Santhali
2. Bhumij

3. Bihard
4. Koda
5. Ho
6. Turi
7. Asuri
8. Agaria
9. Brijik
10. Kora

These languages are sometimes grouped in the following manner:

Munda Languages

A. Western	B. Eastern
1. Korku	1. Korwa
2. Kharia	2. Ho
3. Kanari	3. Koda
4. Juang	4. Bhumji
5. Savar	5. Mundari
	6. Santhali

Since languages are basically acquired, they are not the natural trails of human beings. There are many tribes who are not essentially Kolarian, but they speak Munda languages. This is due to their long association with the Munda speaking tribes. Then, there are tribes who are racially nearer to Munda tribes, but they have either completely forgotten their language or adopted the other ones.

The Munda Tribes, may be divided into following major categories:

I. Munda tribes speaking their own languages. These are: Kharia, Kairwar, Savar, etc.

II. Munda tribes speaking Dravidian languages. These are: Baiga and its Sub-groups.

III. Munda tribes speaking Indo-Aryan languages. These are: Bhils, Saharia, Sonr, etc.

Ho, Munda and Kol tribes have many branches and it is the result of historical migration and geographical isolation. Kols or Mundas still love isolation or wish to live in the villages where only they exclusively live. Dalton writes: "They will not allow aliens to hold land near their villages, and indeed if it were left to them, no strangers would be permitted to settle in the Kolhans".

Kol represents probably the purest forms of the Kolarians. The next comes Mundas and they show racial mixture. Then comes others. Sir Risley includes the Khangar, Kharia, Mohali, Oraon and Savar. The list differs with the authorities on the subject.

KOLARIAN TRIBES

As stated above, Kolarians are found in Madagascar and Malay and in India they are found only in Central India and Chotanagpur. There is no trace of Munda language in larger parts of peninsular India where Dravidian languages are mainly spoken.

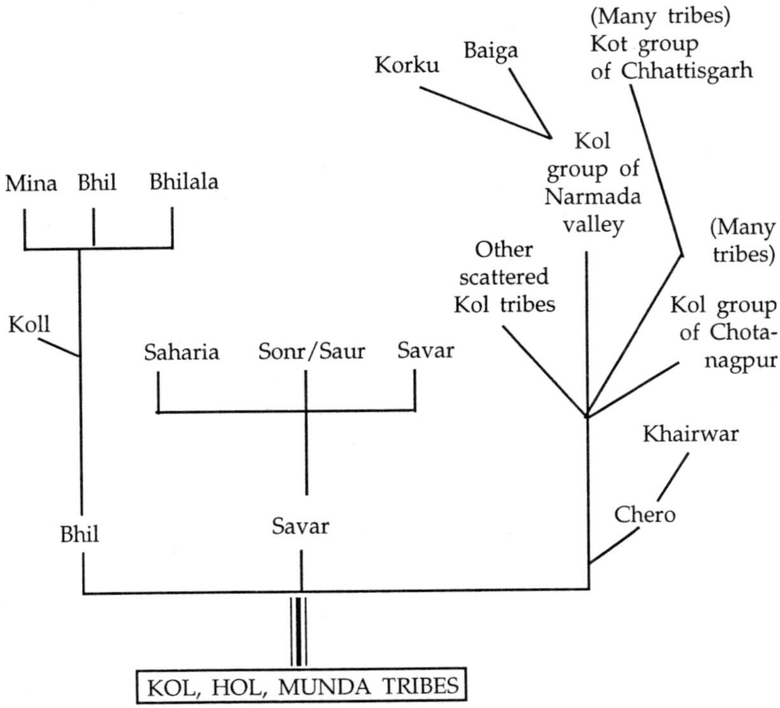

Major Branches of Kolarians

GENERAL PATTERN OF DISTRIBUTION OF KOLARIANS IN CENTRAL INDIA

The general pattern of geographical distribution of the Kolarians especially in Central India is that they have been branched off thousands of years ago in two directions, namely the eastern and the western. The western branch was highly influenced by caucascid racial content of India which seems to have given rise to the Bhils. The eastern branch was widely distributed in Vindhyans and ultimately merged in Chotanagpur. In Chotanagpur due to local isolation and also due to mixing up with the other tribes, many Kolarian sub-groups emerged which in due cause of time identified themselves separately.

It is interesting to note that the Kolarians moved southward of Yamuna river through its tributaries. The Saharias are found all through the valley of river Chambal, Sonr and Saur in the valleys of Beturi and Ken. The Baigas, in fact, seem to have lived all through the Son valley. Most of the Central Indian Kolarians lived in the Vindhyans and when they reached up to the water divide to Yamuna only at few places, they crossed the river Narmada. The Korkus are thus a branch of the Kolarians which moved southwards through the river Betwa.

The Baigas who established themselves in Amarkantak plateau gradually moved toward the West through the southern bank of the river Narmada. In fact, Bharias must have been the early Kolarians who colonised the Satpuras. But both the Baigas and Bharias forgot their language due to their early association with the Gonds.

KOLARIAN TRIBES OF CENTRAL INDIA

A systematic description of Kolarian tribes inhabiting in Madhya Pradesh and the newly-created state of Chhattisgarh many be given as follows.

Kol

In Madhya Pradesh and Chhattisgarh, the Kol zone extends over Rewa, Shahdol, Sidhi, Satna, Panna, Jabalpur, Mandla,

Narsimhapur, Surguja and Bilaspur districts. The Kols are actually a Chotanagpur tribe and because of the size of their population and its influence in historical times, the tribe gave its name to a number of other tribes who were known as Kolarian group of tribes. Some authorities even consider Santhal to be a branch of the Kols. Kharia, Kairwar, Korwa and Korku are believed to be belonging to the Kolarian group.

Their number in Madhya Pradesh is 1,23,810 which is 1.03 per cent of the tribal population of the state.

The Kols have a well-knit 'Panchayat' system. The head is called 'Gontia'. The Kols of Jabalpur division belong to 'Gawathai' sub-group. Those who live in Rewa division call themselves 'Bhumia'. Their main septs are Thakuria, Ratul, Barbar, Chero, Bargiya, Mawasi, Barn, Kothatia, Sonwani, Kumharia, Katharia, Bhuwar, Rakonta, Karpatia and Nathunia, etc.

They worship Suraj Devata and many other gods of the Hindus.

Mawasi

The Mawasi tribe is found in the districts of the erstwhile Vindhya Pradesh region. Venkatachar considered them to be the warrior section of the Kol tribe, and quite a large number of them have started referring themselves as Kol.

In 1981, their number was 11,012, which constituted only 0.1 per cent of the tribal population of the state. Eighty per cent population of the tribe lives in Chhindwara district. They were earlier named as Korku but as they had lived in an area called "Mawas", their name changed. Mawasi mainly worship Lord Shiva of Pachmarhi but they believe in many other gods also.

Munda

This tribe is confined to Raigarh and Surguja districts of Chhattisgarh. Russell and Hiralal considered that those Kols who become civilised are commonly known as Munda. Munda is also the name of a sub-tribe of the Kharia. Actually it was considered to be a group of tribes from which tribes like Nagesia, Nagwanshi, Kharia, Uraon and Sawar got diversified.

This Munda tribe of eastern Madhya Pradesh should not be confused with the Mundas found in Bastar. In Bastar, the Munda was an occupational class of bards and they have no ethnic relationship with the Munda tribe.

In 1981, the population of this tribe in Madhya Pradesh was 1,579. The tribe constituted only 0.013 per cent of the tribal population of the state.

The tribe is divided into a number of *khunts*. Each *khunt* has many *killis* (septs). More important of these are Bhengara, Bodara, Parti, Konraru, Ind, Zirhaul, Mundri, Nimak, Amba, Babul and Gandi, etc.

The Mundas have a Panchayat system which looks after all the social matters. Their religious headman is 'Pahan'. They worship many 'Bonga', the supreme Bonga is 'Sing Bonga' or 'Sin Bonga'. They believe in magic and offer sacrifice to their gods.

Nagesia, Nagasia

This tribe of the Munda group is found in Surguja and Raigarh districts of Chhattisgarh. In Jashpur subdivision of Raigarh district, the Nagesias are divided into three sub-tribes—the Sendurias, the Dhurias and the Telias—whereas these are not found in Udaipur tehsil of the same district. This tribe is also found in Bihar.

In 1981, their population was 14,474 in Madhya Pradesh. The sect is mostly totemic. They believe in magic. The man who is an expert magician is called 'Dwar'. They worship the gods of Mundas and the goddesses of the Gonds.

Kharia

More than 80 per cent of the tribe inhabits Raigarh district of Chhattisgarh alone. They are also found in Raipur and Bilaspur districts. The dialect of the tribe is also known as Kharia. The tribe has two subdivisions—the Dudh Kharia and Delki Kharia.

In Madhya Pradesh, their population was 6,892 in the year 1981.

The Kharia legend of origin resembles that of the Mundas and tends to show that they are an earlier branch of that tribe. According to the legend a pregnant woman while passing through a jungle gave birth to a male child. While she went to fetch a basket to carry that boy, she noticed that the infant was being guarded by a cobra, spreading its hood on the head of the infant. This boy later became 'Nagbansi'. The elder brother of this boy or the elder son of the woman was called the ancestor of Kharias. The Kharias regard Mundas as their elder brother. Nagvansi rajas were really Mundas.

Chotanagpur is the real home of the Kharias. Their best settlements lie near southern Koel river. This river is as sacred to them as the river Damodar is to the Santhals. They throw ashes of their dead in this river. Kharias have migrated up to Bengal to work in tea gardens.

The tribe is divided into totemistic exogamous septs which pay reverence to their totems.

Totems of Kharias are:

1. Kulu = Tortoise
2. Kiro = Tiger
3. Nag = Cobra
4. Konkul = Leopard
5. Kuto = Crocodile

They abstain from killing their totem animal. Kharia dialect is closely allied to Savara and has also some similarity to Korku and Juang. It has some traces of Munda language.

Korwa, Kodaku

The Korwas are from Surguja, Raigarh and Bilaspur districts of Chhattisgarh, the proportionate distribution being 40 per cent in Surguja, 45 per cent in Raigarh and 5 per cent in Bilaspur. The tribe is divided into two sub-tribes, viz. Pahadi Korwa or the Hill Korwa and Diharia Korwa or the Plains

Korwa. The Pahadi Korwa are considered to be one of the six primitive tribes of Madhya Pradesh. The Pahadi Korwas are also sometimes referred to as Beonnia, because of their association with shifting cultivation. In addition to these two subdivisions, the tribe has three minor groups, viz. Kodaku, Binjia and Bhadiya.

Birhor, Birhul

The principal habitat of Birhor tribe is Bihar where 3,464 of the total population of them, 4,300 in India, were found in 1971 Census. Madhya Pradesh had only 738 Birhors in 1971. These are found in Udaipur and Jashpur tehsils of Raigarh and in Surguja districts. The term mean 'dwellers of the forest' (Bir meaning forest and hor meaning dweller). The economy of the tribe is in a bad shape.

Dhanwar

Another name, perhaps a later acquisition, for this tribe is Dhamuhar. The tribe is found principally in Bilaspur, Surguja and Raigarh districts, the main habitat being in Bilaspur district. Here they are concentrated in Katghora tehsil. Russell and Hiralal considered the Dhanwars to be an offshoot of either the Gonds or the Kawars or a mixture of both. It is likely that they are more akin to the Kawars than to the Gonds.

Sawar, Sawara

In Chhattisgarh, the Sawar tribe is principally found in the eastern parts of Raigarh and Raipur districts where about 90 per cent of them are found, the rest being found in Bastar and Bilaspur districts. Like other tribes inhabiting the border areas of Madhya Pradesh and Orissa, the Sawars are also divided into two broad subdivisions—the Laria, i.e. those belonging to Chhattisgarh and speaking Chhattisgarhi and Uriya, i.e. those speaking Uriya. The tribe earns its livelihood as agricultural labourers and farm servants.

According to 1961, Census the speakers of Saora language numbered 2,65,721. Grierson places the Saora language close to Junag and Kharia, all of which belong to the Mundari family.

Thurston (1909) divided Savaras of Orissa in the following manner:

I. Hill Savaras
  1. Jati Savara or Matiah Savara.
  2. Arsi, Arisi or Lombi, Lanjiya (weavers of coarse cloth)
  4. Luara or Muli (workers in iron who make arrows)
  4. Kidnal (basket-makers)
  5. Jadu (Savaras of hill country)
  6. Kumbi (potters)

II. Low-country Savars
  1. Kapu (cultivators)
  2. Saddho (clean or good)

Even in the earliest Sanskrit literature, there are references to Saoras. The worship of Lord Jagannath of Puri is closely related with the Saora religious tradition.

Bhunjia

In Chhattisgarh, the Bhunjias are all confined to Bindranawagarh and Dhamtari subdivisions of Raipur district, the former area being their principal habitat. The Bhunjias are divided into two endogamous groups—Choukhutia Bhunjias and Chinda Bhunjias. The former of these used to have 'arrow marriage' system and they construct their kitchen separated from the main house at some distance. The Cinda Bhunjias do not observe these customs.

Baiga

The Baiga tribe is concentrated in Mandla, Shahdol, Balaghat, Rajnandgaon, Bilaspur, Seoni and Jabalpur districts of M.P. and Chhattisgarh.

The Baigas described by Thomson as "the wildest of the tribes inhabiting the most inaccessible hills and the remotest forest; living on what they can secure with their bows and arrows..'.' The Baigas are known for their shifting cultivation known as Bewar. This has been prohibited now. The tribe is divided into 12 endogamous divisions known as jat. Eight of these are found as follows:

Binjhwar	:	Lamta area in Balaghat district, Narainpur area in Mandla district, Jabalpur district.
Bhumia	:	Baiga Chak and Dindori area in Mandla district, Pandaria area in Bilaspur, Rewa.

The term Bhumia means 'holder of land' and is, in this respect, an honorific term. As such, it is adopted by more than one ethnic groups like Bharia-Bhumia, Bhumia-Baiga and so on.

Bharotia	:	Supkhar area in Balaghat district, Baiga Chak in Mandla district.
Narotia	:	Baihar Tehsil, Balaghat district.
Mundia	:	Niwas tehsil, Mandla district.
Gondwain	:	Balaghat district.
Bhaina	:	Bilaspur and Rewa districts.
Kondwan	:	Balaghat district.

Baigas are enumerated amongst the primitive tribes of Madhya Pradesh (PTG). Their population in Madhya Pradesh in the year 1981 was 2,48,948 which constituted 2.08 per cent tribal population of Madhya Pradesh.

BINJHWAR

The Binjhwars are, actually speaking, a civilized landholding caste who were described by Russell and Hiralal as "a comparatively civilized Dravidian tribe or caste formed from a tribe, found in Raipur and Bilaspur districts and the adjoining Uriya country". In addition to these two districts mentioned by Russell and Hiralal, the Binjhwars are also found in Raigarh and Surguja districts.

Their population in Madhya Pradesh in the year 1981 constituted 0.77 per cent of the state tribal population.

Pl. 12. Baiga ritual dance

Pl. 13. A Kol wearing sacred thread

Pl. 14. Bhil community

Bhaina

This comparatively civilized and acculturated tribe inhabits Bilaspur, Raigarh and Mandla districts. The tribe in all probability is one of mixed descent from the union of the Baigas and the Kanwars.

Their population in Madhya Pradesh in the year 1981 was 39,136, which constituted 0.33 per cent of the tribal population of Madhya Pradesh.

It is said that Raj Bhaina, a sub-group of Baigas of Mandla were in fact, zamindars in Bilaspur, Pendra and Raipur districts. They are said to have been defeated by Kamwars and Gonds but the real history is shrouded in obscurity. They have Panchayat system; the headman is called 'Gontia' They worship Thakur Deo, Bura Deo, Goraiyan Deo and many other goddesses.

Bharia

It is unfortunate to find Bharias, Bhuinhars and Pandos clubbed together, for they are ethnically different and live in separate geographical areas. The Bharias inhabit Chhindwara, Bilaspur, Shahdol, Seoni and Narsimhapur districts. In Chhindwara district, their typical habitat is known as Patalkot which is a bowl-shaped physiographic feature containing 12 villages. In some areas they apply a supposedly honorific suffix, Bhumia, and refer themselves as Bharia-Bhumia.

In Madhya Pradesh, they are widely distributed in Chhattisgarh and Narmada valley. Their number in the year 1981 was 1,95,490 which constituted 1.63 per cent of the total tribal population of the state.

The Bharias of Patalkot are enumerated amongst the primitive tribes (PTG) of the state.

Kanwar, Kawar

The Kanwar tribe is principally found in Raigarh, Bilaspur, Surguja, Raipur, Durg and Rajnandgaon districts, nearly 90 per cent having been returned from Bilaspur division only. The Kanwars are comparatively advanced tribe and Hewitt (1869) was inclined to consider them as "Imperfect Rajpoots who settled in early times among the hills of the Vindhyan range and so failed in becoming Hinduised like other war-like immigrants". The Kanwars have eight endogamous divisions—Tanwar, Kamalbarsi, Paikara, Dudh Kanwar, Ruthia, Chanti, Cherwa and Rautia. Of these Cherwa, Raitha and Tanwar have been included in the List of Scheduled Tribes. It cannot be stated if the Chattri included in the list are the Chanti group missplet. The Tanwar group is the aristocratic division of the tribe.

In Madhya Pradesh, the population of this tribe in the year 1981 was found to be 5,62,199 which constituted 4.69 per cent of the tribal population of the state.

Some of the totemic septs of the Kanwar are:

1. Baghwa = Tiger
2. Chita = Leopard
3. Bilwa = Wild cat
4. Bokar = Goat
5. Bichhi = Scorpion
6. Bhainsa = Buffalo
7. Sua = Parrot

Other septs are Chandrama, Chanwar, Chua, Champa, Dhanguru, Dhenki, Darpan, Gobra, Hudra, Vata, Kothi, Khumri, Lodha, Fulbandhia, Gonga Cochar, Sanwani, Majhi, Nahna, Samund, Kodia Dudh, Adila, Son Pakhar, Vuari, Bhandari, Sikuta, Daharia, etc.

They worship many gods namely Dulha Deo, Bahan Deo, Thakur Deo, Shikar Deo. They also propitiate many goddesses namely Sagai Devi, Matin Devi and Banjari Devi, etc.

Korku, Karku, Bopchi, Mouasi, Nihal, Nahul, Bondhi, Bondeya

The Korku zone extends over Betul, Chhindwara, Hoshangabad, Khandwa, Dewas, Sehore and Raisen districts. The List of Scheduled Tribes shows at serial No. 19, a tribe by the name of KARKU. Apparently, this is a spurious entry in the list, as no such tribe is found anywhere in Madhya Pradesh.

The term Korku simply means "man". Koru being the term for man and Ku simply being a plural termination. The Korkus were formerly divided into two subdivisions, viz., Raj Korku and Patharia Korku. In course of time, this division has become more or less obliterated and instead we find the tribe divided into four territorial groups—Mouasi, Bawaria, Ruma and Bondoya.

The Mouasis are considered to be the highest Korkus. The Bondoyas (Bondhi, Bondeya) are found around Jitgarh in Pachmarhi area. The Bawaria Korku are found in Betul district and Ruma Kurkus are not found in this state but are found in Amaraoti district of Maharashtra. The Bopchis are also not found in Madhya Pradesh but are found in Wardha district of Maharashtra. The terms Nihal and Nahul of the list actually stand for Nahal who are of mixed origin of Bhil and Korku and are found in Khandwa and Hoshangabad districts.

In Madhya Pradesh their population was 6,6781 in 1981 which constituted 0.56 per cent of the total tribal population of the state.

According to Korku mythology, they were given life by Lord Shiva during the time of Ravana.

BHUINHAR-BHUMIA

The List of Scheduled Tribes contains this name. Actually speaking, there is no tribe with the name Bhuinhar-Bhunia though we have two different ethnic groups—Bhuinhar and Bhumia. That the name given in the List is wrong is amply clear from the fact that both words, Bhuinhar and Bhumia mean the same and it is most unlikely to find a name of two words both of which have the same meaning or connotation. Russell and Hiralal also gave Bhuinhar as a synonym of Bhumia. The tribe referred to by this name is actually Bhuinhar. This tribe is found in the eastern region of Chhattisgarh in Raigarh and Surguja districts. The tribe should not be confused with a caste of the same name found in Bihar and West Bengal.

Paliha

In the List of Scheduled tribes, the Palihas are grouped with Bharia, Bhumia, Bhuinhar and Pando. They are confined to Shahdol district and in contiguous areas of Sidhi district. The Palihas appear to be allied to Bhumias or to Bhuinhars but we will have to wait for final decision till more researches are done.

Pando

The Pandos are principally found in Surguja district and in the adjoining areas of Bilaspur district. They are grouped with Bharia, Bhumia and Bhuinhar in the List of Scheduled Tribes. In his Report of 1931, Census (CP and Berar), Shootbet considered that there was a marked similarity between the Pando and the Korwas but he rightly concluded that until further evidence is available, the Pandos should be regarded as a separate and independent tribe. The Pandos have two territorial subdivisions—Uttarha and Surgujiha. Formerly the Pandos used to have youth dormitory known as Bhangra but this system has fallen into decay. The economic life of the Pandos centres round collection of forest produce and labour.

THE KOLARIANS IN REVOLT

The Kol tribes lived happily in their forest habitats without any interference. Banabhatta (6th century A.D.) in his famous work *'Kadambari'* devotes a full chapter on tribals. The chapter *'Sabar varnanam'* gives important information about the life style and culture of tribals. Banabhatta writes *'Rajayam sunyaswatvisu'* or the kingdom of tribal chiefs lies in the forests devoid of common civilized population. The tribals collected the forest products and sold them in cities.

Even the Mughal rulers continued to encourage the establishment of settlements by peasants both belonging to forest-dwelling communities and those already living in villages on the fringe of forests.

However, things changed considerably after the battle of Plassey.

After the Britishers had established their rule in India in the last decades of eighteenth century, they enforced the same laws and regulations in tribal areas which they had promulgated in the non-tribal areas.

The laws were implemented through local population of the Hindus. Thus the Britishers began to use one section of Hindu population against the other section for the purpose of exploitation. Gradually the concept of 'Alienation' was evolved in the academic field. The British authorities exploited not only their material wealth but also their religion and culture.

This normally resulted in agitations all over India against policies initiated by Britishers. In academic terms, these movements are classified as:

1. Agrarian (1858-81)
2. Revivalistic (1881-90)
3. Political (1890-95)

Most of the Kolarian tribal revolts were in neighbouring states of Madhya Pradesh. Some of them are briefly narrated here.

Bhumij Revolt

Excepting the revolts of Santals (1781), Kurriciyars (1802), Khasis (1829) and Kols (1831), the entire community did not participate in the revolts.

Ganga Narain Singh, a Hindu Bhumij chief of Chotanagpur revolted against the British in 1832. He was the first leader of the tribals who was able to take utmost advantage of the frustration and anger of the Bhumjis against the existing system of government by convincing them that their struggle was against oppression. He was a charismatic leader. He realized that local zamindars were groaning under the oppression of Madhav Singh and before embarking on the path of revenge he secured their support. He also appealed to the anti-colonial and anti-diku feelings of the people. He exploited successfully the superstition and credulity of simple tribal folk by claiming to possess supernatural powers.

Non-tribal intruders, police thanas and British officers were the main targets of the attack of the rebels. The most common offence was the plunder of cattle and property.

In the words of J.C. Jha (1967) in 'Bhumij revolts', it was a cry for vengeance on rich and oppressors, a vague dream of some curb upon them, setting right the individual wrongs.

The movement of Ganga Narain Singh can be regarded as belonging to a transitional phase. Before him, no one posed himself as a true leader possessing supernatural powers and demanding complete obedience from his followers. After Ganga Narain Singh, several tribal leaders professed themselves to be the incarnations of God. Majority of them remembered the 'golden age' in which the tribals had lived in the distant past.

The long drawn revolt of Ganga Narain Singh, the participation of a large number of Bhumijs and bloody encounters between the two contestants seem to have led British government to announce its decision to separate the tribal areas from the administrative set-up of non-tribal regions.

Santal Insurrection (1855)

Sidhu and Kanhu were the two brothers who stood against the British. They made elaborate preparations for the revolt. Tribals were intensely dissatisfied by the British policies which enabled 'dikus' to exploit them. The two brothers tried to reform their agriculture and living to make the lives of common tribal happier. For this Santal rituals were observed with new zeal.

But the most important feature of this movement was the use of legal means. For the first time in the history of tribal revolts against colonial rule, an attempt was made to warn the government, zamindars and outsiders. Besides marching to the Legislative Assembly of Bengal for reminding the Government to take adequate steps to end the oppression, they also sent letters to Commissioner, Collector and Magistrate of Bhagalpur, officials of Birbhum, several zamindars and darogas of the Thana of Dighee and Tiku. Subsequently they submitted several petitions to the Government at various levels. They asked the Santals to pay revenue at the rate of two annas on every buffalo plough and half-an-anna on each cow plow per annum. Thus before commencing the revolt, the two brothers adopted constitutional means to get the voice of the Santals heard, but all this had no result.

The Santal rebellion of 1855 known as 'hul' was a messianic movement. Both the brothers claimed to have seen in a vision the Thakur (God), who shall give daily 'darshan' to them in different forms. The God also gave them the message that 'Sahibs' and 'Dikus' should leave the country and go to the other bank of river Gunja. They exhorted the people to send one man from each family to join army being organised by them. Both the brothers demanded implicit faith and obedience from their followers.

According to some British authorities, at the beginning, opposition of the Santals was confined to end exploitation, but soon it flared. During the course of struggle, violence and plunder were practised on a large scale by both the sides. The British forces killed Santals in large numbers, burnt their houses, destroyed their provisions. The Santals also retaliated in the same manner.

Revolt of Birsa Munda

Birsa Munda's revolt began in the last phase of the famous 'Sardar movement' of Bihar. The Sardars, in the last phase of their movement merged it with Birsa's plans. K. Suresh Singh had vividly traced the influences which shaped his ideology from 1890 to 1895. In this period, he constantly changed the emphasis on the ends and means of his movements.

Birsa was originally brought under the influence of Christian Missionaries, owing to his early education in Mission schools. He later on realised that they were not friendly and favourable to the idea of independence for the country and freedom of action for the exploited Munda people. This was evident when the Chaibassa Roman Catholic and German Lutherian Missionaries began to criticise the Sardari movement, which was aimed at ending the exploitation of the tribals.

Birsa, the agitator, by force of events and pressure of circumstances was gradually developed into a prophet. With the adoration of thousands of people constantly surrounding him, he was led into the belief that he was a messenger of God and that he was chosen to redeem his people.

He organised many big meetings of his followers where he condemned the Courts and Laws. He proclaimed himself the Rajan and deputed his chief followers to various parts of Munda country. His followers openly talked of battle, fire and sword.

The revolt of Birsa came to an end with his arrest. While in the arrest, on the morning of 9 June, 1900 he breathed his last at 9.00 a.m. His death remained a mystery, like his life.

Birsa's revolt led the way to other tribal revolts. More, important of them are listed in the following table.

TABLE-17.2

Revolts of Kolarian Tribes in Chronological Order 1778-1947

Year		*Revolt*
1778	:	Revolt of the Pahariya Sirdars of restless Bihar against the British government.
1784-85	:	Koli disturbances (Maharashtra) at the instigation of a Rani of Jawahar.
1789	:	Revolt in Tamar of Chotanagpur.
1794-95	:	-do-
1795-1800	:	Revolt of the Chuari movement in Bihar.
1798	:	Panchet estate sale revolt
1801	:	Tamar revolt in Bihar
1803	:	Koya uprising in the Rampa area of the East
1807	:	Chotanagpur tribal revolt
1808	:	-do-
1809-28	:	Bhil revolt in Gujarat
1811, 1817, 1820	:	Bihar agrarian tribal revolts
1818	:	The Koli revolt (Maharashtra) after a conspiracy

Year		*Revolt*
1831-32	:	The Great Kol insurrection
1820, 1832, 1867	:	Munda revolts in Bihar
1832-33	:	The Kherwar rising under the leadership of Bhagirath in Bihar Hazari Bagh rising of Kherwars—leader Dubia Gossaian—Bihar. Phatel Singh of Palmau was later rising's leader in Bihar
1846	:	Bhil revolt under Kuwar Jivo Vasavo in Gujarat
1850	:	Revolt of Chakra Bisoyi, the Kondh tribal leader in Orissa
1854	:	Kachari chief in North Kachari hills of Assam submitted and permitted the British to annex his territory
1855	:	The revolt of Santals in Bihar
1855	:	Eden's punitive expedition against Mishmis to avenge their killing of two Missionaries
1857-58	:	Bhil revolt (Gujarat) under the leadership of Bhagoji Naik and Kajar Singh
1861	:	The Phulaguri uprising of tribal peasants
1861	:	The Juang revolt in Orissa
1862	:	Andhra Agency Koya tribal revolt against Muttadars (petty tribal zamindars) and their supporters, the British
1868	:	Naik's revolt under Joria's leadership in Gujarat
1869-70	:	Dhanbad Santal unrest (Bihar) against Raja of Tundi subsequently settled by Colonel Dalton
1879	:	Andhra Agency Koya revolt against Muttadars and the British
1880	:	Koya's revolt under Tammandora's leadership Malkangiri, Orissa
1889	:	Sardari (Munda leaders) agitation against the British Government

Year		*Revolt*
27 August, 1895	:	Birsa Munda's arrest
1811	:	Bastar tribal uprising
1913, 1914, 1920, 1921	:	Tana Bhagat rebellion in Bihar
1922	:	Rampa rebellion of Koyas under Alluri Sree Rama Raju against the British
1941	:	Gond and Kolam revolt against the British Government, in Adilabad district of Andhra Pradesh, led by Bhimu
1942	:	Lakshmana Naik's Koraput revolt in Orissa

NOTES AND REFERENCES

1. Chanda, R.P. (1916): *The Indo-Aryan Races*, 1st Published, Rajshahi Reprint 1978, Delhi.
2. Dalton, E.T. (1866): The Kols of Chotanagpur, *Jour. and Proc. of Asiatic Society of Bengal*, XXXV, Calcutta.
3. Grierson, G.A.: *Linguistic Survey of India*, Vol. 1-3, Reprinted, Delhi, 1967.
4. Mitra, P.C. (1988): *Santhali: The Base of World Language*, Firma KLM, Calcutta.
5. Mukhopadhyaya, S. (1975): *The Austrics of India*, K.P. Bagchi & Co., Calcutta.
6. Pande, Ram (ed., 1984): *Tribal Movements*, Sodhak, Jaipur.
7. Raghvaiah, V. (1971): *Tribal Revolts*, Andhra Rastra Adimjati Sevak Sangh, Nellore, Andhra.
8. Risley, H. (1891-92): *Tribes and Castes of Bengal*, Calcutta.
9. Risley, H. (1915): *The People Of India*, 2nd ed., London.
10. Russell and Hiralal (1916): *The Tribes and the Castes of the Central Provinces of India*, McMillan, London, 1-4 Vols. Reprinted in 1997, Delhi.
11. Sachchidanand (1954): *Birsa: The Adivasi Fighter for Freedom*, Vanya Jati, II, 4.
12. Thurston, E. and Ranga Chari, K (1909): *The Castes and Tribes of southern India*, Vol. 1-3, Reprinted, Delhi, 1975.
13. Wilson, J. (1858): *India Three Thousand Years Ago*, Bombay.

XVIII

SCATTERED AND ISOLATED KOLARIAN TRIBES OF CENTRAL INDIA

The wide distribution of Kolarian tribes over northern part of Indian peninsula has influenced the Kolarian groups in two ways. They have either scattered distribution or are isolated in one particular place. However, such distribution is not peculiar to Kolarians only; Dravidian tribes have also more or the less the same distribution pattern, but in general they seem to be less scattered.

In Central India, Kolarians, apart from the Bhils and Savars are mostly restricted to northern part of Chhattisgarh, especially in Surguja and Raigarh districts. In these districts there are certain tribes which are found exclusively there. Then this region in also the peripheral region of Chotanagpur plateau, hence some Kolarian tribes which are found mainly in Chotanagpur plateau are also found in this region. They speak one or the other dialect of Munda language.

The Narmada valley is mainly inhabited by Gonds but Baigas in the upper Narmada valley and Korkus in the lower are Kolarian tribals. Whereas Baigas due to cultural influence of Gonds have altogether forgotten their original language, Korkus still use one of the Kolarian languages.

Among the most scantly distributed tribe is Khairwar. It seems that in the past they had been a more successful tribe and they even ruled some areas in different capacities. With their general decline in political influence, they specialised in Kattha making. The pursuit of Kattha tree enlarged their range.

In Chhattisgarh, Hill Korwas and Birhors have different historical background. But in due course of time, both the tribes became more backward and thus at present they are counted among the primitive tribes of Madhya Pradesh (P.T.G.). Baigas are stratified community, but those living in Baiga Chak are one among P.T.G. The Kolarian tribe of Chhattisgarh are the following:

1. Kolarian tribes of Surguja
2. Khairwar scattered in many states
3. Isolated tribes of Chhattisgarh: Korwa and Birhor
4. Isolated tribes of Narmada valley: Baiga and Korku

The history of the Korkus is obscure. They speak their own language but to what an extent they are related to Kodakus of Chhattisgarh, a near relative of Korwas, is not known.

1. KOLARIAN TRIBES OF SURGUJA

Surguja and Raigarh are the easternmost districts of Chhattisgarh. The hilly terrain of these districts was ideal for survival in isolation. The districts are inhabited by number of Kolarian tribes as given in Table 18.1.

TABLE 18.1

Tribal Communities of Surguja District

A. Dravidian Tribes	*Population*
1. Gond	2,37,885
2. Bharia, Bhumia or Bha	36, 933
3. Oraon	1,06,186
B. Kolrain Tribes	
1. Kol	2, 857
2. Kodaku	14,768
3. Korwa	20, 414
4. Majhwar	10,096
5. Nagesia	28,172
6. Saonta	4,633
7. Baiga	7,480
8. Bhinjwar	671

9. Dhanwar	1,920
10. Kawar	92,132
11. Khairwar	19,460
12. Bharia Bhumia or Bhuinar Bhumia (including Pando, etc.)	36,933

It is evident that the Gonds (including Agarias, etc.), Korwas, Oraons, Majhwars and Kawars are numerically the most populous tribe. The total number of Scheduled Tribes in the district according to the Census 1971 was 741,894, out of which only a very small number (9,501) was reported to be living in urban areas.

A brief description of some of the tribes of Surguja is noted below.

KAWAR

The Kawars (Kanwars) trace their origin from the Kauravas of the *Mahabharata*. The home of this tribe is the hilly tract of Chhattisgarh region, North of the Mahanadi, in the districts of Bilaspur, Raigarh and Surguja. According to a tradition, after the defeat of Kauravas in the battle of Hastinapur, two pregnant women fled to the hilly area of the region and took refuge in the houses of a grazier and a washerman, respectively. There they gave birth to a son and a daughter who became the ancestors of the tribe.

Due to the legend of descent form the Kauravas, they consider military service as their traditional occupation. They are, however, engaged in agriculture, collection and sale of forest produce and in large scale industries. They are divided into eight endogamous divisions, viz., Tanwar, Kamabansi, Paikara, Dudh Kawar, Rathia, Chanti, Cherwa and Rautia. They have a large number of exogamous septs, which are generally totemic. Marriage within the same sept is prohibited, so also between the children of brothers and sisters. A man can marry his wife's younger sister during her lifetime. The system of bride-price is common and is known as *suk*. Widow remarriage is permissible except in the Tanwar sept. The dead are usually buried, though well-to-do people have adopted cremation.

Kanwars are very much advanced as compared to other tribal groups. In the rural areas, they are mainly cultivators. In the urban areas, their predominating occupation is service.

Nagesia

The Nagesias are residing principally in Jashpur tehsil of Raigarh district. They also refer themselves as Kisan. The tribe derives its name either from two words Nag (cobra) or from Nag and Oasis meaning original settlers of Chotanagpur. They are considered to be an offshoot of the Mundas.

They are divided into three groups, viz., Telha, Dhuria and Senduria. The Sendurias are so named on account of using different material for making the forehead of the bride at the time of the marriage ceremony. The Telhas and Dhurias marry among themselves but not with the Sendurias who consider themselves superior to the other two. The Telha and the Dhuria women do not wear glass bangles and armlets above toe elbow. The Telha women do not wear nose-ring nor tattoo their bodies while the Sendurias do both.

Kodaku

The Kodakus are regarded as an offshoot of the Munda or Kolarian tribe akin to the Korwas. They, however, consider themselves a different people from the Korwas but admit that the difference is not great. As a matter of fact, the Kodakus are somewhat better clad than the Korwas and have perhaps a slightly more civilized appearance.

The tribe is usually divided into two groups, viz., Raj Korku and Potharia. But these two divisions are being replaced by four sub-castes with territorial names, Mauasi, Bawari, Ruma, and Bondeya.

Marriage within the same sept or between first cousins is strictly prohibited. Bride-price is paid, out of which a certain amount goes to the Panchayat. Some septs of the tribe give away their daughters in marriage without any ceremony. Other forms of marriages are, by service, elopement or intrusion. Polygamy and widow marriage are permissible.

The district Gazetteer mentions 'Korku' as an alternate name of this tribe.

2. KHAIRWAR

The term 'Khairwar' has two different origins. According to one, the term is derived from 'Khair' (*Catechu*), thus those who make Kattha from the Khair (*Catechu*) tree are Khairwars. Khairwar, Khairwas, Kathakaris and similar words are often used for tribal 'Kattha' makers of Central India and Maharashtra. The tribal 'Kattha' makers are found from West Bengal, Jharkhand, Chhattisgarh and Madhya Pradesh to Maharashtra.

The term Khairwar is also said to have been derived from 'Khairagarh'. The Khairwars associate themselves with a place called 'Khairagarh'. There are two such places, one is situated in Hazaribagh district of Jharkhand state and the others in Chhattisgarh. There is one more place, the old 'pargana' of Allahabad district.

It seems that both the derivations are significant. It is a fact that the larger number of Khairwars till recent past had been mainly the Kattha makers. But these Kattha makers might have descended from the ancestors who lived in one of the 'Khairagarhs'. Again there are two mythological traditions about the origin of the Khairwar tribe.

Mythological Origin of the Tribe

According to one of the stories, thousands of years ago when the earth was without human beings, a wild goose coming from the great ocean alighted at Ahiri Pipri and there laid two eggs. From these two eggs, a man and a woman were born, and these were the parents of the Santal race. From Ahiri Pipri, the descendants migrated to Hara Dutti where they multiplied and got the new name of 'Khairwar'.

This story leads us to believe that the tribe came into existence when Cheros and Santals began their matrimonial relationship. If this tradition has to be believed, the Khairwars had their origin in 'Khairagarh' of Hazaribagh district. It is to be remembered that in tribal languages, 'Garh' means a fort and also a well-defined tract.

Risley states that 'the Khairwars declare their original seat to have been fort of Rohtas, so-called as having been the chosen abode of Rohitaswa, son of Harischandra'.

It is well-known that the famous king Harischandra belonged to Solar dynasty (*Suryavansi*). It is not surprising that the Khairwars who call themselves *Suryavansi* belonging to Rohtas trace their history from king Rohitaswa. Since they think themselves Ksatriya, they wear the sacred thread or *yagnopavit* like the Rajputs.

'sun' seems to be pivotal in the Khairwar legends, may it be, the solar dynasty or the 'sun' in the anthropomorphic form. According to another legend, a daughter of goddess Lakshmi lived in the town of Sara. She was very beautiful and a son was born from the union of this girl and the sun-god. The son was born from her arm and thus named Bhujbal Rai; a daughter was also born from her thigh, hence her name was Janghrai. Bhujbal Rai became the king of Rathgarh. Hiralal identifies the Rathgarh of this story with the tract of Rath in the North of Raigarh state and the town of Sara, where Lakshmi's daughter lived and her children were born, with Saria in Sarangarh.

If these legends are not taken verbatim, we find that the Khairwars had been an offshoot of old Ksatriyas of solar dynasty. They married with the local tribals in their distributional areas and the tribe got its new name of Khairwar. Then they were rulers, soldiers, statesmen, traders but with the time, the larger section of the tribe was forced to live in the forest where they specialised in Kattha making. This section of Kattha makers established marriage relationship with many more tribes who were more backward and primitive than them. The result was that the larger number of Khairwars formed the least developed communities.

General History of the Tribe

Colonel Dalton considers the Khairwars or Kharwars to be closely connected with Cheros. He relates that Cheros, once dominant in Gorakhpur and Shahdol, were expelled from these tracts many centuries ago by the Gorkhas and other tribes and came into Palamau. At the commencement of Chero rule in Palamau, they numbered twelve thousand families and Khairwars eighteen thousand. If an individual of one or the other tribe is asked to which tribe he belongs, he will say he belongs to the twelve-thousand (Chero) or eighteen-thousand (Khairwar) as the case may be.

It is said that the early Palamau population consisted of Khairwars, Gonds, Mars, Korwas, Pahariyas and Kisans. Of these the Khairwars were the people of most consideration. The Cheros conciliated them and allowed them to remain in peaceful possession of the hill tracts bordering on Surguja.

Intermarriages between Chero and Khairwar families have been taking place.

A relative of the Palamau Raja married a sister of Maninath Singh, Raja of Ramgarh. The Rajas of Ramgarh and Jashpur were the members of this tribe. Later on, a Jashpur Raja was married to a lady of pure Rajput blood.

There has been close connection between the Cheros and Khairwars.

There has been two different viewpoints regarding the identity of Khairwars. Khairwars sometimes are regarded as an occupational offshoot of Cheros and Santals in Chotanagpur, but Khairwars of Kaimur hills are said to have derived from the Gonds and Savars. Thus ethnologically there are three views regarding the existing Khairwars—first, as an independent tribe; second, as a mixed tribe of Cheros and old Khairwars; and the third, as a mixed tribe of Gonds and Savaras.

Sometimes Khairwars are said to be the offspring of diverse elements held together by the common occupation of Khair making.

Cultural history of Khairwars has essentially exhibited two types of development.

In one of the streams of development, the Khairwars are Surajbansi, Dualbansi, Patbansi and Beldar or Matkora—these divisions are parallel to the Brahmin, Ksatriya, Vaisya and

Sudra castes. Among this group none of the sub-groups make Kattha. Kattha makers are 'Khairchurias' or the 'tribals' among the tribe. The tribals among the tribes have their own geographic distribution. No one knows how closely they are related to each other. These are:

1. Khairaha of Uttar Pradesh
2. Khairi of West Bengal
3. Khairwars of Chotanagpur
4. Kondars of Bundelkhand
5. Khairchurias of Baghelkhand
6. Kathkarias of Maharashtra

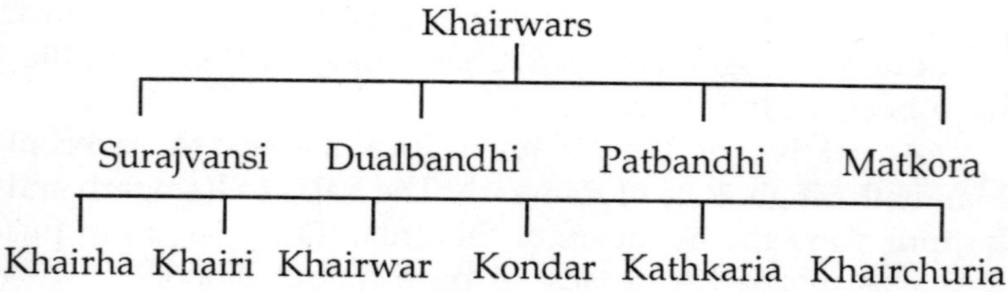

The Khairwars are a stratified society. They are classed in the following way.

1. *Surajvansi*

Surajvansi Khairwars trace their origin from sun-god. Surajvansi Khairwars wear sacred thread or *yagnopavit*. This is the aristocratic division of the state. This group of the tribe consists of zamindars and the chiefs. According to their usual practice they have consolidated their higher position by marrying only in their strata.

2. *Dualbandhi*

According to some philologists, the word 'Dual' is derived from 'Diwal', thus Dualbandhi Khairwars were those who made their livelihood by earthen walls (*dewals*) for houses. Another meaning of 'Dual' is leather belt and many tribals trace their tradition with the belt. The belt is supposed to have been uniform of their forefathers working as soldiers.

3. *The Patbandhi*

The Patbandhi Khairwars are those who either reared tsar silk cocoons or traded the silk. They were thus either the agriculturists or the traders. According to their folklores, they were, a rich community, the members of which wore costly silken clothes.

4. *The Beldar or Matkora*

They are also known as Kawarvansi or descendant of Kawars, another tribe of the locality.

The last of the strata constitutes only those who actually made their subsistence by catechu-making from Khair trees. This group is called 'Khairchura'.

5. *Rebellious Tribe*

In fact, once Britishers suppressed the tribe in the forests. They had only two options—either to die of hunger or subsist on fishing and hunting. Britishers never allowed them to occupy forest land for the sedentary agriculture. The poor and the primitive people in some cases showed their anger against repression. An instance as narrated by Dalton is cited here:

> In the hills of Palamau skirting Surguja, in Tori and Bhanwar Pahar of Chotanagpur and other places, they have always had an indifferent reputation. The head of the clan in Palamau was a notorious freebooter, who, after having been outlawed and successfully evaded every attempt to capture him, obtained a Jagir on his surrendering and promising to keep peace. He kept to his engagement and died in fair repute, but his two sons could not resist the opportunity afforded by the disturbances of 1857-58. After giving much trouble they were captured-one was hanged, the other transported for life and estate was confiscated.

The recent history of Khairwars thus shows that whensoever tribals showed any self-respect and claimed their ownership, they were soon outlawed by the Britishers. The instance cited shows that Britishers, then world power, accepted the second or third grade ruler status of any tribal chieftain for the time being only, for a period they could not successfully and brutally kill the man in real command.

Colonel Dalton considers the Khairwars to be closely connected with Cheros. He relates that Cheros, once dominant in Gorakhpur and Shahabad were expelled from these tracts many centuries ago by the Gorkhas and other tribes, and came into Palamau.

1. *Khairwars of Chotanagpur*

Khairwars of Chotanagpur are an occupational offshoot of Cheros and Santals and those of Kaimur hills are one of the Gonds and Savars. Khairwars of Chotanagpur have everywhere a sub-group which makes catechu.

2. *Khairwars of Kaimur Hills*

Captain J.P. Blunt (1794) met with the Khairwars of Kaimur Hills in the Mirzapur district, in the North of the Son river. His description of these tribes in the Seventh volume of *Asiatic Researches* is as follows:

> The women were seen, assisted by the man carrying off their children and moving with speed to hide themselves in the woods. It was observed that they were nearly naked, and only articles of domestic use found in the deserted huts were a few gourds for water vessels, some bows and arrows, and some fowls as wild as their masters. With great difficulty, by employment of Kols as meditators, some the men were induced to return. They were nearly naked, but armed with bows and arrows and a hatchet.

3. *Khairwars of Panna State*

To extract Kattha, they cut down a tree, strip off the bark and cut the inner and tender wood into small pieces. These are boiled for two or three days until a thick black paste is obtained. From this, water is allowed to drain off and the residue is made into cakes and dried in the sun. Khairwars in the erstwhile Panna state of Bundelkhand appear every year during the winters when they extract Kattha and move back at the beginning of summer.

4. *Khairwars of Chhatarpur State*

Khairwars of erstwhile Chhatarpur State of Bundelkhand have the same annual schedule. In Chhatarpur district they are also called 'Kondar'. In a survey it was found that Khairwars lived in dense forests. In recent years, some of the families living near Panna National Park were located (Tiwari, 1997).

5. *Khairwars of Damoh District*

In Damoh district, the Khairwars are said to have come from Panna state. During working season, they live in temporary sheds of forests and migrate from place to place as the supply of trees is exhausted. Now the felling of trees is totally banned. But when the practice of *Kattha* making was prevalent, duty was levied by the Forest Department at the rate of one rupee per *handi* or the pot in which boiling was carried out.

6. *Khairwars of Maharshtra*

In Maharashtra, the tribe is known as Kathakaris. Crooke in Bombay Gazetteer writes about them as follows: 'The Kathakaris represent themselves as descended from the monkeys of Rama. Now that their legitimate occupation of preparing catechu (Kattha) has been interfered with, they subsist almost entirely by hunting, and habitually kill and eat monkeys, shooting them with bows and arrows'.

It is simply clear from this description that once the Britishers began to interfere with the traditional occupation of the Indian tribes, they were further dragged to the abyss of the poverty and were forced to subsist by hunting.

3. ISOLATED TRIBES OF CHHATTISGARH

Korwa

The dialect of the Korwas is most closely related to Asuri and resembles Mundari and Santhali. The principal subdivisions of the tribe are—the Diharia or Kisan Korwas and the Paharia, Korawas of the hills. The tribe is also divided into totemic exogamous septs.

Korwa tribal community is found in the eastern tribal zone of Chhattisgarh in Raigarh, Sarguja and Bilaspur districts. According to a special survey, total population of this tribe in these districts is 16,860.

The separate Census for this group is not available. As per survey conducted by the Pahari Korwa Development Agency in the year 1982, the total population of Pahari Korwas in all the three districts of Raigarh, Surguja and Bilaspur was 16,860. The district-wise break-up of the population and the percentage of Scheduled Tribe population inhabiting the Pahari Korwa villages is given in the Table 18.2.

TABLE-18.2

Distribution of District-wise Pahari Korwa Population (Survey-1982)

Name of District	*Pahari Korwas*	*Percentage to ST Population*
Raigarh	5,393	17.7
Surguja	10,361	10.9
Bilaspur	605	21.7
Total	16,860	12.9

The history of this tribe reveals that they moved Westwards into the old Khudia zamindari (present Sanna and Bagicha revenue circles of Jashpur tehsil of Raigarh district) from Chotanagpur region at a date which cannot be fixed. They are the original settlers in the Khudia region of Jashpur. From Khudia, in due course of time, they further migrated to the adjacent parts of Surguja district and settled there. From Surguja, a group of the community gradually migrated to Palamau highlands and further into the hills of Vindhyachal near Dhudhi in Mirzapur district of Uttar Pradesh. During the course of migration and settlement those who remained on hills and in dense forest were called Hill Korwas or Pahari Korwas and those who settled down in the plains were called Deharia Korwas. So, the dense forests and hills became the abode of Pahari Korwas.

Thus, being one of the sub-groups of the Korwa tribe, Pahari Korwas are dispersed in Raigarh, Surguja and a few in Bilaspur district. In Raigarh district, they are found in Jashpur tehsil which is also an Integrated Tribal Development Project. In Surguja district, they are found in three tehsils viz., Samar, Ambikapur and Pal. In Bilaspur district, they are found in Katghora tehsil which is also an Integrated Tribal Development Project. As per the survey their numerical strength in these district is as follows.

In Samari tehsil of Surguja district, they are concentrated in two Tribal Development Blocks namely, Sankergarh and Kusumi, whereas in Ambikapur tehsil they are spread over in seven Tribal Development Blocks but their major concentration is in two blocks, i.e. Lundra and Rajpur. According to the district administration, it is said that Pahari Korwas are concentrated only in Wandrofnagar Tribal Development Block of the Pal tehsil. But during the preliminary investigation it is found that Kodaku tribal community inhabiting this Block claims itself to be Pahari Korwa. Block-wise break-up of the families of Pahari Korwas inhabiting these three tehsils of the district is shown in Table 18.3.

TABLE-18.3

Block-wise Population of Hill Korwas

Sl. No.	*Tehsil*	*Block*	*No. of Villages*	*No. of Families*
1.	Samari	(i) Shankergarh	42	634
		(ii) Kusumi	23	289
2.	Ambikapur	(i) Lundra	48	418
		(ii) Sitapur	6	78
		(iii) Mainpath	15	182
		(iv) Lakhanpur	12	107
		(v) Ambikapur	6	120
		(vi) Batoli	9	130
		(vii) Rajpur	23	270
3.	Pal	(i) Wadrofnagar	22	196
		Total	210	2502

In Bilaspur district, Pahari Korwas are found only in nine villages of Korba Development Block of Katghora tehsil. Total number of families of Pahari Korwas in these nine villages is 117.

Habitat and Dwellings

The area of habitation of Pahari Korwas is spread over in Jashpurnagar tehsil, Raigarh district, Samari, Ambikapur and Pal tehsils of Surguja district and Katghora tehsils of Bilaspur district. The topography of these areas is characterised by hilly and undulating terrain with a fairly good forest cover. These topographical conditions of the area appear to be responsible for keeping these people (Pahari Korwas) at the stage of hunting, food-gathering and primitive agriculture. Thus, the eco-system has been inextricably bound with the life of Pahari Korwas.

Jashpurnagar tehsil is divided into upper and lower ghats. The upper ghat previously under Khudia zamindari now consists of Baghicha and Manora Tribal Development Blocks. This is an extensive plateau rising to about 1,200 metre above sea level and is covered with dense forests. This is bound on North and West by the Samari tehsil of Surguja district. The elevated plateau called 'pat' is the main abode of Pahari Korwas. Samari which is adjacent to the region of Jashpurnagar tehsil is separated by Kanhar river which is hilly, undulating and is covered by dense forest especially. The western region is inaccessible and remains cut off during the rainy season. Pal tehsil is in the northwest while Ambikapur is in the southwest of Samari tehsil. The southeastern border of Ambikapur tehsil touches the southwestern border of Jashpurnagar tehsil.

Society and Culture

The tribe bury the dead, placing the corpse in the grave with head towards the South. A little rice is buried with the corpse. In Bilaspur, the dead are buried in the forests and the graves of old men are covered with branches of the sal (*Sorea robusta*) tree. Then they go to a little distance and make a fire, pour 'ghi' and incense on it as an offering to the ancestors, and when they hear a noise in the forest they take it to be the voice of the dead man. When a man dies, his hut is broken down and they do not live in it again. The bodies of children under five are buried either in the house or under the shade of a banyan tree, probably with the idea that the spirit will come back and born again. They say that a banyan tree is chosen because it lives longer of all trees and is evergreen, and hence it is supposed that the child's spirit will also live its proper span instead of being ultimately cut off in its next birth.

Other Customs

The Korwas do not admit outsiders into the tribe. They will take food from a Gond or Kanwar, but not from a Brahmin. A man is permanently expelled from caste for a liaison with a woman of the impure castes, and a woman for adultery with any person other than a Korwa. Women are tattooed with patterns of dots on the arms, breasts and feet. Neither men nor women ever cut their hair.

Marriage within the sept is forbidden and the system of paying price for a bride is prevalent. Polygamy is permissible. Among the Paharia Korwas of Surguja, the boys and girls arrange their own marriage. Divorce and remarriage of widows are permitted and a widow often marries her late husband's younger brother. It is customary for a husband divorcing his wife to give feast to his tribesmen for five days.

They worship Dulha Deo, the Chief god of the Gonds. In Surguja district, their principal deity is Khuria Rani. Thakur Deo is considered to be their corn god and it is believed that the god protects the village from diseases and epidemics. They observe three main festivals—Deothan, which is observed on the full-moon day of Pus (December) when all the gods are worshipped; the Nawanna or the harvest festival and Faguwa or Holi. They are engaged mainly in agriculture and 'other services'.

Economy

The economy of Pahari Korwas is forest-based. Now the forests are gradually vanishing and shifting cultivation has been stopped. This has torn the fabric of the economy of the tribe and the result is that they are neither shifting cultivators nor yet settled cultivators. They are in a process of economic transformation in the context of disturbed eco-system. Above 55% families of all the three districts are landless. All the 117 Pahari Korwa families of Bilaspur district are landless. In Raigarh and Surguja districts, the percentage of landless, Pahari Korwas is 52.94 (321 families) and 55.55 (1,390 families) respectively. The size of holdings in Raigarh and Surguja districts are given in Table 18.4.

TABLE-18.4

Landholdings of Hill Korwas

S.	*District*	*Size of Landholding in Acres (Percentage)*			
		Less than 2	*2-5*	*5-10*	*10 & above*
1.	Raigarh	13.00	40.3	22.2	24.5
2.	Surguja	30.0	37.8	9.8	22.4

Shifting cultivation or 'Beora' continues to be the main source of sustenance which is being regulated on ecological considerations. Hill Korwas raise various inferior crops through 'beora' cultivation, which is a kind of shifting cultivation in the hilly parts in the sides of 'pats'. In these areas, a kind of rahar crop, locally known as 'beora rahar' was grown for one year followed in the succeeding year by 'gondli' and 'maker'. After this, the area was allowed to revert to jungle and a fresh portion of jungle was cut. The local business community comprising Goalas/Ahirs/Jains/Banias, etc. used to instigate the Pahadi Korwas to grow rahar in the above manner and sell them in exchange of equal quantity of rice through barter system. These local businessmen also supplied them with rahar seeds at the time of sowing and they used to charges 6 to 10 times of the seeds supplied at the time of harvest. This practice continued for about six to seven decades.

As usual, during the year 1980-81, the Pahadi Korwas took Arhar seeds from local businessmen and sowed the crop. However, the forest authorities also became cautious and the Project Officer, Pahadi Korwas Development Agency took keen interest. Due to their joint efforts, the entire produce of arhar of the Pahadi Korwas was purchased by the Forest authorities.

Out of 3,602 Hill Korwa families, about 2,000 families are either landless or are only marginal cultivators who at the moment mainly depend on wage earning, which is also not always available. They have to be provided with some alternative source of livelihood. They have been traditionally shifting cultivators and rearing the cattle of Ahirs as wage earners and therefore, posses the necessary know-how for keeping the cattle. Landless or marginal families can be provided productive employment.

The collection of minor forest produce is done but all the produce is not sold in the market. Sal seed, mahua and imali are sold to nearby sahukars or Ahirs and they do not get fair price for these commodities. They go to sahukar to sell these produce because they need immediate payment. Besides, there are certain minor products like roots, char, fruits and mahua flowers and seeds which are still exchanged with salt and chilli, etc. They do not get rice and other items of consumption at a reasonable price for want of proper agency. They are indebted to 'sahukars' and Ahirs or other dominating castes due to debt obtaining for consumption and social needs as well as for getting seeds at the time of sowing operation.

The Pahari Korwas of Surguja also possess these skills except that of weaving the fishing nets. Even making these things for domestic use is becoming difficult due to scarcity of raw material like bamboo, chhind and date leaves. These raw materials are not available in forests of 'pat' areas of Jashpur tehsil but in Samari and Ambikapur tehsils, these are still available.

A Pahari Korwa is always busy about the site selection

of his homestead. The place where a homestead is to be constructed carries great importance to him. It can be built anywhere in the forest but only after observing and performing certain rituals. It is a belief of the Pahari Korwas that a cooler place is better to live and that maize, mustard, etc. grow better. Pahari Korwas prefer to live aloof on hills in the midst of forests so that they many not be disturbed in their day-to-day life by other communities inhabiting the nearby villages.

Traditionally, the house of a Pahari Korwa is not permanent and well-built but a temporary and weak structure. It can be built within a few hours and can also be dismantled within no time. A homestead must always have a 'bari' land. Normally the houses are made of mud with thatched or tiled roof. They are grouped together on a raised ground. The houses are generally partitioned with about one metre high wall into two portions. The small portion is used for kitchen purposes and the big one is for living.

In all the homesteads, the trellis work of the roof is constructed with 'Sal' rafters. In case of tiled roof, after trellis, tilting is done. Thatched roof is not so common now. The four low side walls are made of mud or twigs plastered over with mud and cow-dung. There is no open space in the interior for courtyard. The 'bari' is fenced during rainy seasons to protect from animals the maize and vegetable grown.

Food and Drinks

The staple diet of the tribe is coarse rice-maize or kodo. They supplement their diet with fruits, various kinds of roots, tubers, leaves, ants and animals. The roots, leaves, fruits and flowers are collected from forest. Besides these, various tubers, leaves, mahua seeds, flowers and fruits are also collected from the Bahera seeds for consumption. It is found that for the months of April, May and June, they entirely depend upon different kinds of fruits and roots, when these are found in abundance. This is also the season for hunting, but now due to the scarcity of game, they hardly go for hunting.

During rainy season, the tribe is fully dependent on buttermilk, mango, seeds, 'gate kanda', 'hakbakanda', 'patal kanda' and small fish. A kind of bread is prepared from the powder of mango seeds called 'teak'. Winter is supposed to be the best period for them. During the season, maize, kulthi, urda and tuar pulses, gondali, and gora dhan are harvested and they get sufficient food. During this season, they celebrate various festivals connected with harvesting. Maize is their principal diet of this season. Pulses of kulthi, urad and tuar are also consumed. Rice is consumed by those who cultivate gora dhan. January to March are also the months of comparative plenty when they consume their harvested crops and vegetable grown in the 'bari' land. The availability of maize, madia, kulthi and tuar pulse depend upon the yield of these crops. In case the yield is sufficient, it is still available for consumption during this season.

They drink Mahua liquor and also Haria, an alcoholic drink made at home by fermentation of cereals.

Fragmentary History of the Korwas

De Brett in the beginning of twentieth century depicts the Korwa in the following words:

> The Korwas are liable to outbreaks of crime, which usually take the form of an attack on an Ahir, a class of men, who by their reckless manner in which they allow their cattle to damage the cultivations of these aborigines, often excite the latter to reprisals. Occasionally they also attack the passing traders to get salt or cloth, or a liquor shop to get a supply of drink. These men are usually armed with bows and arrow, spears and axes and since they do not hesitate to use their weapons and are usually in considerable force, they are formidable opponents to unarmed people.

Risley, Hutton, Crooks, Driver, Russell and Hiralal and Prasad have made only passing reference to the Hill Korwa. Thus, their accounts shed little light on the life and culture of the people. Majumdar did fieldwork among the Korwa in the tri-junction of Mirzapur, Surguja and Palamu. Bhandari has studied kinship organization of the Korwa of Mirzapur (U.P.) only. Prasad's brief account of the people is based on the Korwa of Palamu (Bihar) and Singh has made a brief mention of Korwa while bringing into relief the past and present of the Surguja district. His accounts are based more on hearsay than any genuine fieldwork. Ahmad has mainly dwelt upon the physical aspect of the Hill Korwa of Surguja.

Dalton feels that the Korwas were the first inhabitants of the area and were at one time masters of the whole country, ..."the savage and almost nomadic life they lead is not favourable for increase of population...they were at one time more numerous and powerful and it is possible that many of the broken tribes now found scattered throughout this part of India once formed with the Korwa people united under some rude form of Government".

Risley and Gait in the *Census of India 1901*, furnish the following information regarding the Korwa and distribution of their population in Central India: "The only considerable tribe of western Bengal who speak Munda languages are the Korwa... who appear to be related to Mundas, inhabit the West of Chotanagpur especially the states of Surguja and Jashpur, the Dewan of the latter being the member of the tribe. They are even found in that part of the district of Mirzapur which lies South of the Son (river), being the only Munda tribe speaking a Munda language in the United Provinces. Here, their language is called Korwari, Singli and Ernga are said to be the dialect of Korwari".

Language

The Hill Korwas of Surguja speak a dialect known as Korwari which is closely related to Mundari. They are gradually abandoning their old dialect which has been replaced by Kurukh. The Chattisgarhi spoken by Hill Korwas in Jashpur tract is known as Sadri Korwa.

According to Captain Samuels, Assistant Commissioner quoted by Dalton,

> The first human being settled in Surguja was very much troubled by the depredations of wild beasts on their crops. He put up scarecrow in his field, figures made of bamboos dangling in the air to frighten the animals.
>
> When the 'great spirit' saw the scarecrow he hit on an expedient his trouble of reconstructing them. He animated the dangling figures,

thus bringing into existence creatures ugly enough to frighten the birds and beasts.... and they were the ancestors of the Hill Korwa.

In Rakaiya, the hill Korwas narrated to this author the following story of their origin: "A scarecrow (druna) holding a bow and arrow was installed to frighten birds (viz. *pandki*). Rama's wife (Sita) asked her husband to animate the figure. Rama asked Sita, 'What for I should give a new soul to it?' (thinking it is something insignificant). Rama's wife replied, 'If you do not animate the scarecrow (*druna*) I will cease living with you, and will request you to pass your life the way you like and I will be passing mine (separately)'. Hearing this Rama conceded to her wishes, animated the figure and transformed it into a human figure holding a bow and arrow. He was the first Korwa from whom the present Korwa came into being and never parted with a bow since then".

In Sardapath (Raigarh), the Hill Korwas gave the version similar to the above story excepting the variation that instead of 'Rama and his wife', they held Sankar and Parvati responsible for animating the scarecrow. The above version differs only on the point as to who animated the scarecrow whether the 'great spirit' (Dalton), Rama and his wife (Rakaiya), or Sankar and Parvati (Sardapath).

A different version regarding the origin of the people was given by Sri A.L. Dubey (the then Deputy Director), Social Welfare, M.P. Government (personal communication). It runs as follows: "Parvati had two sons. Once both of them were sitting on her lap (*kor*). One of them fled from there and the other remained sitting thereon. One who fled from the Parvati's lap (*kor*) was called Kodaku and one who remained sitting her lap was named Korwa". The Korwa informants did not lend support to this story.

The Place of Origin

A consensus among all Korwa informants was that the place of their origin was Khuria in Jaspur tehsil of Raigarh district. The area under the erstwhile Khuria zamindari is treated as a Scheduled Area specified in Scheduled Area (Part A-States) Order, 1950, *Census of India*.

We find the following description of the erstwhile Khuria zamindari furnished by Dalton:

The present Raja of Jashpur fully admits that the Korwa Dewan's ancestors were the original rulers of the country. His own family counts only seventeen generations since assuming the throne, and were first established in the low-lands where the remains of their ancient strongholds may still be seen. They were Khairwars, whom, I suppose to have been an offshoot of the same race and their tradition that they were driven out of Belonja in Bihar may refer to the break of the Chero-Kol-Khairwar nation formerly located in Magadh. The family having established themselves in the lowlands gradually brought the highlanders under subjection, but the great highland chief only yielded on condition that he was to be acknowledged as the second person in realm, the lieutenant or Dewan. This was conceded and from generations there was no breach of the contract till the grandfather of the present Raja, disregarding the ancient policy of his family confided the affairs of the Raj to his foster-brother, a Kahar named Anant Ram. The hereditary Korwa Diwan Munawar Singh, resented this and a small war ensued which lasted for many years and was still in active operation when Jashpur with Surguja and other territories ceded to the British Government by Appa Sahib. Some of the Government troops were sent to co-operate with the Raja against his refractory vassal but they made very little impression on the Korwas, and Munawar Singh fought till he died in A.D. 1821.

His son Maniar Singh, who had been captured during the hostilities and under the guarantee of the British Government was reinstated with all the hereditary honours and possessions of the family, since when the Jashpur Korwas have always conducted themselves peaceably and loyally. Village of Bharatpur tehsil, it appears probable, that in early times, the district was occupied by a civilized race. Who the people were and what was their period of stay is however, unknown (D.C.H. Surguja: XII).

In 1759, a Maratha army overran the eastern half of the district and compelled the chief to acknowledge himself as a tributary of the Berar Government. Beyond this, the Marathas did not take interest in the affairs of Surguja. In 1792, the three erstwhile feudatory states which constitute the present district ceded to the British Government. The British force appointed Amar Singh as the Chief of Surguja. Amar Singh's rule lasted till 1852. On his death, his eldest son Indrajit Singh succeeded to the throne in 1853. Indrajit Singh died in 1897 and his son Raghu Nath Singh was declared the ruler of Surguja. He ruled Surguja till his death in 1917. After his death Maharaja Ramanuj Sharan Singh came to the throne and ruled the state till 1942. The last Maharaja adopted modern techniques of administration.

The new Maharaja himself killed many tigers during various hunting expeditions and imposed heavy penalties on the Korwas and Kodakus. He made the Korwa chiefs responsible to control their people and granted them allowances and red-turbans.

There were in existence within the last twenty years as highlanders, chiefs and holders of manors four Korwa notables, two in Surguja and two in Jashpur; all four estates were valuable as they comprised substantial villages in the fertile plains and great tracts of hilly country on which were scattered the hamlets of their more savage followers. The Surguja Korwa chiefs were, however, continually at strife with the Surguja Raja and for various acts of rebellion against Lord Paramount, lost manor till each but one or two villages remained.

This was the position when the mutiny of 1857 broke out and like many others, they thought the disturbances and anarchy that supervened afforded them an opportunity of recovering what they had lost. Placing themselves at the head of their clansman, they committed a series of raids on the lowland villages and wholesale plundering and murdering were restored to for a time but ere long the insurrection was cut short by capture of two chiefs: one of them who was convicted for murder was hanged, the other was amnestied and died.

The two Jashpur thanes conducted themselves right loyally at this crucial period and they are now prosperous gentlemen in the full enjoyment of their estates... one of them is the hereditary Dewan of Jashpur, lord of the whole tribe of Korwas. The other holds an estate called Kakia, comprising twenty-two villages in the lowland and some hill country.

It can be derived from the above account that the Korwas of Jashpur were actual rulers of the land till the middle of fourteenth century. They were later subjugated by the Kharwar rulers. The Dewanship was granted to Korwa highlanders. This system remained in practice till the beginning of the nineteenth century. In the second decade of nineteenth century, there were clashes between the Raja and the Korwa Dewan. This perhaps attracted Britishers and the state of Jashpur was ceded to them in 1818.

These tribals have more concentration near Sanna. Ethnically they are a branch of the Munda tribes, and are akin to the Korkus. There is some similarity in the political organization of the Hill Korwa and the Korku. Like the Korkus, the Hill Korwas also lack a hierarchical structure with a centralized authority. The Diwan of Khuria who was a zamindar was respected by the Hill Korwas as king. He was a Rajput by origin, and was a Baghel Kshatriya.

The only tribal chief among the Hill Korwas can be found at the village level. Mukhiya is the village chief and is greatly respected and obeyed by all. He issues dictates which are assiduously followed by all. During the regime of the Diwan at Jashpur, the Mukhiyas were elected by villagers. Of late, there is no election and a brother or nephew of the old Mukhiya assumes the post. The panchas from the village may also select a person for the post. He plays an important role in settling disputes.

The *Sayanas* (the wise) or the panchas are selected from among the elders from the village for settling disputes. But the traditional panchayat is not in vogue. It is ad hoc arrangement. Mostly on Thursdays, five elders (*Sayanas*) are called, who sit together and after hearing the parties give decisions.

Baiga is their spiritual chief who guides them in social and religious matters. He is usually a man of character and is a well-informed person. He acts as a friend, philosopher and guide for the villagers and hence assumes informal leadership. The post is hereditary and goes to the son.

Mukhiya and *Baiga* are the two chiefs and at times the same person may hold both the posts.

Birhor

Birhor is one of the smallest tribes of Central India. In 1911, their total number in Bihar and neighbouring provinces was 3,805, out of which 1,093 used their own dialect belonging to the Mundari family. They rapidly accepted other languages, as in 1961, the number of persons using their own dialect came down to 590 only.

The Birhors live in the districts of Hazaribagh, Manbhum and Singhbhum of Bihar and in Palamau and in Mayurbhanj in Orissa.

Table 18.5 gives details of Birhor population in Bihar from 1871 to 1971.

The most important feature of Birhor life is their nomadic habit. They live on forest products and small games in which animals are trapped, snared or killed in the forest. They make durable ropes for which they collect particular kind of fibre from the jungle creeper and process it. These ropes are in great demand amongst peasants.

Sarat Chandra Roy (1925) studied the tribe. He has described their hunting of monkeys and given account of hunting expeditions. They pray to Sing Bonga thus: "Thou in the sky, O Sin Bonga, king should anybody (of our tanda) have cost an evil look, and (his or her) evil eye, evil tooth or evil mouth, has fallen (on our party) may that be withdrawn.(S.C. Roy, *The Birhor*, pp. 74, 79)

They had system of separate dormitories for bachelors and maidens. Now this system is not observed.

The Birhors are simple-hearted, affectionate, peace loving and shy. Birhor (man + forest) is a name given to them by their neighbours. They call themselves Chopdar. In their language 'Chop' means any kind of 'Rope'. They make a variety of 'Chop' (ropes). Some of the ropes are fine. On certain religious occasions the religious head bears sacred thread (*yagnopavit*) made of chop fibres like a Brahmin priest.

Ethnically, the Bihors belong to proto-Australoid group. Roy (1925) narrates their physical features as:

'Ethnologically the Birhors belong to dark-skinned (Melanodrms). Regarding the racial history of the Mundari speaking people, different schools have given different views.

(a) According to Risley (1901) Birhors are Dravidians.
(b) Rougree (1921) puts them under Australoid Group.
(c) B.C. Guha (1931) classified them under proto-Australoid.
(d) Bradley Birt (1903) describes them as 'Wildest tribe in Chotanagpur'.

Linguistically, Birhors belong to Austro-Asiatic Mundari group. The Birhors speak a language, which is commonly classed under the Austro-Asiatic sub-family of the Asiatic Linguistic Family which extends through Malayasia and Indonesia. The Birhor dialect is more closely connected with Mundari than that of Santhali.

With non-Birhors, the Birhors speak Khortha Sadani, a lingua franca for Chotanagpur tribals.

The Birhors are one of the primitive tribes of Madhya Pradesh. Their original home, where they live in large numbers lie beyond the limits of Madhya Pradesh. The tribe is native to Chotanagpur Plateau of Bihar. In 1915, Haddon, then Reader in Ethnobotany in the University of Cambridge, took note of Birhors as 'nomads... who had no fixed habitation'. Later S.C. Roy, in 1916, found them to live in small bands, roaming about in Chotanagpur and Orissa hills. Roy wrote a comprehensive account of the Birhors.

Population

The 1961, Census recorded the total population of Birhors in Bihar at 2,438 which went up to 4,377 in 1981. The Birhor has been numerically one of the minor tribes of Bihar. In the year 1971, as per Census Report, their total population was 3,464 only. This means the tribe had registered less than 50% growth of population in three decades. However, the growth rate accelerated in the period between 1971 and 1981. Maximum concentration of the Birhor population is found in Hazaribagh and Girdih districts and their number is small in Palamau and Gaya districts.

In the pursuit of game and food, a few Birhors have migrated beyond Chotanagpur division and reached other parts of West Bengal, Orissa and Madhya Pradesh. In the year 1971, total population of the migrated population was less than 1,200.

TABLE-18.5

Birhor Population in Bihar over 100 Years

Census	District							
	Hazari	Ranchi	Singh	Pala	Purnia	Gaya	Dhan	Total
1871	132	277	-	-	-	-	-	1221
1881	Not Available							
1891	717	504	-	-	-	-	-	1,221
1990	506	504	342	-	-	-	-	848
1911	506	1,024	927	48	27	-	-	2,026
1921	582	374	380	46	-	-	35	1,417
1931	1,143	441	12	141	-	-	133	1,870
1941	1,623	561	335	11	-	-	-	2,530
1951	Not Available							
1961	1,233	947	257	01	-	-	-	2,438
1971	1,872	876	319	87	106	96	108	3,464

Population in Madhya Pradesh

As per Government of Madhya Pradesh Reports in the project plan on Birhor, their population in 1992 in the State was 938 and they were spread over 32 village in seven Development Blocks of district Raigarh. There are less than 300 Birhor households.

They are mainly found in Raigarh and Surguja districts. Their maximum concentration is at Bagicha, Kasabel and Kankuri. A survey of the Government of Madhya Pradesh has revealed that this primitive tribe is found in 26 villages of Dharamjaygarh and Jashpur project areas of Raigarh district. The total population of the tribe is 938, spread over in seven Development Blocks viz., Lailoonga, Dharamjaygarh, Tamnar, Pathalgaon, Bagicha, Kasabel and Kunkuri. In all, there are 281 families of the Birhors out of which only 27 families had some land (9.6%). They are mainly engaged in rope-making, labour and collection of forest produce. Majority of the population works as agricultural labourer.

Household characteristics

The average number of persons per household was found to

be 3.5 persons among the Birhors and 4.8 among the non-Birhors. The percentage of nuclear households was higher (87%) among the Birhors compared to the non-Birhors (59%). The difference found statistically is highly significant.

Age-sex Composition

The medial age of the Birhor population is 23.7 years and it does not differ significantly from the non-Birhors (23.6 years). Among the Birhors, the medial ages for males and females were 22.5 and 24.6 years respectively, which did not differ considerably from the non-Birhors.

As regards the age composition of the Birhors, 36.7 per cent population was below 15 years of age and 6.5 per cent population was reported to be in 60+ age group. The figures for non-Birhor population were 34.1. and 7.6 percents respectively. The dependency ratio indicated that the Birhor population was young compared to the non-Birhor population.

Settlement Pattern

The tribe lives in clusters of villages often known as Tandas. Each cluster may have one or more Tandas. For instance, Chalkari Birhor cluster has Chalkari, Banaso, Chalanga, Khambhawa, Jaranga and Amnari Tandas; Tulbul Birhor cluster has two Tandas, i.e. Tulbul and Dumari. But Sidhabara cluster has only one Tanda, i.e. Sidhabara.

A Tanda may be a full village or part of village. It consists of 2 to 24 families of Birhors belonging to one class or more than one class.

The village may have a Tanda and habitation of other communities also.

House

The Birhors live in small houses, which are locally called 'Kurhas'. The houses are mostly identical in shape, size and form. These are conical umbrella type structures made of dry sal leaves. Each house measures about 8 feet in height and 160 sq. feet in diameter. The houses have no windows or ventilators to provide fresh air. Every house has one small exit. Its shape is oval and size is only 12 sq. feet. Even a boy of 8 years cannot enter straight in the hut. Every adult has to bow down considerably at the door of the house. In fact, they all crawl while entering the house.

The houses are properly thatched, and as the Birhors living in them claim, rain-water does not enter the hut. They also claim that the interior of their hut is warm in winter and cool in summer.

The interior of the house is divided into two sections, the bigger section is used as a bedroom. The other section is kitchen. The floor of the hut is usually clean. The surface is freshly laid with a thick mixture of earth, cow-dung and water.

Economy

The Birhors are mainly hunters and gatherers of Chotanagpur plateau. In Madhya Pradesh, majority of Birhors are engaged in rope-making (93%). Only 3% are engaged in agriculture and other activities. But those living in Bihar and Orissa hunt small games like hare, pea-fowl, jungle food, etc. On the organisational level there are two main sections of Birhors.

1. Uthlu Birhor or Nomadic Birhor, and
2. Jungh Birhor or Settled Birhor.

Shahu (1995) suggests one more type of Birhors-'Biasalu' or Semi-nomadic Birhor. This third type has only recently emerged.

Uthlu Birhors are those who are nomadic and roam about from one forest to another in quest of food, game and edible products. They follow a peculiar migration pattern.

In summer and monsoon (June to October) during which hunts go waste, it is difficult to find them in forests. These hunters take up subsidiary occupations like making bowls, ropes and pattal and donas of leaves and selling or bartering them at village markets for grain. They work only occasionally as labourers in the neighbouring villages.

The Birhor migration is mainly due to exhaustion of resources from the neighbouring forests. Normally a patch of forest where they live provides food for three months.

Migration is also due to death, epidemic or personal cause.

Jungh Birhors are known to live in a place for more than 50 years, but this span of time is rare.

In Madhya Pradesh, they are not reported to be engaged either in service or in business. In the distributional areas of Birhors, other tribals are engaged in agriculture and other activities. The percentage of their activities differ with places.

TABLE-18.6

Economic Characteristics and Health Care among Birhors

Birhors	*Others*	
No. of households studied	112	137
Average size of household	3.2	5.4
Landless households (in percentage)	44.6	11.7
Size of land per household (in Acres)	1.6	5.3
Source of Income (%):		
Rope-making	70.9	0.0
Cultivation	6.9	36.5
Forest Products	9.7	28.1
Labour	9.6	16.9
Service	0.0	13.4
Others	2.9	5.1
Average household income (Rs. per annum)	4,582	8,098
Average household expenditure (Rs. per annum)	4,611	7,502
Pattern of expenditure: (in per cent)		
Food pattern	81.5	70.8
Clothing	10.1	15.2
Alcohol & tobacco	2.7	3.0
Others	5.7	11.0

Food

Birhors still live in hunting and gathering stage of culture. Twentieth century had only small effect on this tribal group.For instance, all of their belongings are related to the hunting activities but for the exception of small loin clothes. Their houses have leaf mats, spears, hammers and axes to hunt and cut wood, aluminium glasses and plates to drink and eat. They wear 'tyre sandals', but these are rarely, if ever used, because on wearing them they cannot chase their hunt. They have to walk a minimum of 10 to 12 km daily for hunt, because the forests are not just close to their settlements. Then, there is a growing scarcity of wild animals, small or big in all the forests. The man goes to hunt birds and animals, and the women and children move around picking fruits, flowers, herbs, yams and tubers.

The Birhors are known monkey-hunters. They are hunting monkeys by tradition and eat them.

Even though each family maintains a separate kitchen, they all share the hunted and gathered items. It is to be noted that the use of kitchen in Birhor family is mostly restricted when they eat vegetable food. In most cases when an animal is killed, it is put in kitchen only up to the time meat has not been cooked. Generally, meat is cooked in kitchen in the open. Open air cooking sites provide ample space for sitting.

The kitchen serves more the purpose of a storeroom; it is used mostly in the rainy season. The ideal condition of their kitchen is that when it is full of hunted wild rats, rabbits, etc. Rice is their main cereal, other items of food are salt, mustard oil, chillies and sufficient wood for fire.

The Birhors are monkey-eaters, which they hunt in the nearby forests. They were thought of hunting monkeys only when other animals were not available in forests. This concept took political twist in the year 1997, when some observers reported in local newspapers that these tribals were compelled to subsist on food which was not fit for human consumption. The monkey-eating habit was said to be related with the starvation of these tribals due to famine. However, some of the tribals denied such assumptions, they established that there was nothing bad in the tradition of eating monkey meat. According to them, they never hunted langurs (*Presbytis entellus*) beyond a certain point. The monkey population was never in danger. They also keep hens.

Haria (rice beer) is an essential part of their food. Haria is brewed in earthen vessels. Everyone above the age of five years is permitted to drink this beer. They cannot think of a life without haria. When they drink too much, they may quarrel with each other but for a very short spell of time. It is interesting to note that Birhors never let the members of their tribe remain hungry. In times of emergency, food is shared even out of family, but in doing so they are partial about drinks.

Usually, Birhors take two meals when available, one in the Seta Kalwa Joma (lunch) and another Ayub Panadan (dinner) but they keep some food for their children's breakfast. Generally their meals consist of rice and vegetable or rice and meat of trapped game. During festivals like Sarhul, Holi, Sohari, Dashahra, they prepare special food items which include rice, pitha, meat, chicken and haria. Other food items are wheat, potato, jack-fruits, leafly vegetables, fish and mustard oil.

Sex Ratio

Sex ratio among the Birhors was 904 females per 1000 males, lower than the non-Birhors (929). It indicates poor health status of women in the tribe.

Literacy

General literacy rate among the Birhors was 14.3 per cent which was lower as compared to the non-Birhors (34.7%). In 7+ yrs. population, 18.8 per cent were literate and out of them only 2 per cent had education above Higher Secondary level. Among Birhors, more than 91 per cent females were illiterate.

Age at Marriage and Marital Status

In Birhors, the mean age at marriage, of males and females, was 17.6 and 14.8 years respectively. It may be noted that 83 per cent of the Birhor females got married before the prescribed legal age of 18 years and 85 per cent of males got married before the legal age of 21 years. The mean age at marriage for males and females were higher in non-Birhor population (18.4 yrs. males and 16 yrs. for females). The proportions of marriage below the prescribed age were 73 per cent and 77 per cent among the non-Birhor females and males respectively. The mean age at marriage for males and females differ considerably between the two ethnic groups. Among the Birhors, 52 per cent population was found married, 6.3 per cent widowed/divorced, one per cent separated. The figures differ considerably for the non-Birhors.

4. ISOLATED TRIBES OF NARMADA VALLEY

Baiga

Writing about the Baigas of Baigachak, D.N. Tiwari (1985) gives the following graphic picture:

> Baigas are fine manly race. His almost nude, the black figure, sturdy looks, well chiselled body, long tanglied hair-locks hanging like pendulum on the left shoulder, rough but as refreshing appearance as the forest in which he lives, mark him out at once in many crowd gathered in a weekly market of the tribal tract. Though rustic in appearance he is extremely mild, hospitable, a humorous, simple and large hearted friend. He is a rare example of finer qualities embodied in a rough weather have made him hard like rock, and courageous like the king of the forest. It is a pleasure to meet a Baiga whether in youth or ripe in age.

Baiga has better looks and possesses fine physique than his brother tribesman, the Gond. The hair is black and thick and long on the head, but generally speaking scanty elsewhere. As no survey has been made of their anthropometric characters, it is difficult to describe their physical features with accuracy. However, Elwin divides them into two categories: the first type has a long head, high cheek bones, a fine pointed face and chin, small almost delicate nose, not depressed at the root, narrow eyes, and straight eye-slits, lips of medium thickness, and a slightly emphasised under-jaw. The second type is mixed by a square head, and much coarser feature. The cheek-bones are not so high, the nose is large with wise nostrils and is slightly depressed at the root. The eyes are larger, the lips of medium thickness but coarser, and there is marked retreating chin.

The Maikal hills are the backbone of the Baiga region. The range of hills lying between 21.11° and 22.40° N. and 80.46° and 81.46° E. is the connecting link between the great hill systems of the Vindhyas and Satpuras. D.N. Tiwari (1985) has given a vivid description of Baiga region.

The catchment of the Narmada and its tributaries with Maikal range at the bottom is the real home of the Baiga. The area is shared by five districts-Mandla, Bilaspur, Balaghat, Rajnandgaon and Shahdol. But Baigas are not spread all over the districts, they reside in forest-covered hill tracts. Their preference for isolated places has carved out a region comprising tehsils of Dindori, Niwas, Mandla, Bilaspur, Gourela, Maungeli, Kawardha, Balhar and Pushparajgarh with Dindori tehsil as their main concentration. The region has the shape of human foot. Let the toe ascend over three thousand feet, high southern hills of the Amarkantak and the heel tall on Narmada where Silgi joins it and the ankle rest on the Saletekri hills in Baihar tehsil, the foot is complete.

The northern boundary of the region is guarded by river Narmada beginning from Amarkantak hill until it takes a southward course at Silgi junction. Irregular hillocks, forests and plains between Mandla and Baihar form the western line. Saletekari hills of Baihar provide the southern base which stretches though Maikal range and joins Eastern boundary at Amarkantak.

The region can be roughly divided into four physical divisions. The first division in which the largest number of Baigas reside, stretches along the Maikal range from Chauradadar in the East to Motinala hills in the southwest. The tangled confusion of peaks and ranges of the Maikal hills divide the face of the country into a number of valley and table lands which, gradually increasing in height from southeast to East, culminate at last in the plateau of Charradadar and form a barrier between the highlands of Raigarh Biochua and the lowlands of Chhattisgarh.

The second division is the highland of Saletekari, which gradually slopes down towards the central plains of the Baiga region. The tract is partly hilly and partly tilted giving an appearance of a plank inclined towards the heart of Mandla district.

The central part, which is less rugged and irregular, forms the third division. It is a cobweb of rivers and streams, all draining into the great Narmada. Fertile valleys and wild vegetation of the region give an appearance of nature's garden. The rising ranges of Satpura hills open the fourth divisions in which more than three thousand Baigas have found shelter.

The Baiga region is a hilly tact. Its elevation is very irregular. Peaks and ravines, hillocks and hollows render the whole area uneven chain of small plains and rising hills. The Katha hills 9.6 kilometres northeast of Lormi in the Eastern corner of the region, stand as 760 metres high sentinel above the sea level. Lormi, Lilapur, Setaganga and Desrangpur, other peaks in the neighbourhood have elevations of more than 300 metres. The northeastern portion of Bilaspur district, which forms the Eastern part of the region, is wild and hilly.

The climate of the region is typical monsoonic, with 3 distinct seasons.

Baiga Population

Baigas are not distributed evenly in the five districts of their distributional area. They are also not 'primitive' in all of their distributional area. In fact, in some of the villages neighbouring districts of Mandla they can be compounded with Gonds and other tribal communities as per their income and development. The primitive Baigas live in Dindori and neighbouring areas, where they practise shifting agriculture.

The primitive Baigas live in Dindori tehsil (now district) of Mandla district. The villages of Primitive Baigas are listed given in Table 18.8.

TABLE-18.7

Major districts of Baiga Population

S. No.	*Name of the District*	*Baiga Population*	
		1961 Census	*1971 Census*
1.	Mandla	31,769	48,803
2.	Balaghat	8,738	12,379
3.	Rajnandgaon	2	21
4.	Bilaspur	2,916	2,950
5.	Shahdol	71,061	74,473
		1,14,486	1,38,626

TABLE-18.8

Villages of Primitive Baigas

S.No.	*Village*	*Baiga chak*
1.	Ajgar	These eight villages were the forest settlements of the Baiga tribe, hence the area was termed as 'Baiga chak'
2.	Dhaba	
3.	Dhurkutta	
4.	Kandwari	
5.	Rajnisarai	
6.	Silpendi	
7.	Tantor	
8.	Lamota	

In the year 1890, the area now known as Baigachak was earmarked by British administration. There Baigas could practise shifting or Jhum agriculture. The area of this forested zone was 22,858 acres. These villages were situated in Dindori tehsil of Mandla district. In 1964-65, as many as 43 Baiga households practised shifting agriculture.

Baiga Agency

In course of time, especially while finalising the Tribal sub-plan, planners decided to provide the benefits of modern public facilities to the entire habitat. Thus the distributional area of the entire community is developed in a planned manner.

With this new approach, the area of Baiga Agency was considerably enlarged. In this larger area, Baiga Agency was considerably expanded and there lived many other tribal communities like the Agarias and Gonds.

Thus in the sub-plans as many as 1,219 villages were included in the Baiga Agency. This is a significant change. We now see that from mere eight villages, the number has increased to several hundred per cent. The new strategy has benefited more than 1 lakh 20 thousand tribals. A large percentage of this population is obviously of Bagia tribe. This large population lives in forest and Raiyyatwari Villages. But there is a change, the Baigas now no more live as bonded labourers. Almost all of the families are now cultivators. Of course, their landholdings are very small and they still have to depend upon forests to some extent.

It seems that while selecting a place for establishing a village, Baigas had only one consideration viz., that the place must be in thick forest. The Baiga villages are situated not only on the top of the hills but also on the flat level lands. Their villages are not necessarily near rivers hence most of the villages have constant water problem. The Baiga women have to go 20 to 25 kilometres to fetch water. When the village is situated on the top of the hill, the toil of the women-folk increases. The villages are unplanned and the houses are very close. Only some of the villages have space in the centre where children play for most of the day time. A village may have only three or four houses but there are bigger villages comprising 100 or more houses.

In fact, originally, only eight villages mentioned in the text had nearabout 100 per cent Baiga population but now things have changed. Fifty-two villages have larger proportion of the Baigas, the rest belonging to other tribes. Sometimes a village is of fragmented type; its parts are situated at considerable distances, these are called Tola. In most cases these tolas are inhabited by other tribes. With increase in area, the Baiga villages have now become more diverse in the context of ethnic composition.

TABLE-18.9

Villages of Baiga Development Sub-Plan

S. No	*District*	*Tehsil Sub-plan*	*Dev.Block*	*No. of Villages*	*Population*
1.	Mandla	1. Dindori	1. Samnapur	32	3,280
			2. Karanjia	33	3,190
			3. Bajag	23	4,344
			4. Dindori	42	1,865
			5. Amarpur	38	1,655
Total Dindori sub-plan				168	14,334
		2. Mandla	6. Nainpur	05	183
			7. Bichhia	56	4,072
			8. Mawai	33	1,401
			9. Ghrgi	38	2,782
			10. Mohangaon	35	3,353
			11. Mandla	15	1,434
Total Mandla sub-plan				182	13,225
		3. Niwas	12.Mendwani	38	1,882
			13.Shahpura	22	1,527
			14. Niwas	07	324
			15. Narayanganj	31	2,906
			16.Bijadandi	15	1,559
Total Niwas sub-pan				113	8,198
2.	Raj-nandgaon	4.Raj-nandgaon	17. Bodkha	98	7231
			18. Kawardha	64	7,422
			19. Sahaspur	19	1,517
Tota Rajnandgaon sub-plan				181	16,170

3. Balaghat	5. Baihar	20. Baihar	78	3,080
		21. Birsa	64	4,884
		22. Paraswada	68	4,493
Total	Baihar		208	1,248
4. Bilaspur	6. Bilaspur	23. LormI	34	3,091
	7. Mungeli	24. Padaria	32	1,889
	8. Gorels	25. Gorela	10	2,425
		26. Kota	76	50
Total (Bilaspur, Mungeli and Gorela sub-plan)			82	8,255
5. Shahdol	9. Sohagpur	27. Paln	34	8727
		28. Sohagpur	108	28,711
		29. Gohparu	87	6,782
Total Shahdol sub-plan			229	44,221
6. Pusharajgarh		30. Pusharjgarh	5	3,610
Grand Total			1,219	1,20,470

Dress

The wilder Baiga is almost nude except a 'lungoti' with a flap which hangs down in front. It is traditional belief of the Baiga to wear less. But the more civilised section among them know how to wear a dhoti, shirt, or bundi or jacket and a turban. In cold, they tie a thick double cloth, known as kapchi, round their shoulders. The Baigas of Niwas, Banhar and Mandla tehsil have adopted ordinary village dress. However, the Baiga women are more fully covered even in the wilder tracts. They wear a long strip of cloth commonly known as 'Kapra' or 'Lugra' tied round the waist, carried up across the breasts and fixed in at the back end. The strip does not reach even the knees. A Baiga woman is known by the way in which her single garment is arranged so as to provide a safe sitting place in it for the child. The Baigas usually do not use footwear of any kind. They believe that it will render their feet soft and thereby disable them for quick walking in the forest or climbing trees and rocks. Blanket or other woollen clothes do not form a part of their clothing. In the cold season they sleep round the fire kept burning or smouldering all night, stray sparks from which may alight on their tough skins without being felt. For protection from rain, the Baiga wears on his head a sort of indigenous umbrella known as Chhatri made of bamboo frame lined with Mohlain leaves. Sometimes, they also wear wooden slippers which keep them slightly above the mud. For carrying money or tobacco, Baigas use purse (Basuri or thailli) made of yarn or sambhar skin. Pissari (pouch with strings) is a sort of hold-all for smoking materials.

Though, forest-dwellers are the Baigas not devoid of aesthetic sense. Even men wear ornaments. Iron or silver bracelets (*chura*) on wrist, ring on fingers, ear-rings and sometimes a necklace of beads are the common ornaments of the Baiga youth. The older ones discard ornaments with the advancing age. But the taste for decoration finds full expression at the time of dance when the dancer's turban is decorated with a kalgi of peacock's feathers and chutta of gay coloured beads shines on his neck. *Paijan* (anklets) tinkle on the ankle. A younger Baiga will not miss a Hawel at the dance party. The Baiga women wear the Dhar (ornament of ear) without chains or a Tarki (ornament for ear) may be inserted in its place to keep the hole of the ear lobe open. Absence of nose ornament is a distinguishing feature. Kanthi, Latkania, Guria Biculi decorate their necks or the upper part of breast. Rings and bangles are less commonly used by the younger Baiga women. On the feet-Chura, Tinkor or Pairi and Chutki on the toes are also worn. Local tastes and visits to bazars greatly affect their choice of ornaments. The Baigas including women take extraordinary interests in tending and dressing their hair. Males are in the habit of either wearing it long or shave a little beyond the forehead. But in both the cases the rear part is allowed to grow and tied into a long Jura hung usually on the left side of the shoulder. More civilized among them have begun to shave like ordinary villagers or keep a small Chutti-like Gonds. But no barber can touch a Baiga's head for it is tribal custom to shave one another with an indigenous razor supplied by the local blacksmith (Agaria).

Women allow their hair to grow as long as possible. While dressing, they divide it in the middle and give two or three knots before folding them upwards. The folded lock are hung to cover the neck. Young girls put two or three combs.

Social Institutions

The Baiga tribe is divided into endogamous groups known as jat. Since each jat has occupied a separate block of country, there is little chance of intermarriage between any two jats. There are, however, certain areas in which the problem is not so simple as two or more than two endogamous jats live as neighbours. In such places, the social relationship among different groups is governed by a set of rules. Bhumia, Binjhwar and Bharotia may interdine in Shahdol, Mandla and Balaghat. In Dindori and Niwas, Binjhwar may eat at the hands of Bhumia and Muria, but nowhere else. Similarly, Bhaina and Baiga eat food served by Bhumia and Binjhwar sub-tribes in Bilaspur. Similar restrictions regarding dining are in force in different areas which further subdivide the septs for purposes of dining. But nowhere woman of one jat is permitted to eat at the hands of any other jat, for the Baiga believes that woman is the custodian of jat's purity, which, if once spoiled, is likely to affect further generations. But intermarriages are not uncommon. Member of one jat can marry the virgin girl of another jat provided the girl severs all her connections with the parents and their relations. The rules of intermarriage vary from one region to another. Strictness or flexibility in their observance largely depend upon local customs, inter-divisional relations and the influence of other tribes and Hindu castes.

The jats are further subdivided according to their garh and *got*. They believe that originally each group belonged to a particular territory, hill or jungle and that they must give their girls to the people of other territory. Garh is a territorial division of the jat and constitutes an exogamous sept. There are mainly twelve garhs—Binjhwar, Sawat, Chituria, Damgharia, Ghangaria, Dawaria, Pachgaita, Salgaina, Kumaria, Massania, Chanania and Chandgaria. But these garhs are not observed strictly now. Due to the influence of Gonds who have no territorial exogamous divisions, Baiga seems to have taken to the got system. The main gots are—Marawi, Dhurwa, Marka, Parteti and Takam. Sagotra marriage is not permitted, but breach of the rule is well atoned with a bottle of liquor to the elders. It will be safe to say that in recent years all rules regarding got and garh have become loose and are not strictly observed in any part of the Baiga region. Although Baigas have adopted the totemic gotra system of the Gond, there is no real totemism among the former. One may hear some reference to totemic faith in certain villages or families. But in general the Baigas are not a totemic tribe.

Baigas do not observe untouchability but they are still very particular about their food and drink. They will not eat with any other tribe or Hindu caste. Even a touch to their water or cooking utensils is not welcome. But exception is made in case of dry food, fresh fruits, tobacco or milk. Unmarried boys and girls enjoy more liberty. But a married woman must observe all the rules regarding food and drink. On the whole, there are now two schools of thought among the Baigas, one insisting upon maintaining tribal purity by strictly observing the rules of marriage and dining, and the second believes in liberalising tribal rules so as to broaden the jurisdiction of the tribe. A compromise is invariably arrived at in the form of a penalty feast to the tribesmen whenever there is a breach of these rules, and the irregularity is then treated as legalised.

Economy

It has been stressed that Baigas were originally the cultivators of shifting agriculture. From time to time Baigas were persuaded to take the plough, but their deep-rooted conviction that ploughing was something which harmed Mother Earth, did not allow them to switch over to the better farming techniques. Caption wrote in desperation: 'My efforts to persuade them to take to plough cultivation were unsuccessful'.

It was noticed during the survey that forest-dwellers burn the Sal (*Shoren robusta*) forest floor to get more 'Puttu', a fungus (*Astraeus hygrometricus*). Actually, this is an edible fungus forming mycorrhizal association with sal trees and burnt soil/leaf litter favours the growth of many corrhizal fungus. Tribals' belief on burning forest floor for getting more fruit body of this fungs is simply based on saving man-power used in collecting this fungus which grow scattered on unburnt forest floor. But they are totally unware about the fact that these practices may lead to extinction of her because of genome flourishing in leaf litter. This practice can be checked only by training in the field of mushroom growing because most of the primitive societies are mycophagist.

In a sample survey conducted during 1976, it was found that 31.34 per cent (21 out of 67) of the families who have been allotted land by the Forest Department do not have their own bullocks for ploughing their fields. They were borrowing bullocks from others or offering land to a farmer owning bullocks for cultivation on a 50/50 crop-share basis. The main hindrance in the way of agriculture development is that the Baigas live in forest villages which cannot be brought within the pale of planned development.

Cattle Wealth

The cattle wealth of the area presents a very gloomy picture. The cattle of this area is poor in health and breed and is usually under-fed for seven months in a year, due to fact of poor pasture and fodder. Rearing of poultry birds in their backyards is time old practice among the Baigas. Birds are kept as a matter of habit rather than as an economic activity. These birds are of indigenous breed, and are not only poor egg-layers but also produce eggs of very small size. The tribal farmers in the area are in the habit of keeping local non-descript cows and buffaloes for milk and other purposes whose average daily milk yield varies from 0.200 litre to 0.500 litre for cows and 0.500 litre to 1.0 litre in case of buffaloes. Poor nutrition and lack of proper management are the two important factors contributing to this low productivity rate. Piggery is also very popular among the Baigas. Pigs are of indigenous type and are primarily kept for consumption, occasional sale and offering to deities.

Forest Produce

The Baigas live in forest villages and in revenue villages surrounded by the reserve forests. One or the other forest produce is available to them throughout the year. Months of collection of forest produce are given in Table 18.10.

TABLE-18.10

Minor Forest Produce Collected by Baigas

Name of Forest Produce	*Months*
Hara and Balharra and Bahera	Januuary–April
Chiraunji	May-June
Honey	October-November, March-April
Satkatha & Kullu, gum	November-March
Sal seeds & Tendu leaves	April-June
Mahuline leaves & bark	July-September

The Baigas collect minor produce, vegetables, leaves, roots, fruits and tubers for their own consumption and for occasional sale. Sal seed, tendu leaves and chiraunji are the main items sold by them. The Baigas continue with age-old practices. The main problem is supply of raw material. In olden times, 'Mowa' grass was found in abundance; the growth of 'Mowa' grass has since been significantly reduced. It being the raw material used for rope-making, the preservation of 'Mowa' grass should be done. Besides this, Sisal plant also provides raw material for rope-making. The Forest Department may be impressed upon to take up a scheme to increase the growth of 'Mowa' grass on a large scale. As a worthwhile alternative the plantation of Sisal plant on the periphery of forests in three alternate rows and in the patches of the degraded forests may also be raised. The Baiga families may be equipped to exploit this resource for rope-making.

Food and Drink

Staple food of the Baigas is maize and minor millets. It is consumed in the form of "Pej", a gruel prepared from "Kodo",

"Kutki" and "Manda" (minor millets) and sometimes from coarse rice. This is often supplemented with vegetables cooked from leaves, roots, tubers and jungli fruits. Fish available in local ponds and streams, is also consumed. The past practice of getting meat supply by hunting animals in the forest has vanished. Occasional killing of pigs, goats and birds only and poultry birds provide protein supply. By and large, the Baigas are dependent on forest produce, fruits, roots, tubers and bulbs for their food supply. Baiga's daily time table of food starts with a light drink of Pej early morning at about 8 called Juara.

The Baiga settlements are generally located on high altitudes and their agriculture fields are either on the slopes or in the valleys. The schemes to dig wells may be taken up only in a few villages and hamlets which are likely to yield positive results. Only the tube-well scheme of Public Health Engineering Department can solve their drinking water problem to a large extent.

History

Baigas are known for their expertise in herbal medicine. Since how long they have known the properties of plants is a matter of research. It is likely that Baigas have contributed significantly in the knowledge of indigenous methods of treatment and medicine. If this is proved, their contribution towards mankind will be invaluable.

No written document in any form tells us about the history of the Baigas; we do not know if they ruled some parts of Central India. But then indirect evidences are there. Baiga heads traditionally put tilak on the foreheads of Gond kings. Normally such practice is found in tribal India when the old and defeated ruler confirms the royal authority of a new king.

The Baigas in their folklore narrate about a great war when many of their legendary heroes were killed and a big army with horses and elephants was wiped out.

In some of the festive occasions, they use a palki which they identify with elephant. We do not know if they once rode on elephants. Elephant has been the sign of royalty in India.

Korku

Korku is a Munda or Kolarian tribe numbering several thousands and confined to the districts of Hoshangabad, Nimar, Betul and Chindwara and the adjoining Berar districts of Maharashtra.

The appellation Korku is derived from the Kolarian language meaning 'men' or 'tribes men'. 'Koru' in this language means a man and 'ku' is a plural termination. Korkus are commonly held to be racially akin to the Kols and Korwas of Chotanagpur. The present-day ethnologists consider them to be closely related with the Sabras, despite some superficial changes that have been brought that the Mahadeo and Maikal Hills and the Satpuras in the middle India were once populated with Korkus and Sabaras and when the Gonds came into power in these areas during the rule of the Hindus, they replaced the Korkus and Sabaras altogether. Venkatachar, writing of the Korkus of the Central India Agency in 1932 says, "In these parts they appear to have been ousted by the Gonds who held the Narbada valley till they in turn were subdued by the Muslims and the Marathas". As a matter of fact Korkus are the only tribe speaking the Austro-Asiatic language in the Madhya Bharat. During the Census of 1931, the number speaking the Korku language was very small and "indigenous to Central India and merely a spill-over from the Satpuras".

Korkus, like Bhils and Gonds trace their origin to the Mahadeva. Russell and Hiralal have quoted at length a legend of their genesis as recorded by Crosthwaite. This legend tells us that Ravan the Asura king of Lanka found the Vindhya and Satpura ranges to be uninhabited. He requested Mahadeo to populate them. Mahadeo discovered the suitable soil to make images of a man and a woman, and as soon as he tried to put life into them, Indra sent two fiery horses to trample the images to dust. Then Mahadeo made the image of a dog and succeeded in putting life into it. This dog kept the horses away and allowed Mahadeo to put life into the images of a man and a woman. These two became the ancestors of the Korku tribe. Korkus tell another tale of their origin which speaks of Dharanagar (modern Dhar) as being the seat of their forefathers. The tale runs like this: Once these forefathers went out hunting and followed a sambhar which ran on and on ultimately entering a cave in the Mahadeo or Panchmarhi hills. There Mahadeo appeared before them in the form of a hermit and revealed that he had lured them there to settle in that region and worship him. A Korku zamindar continues to be the hereditary guardian of Mahadeo's shrine at Panchmarhi. The tale as such is regarded as merely an effort to connect the ancestry of the tribe with the Rajputs.

Funeral Rites

Korkus generally bury their dead. The body is laid in the grave, face upwards with head pointing to the south.

Political Organisation in the Korku Tribe

The Korku tribals from the Melghat area (Dharni and Chikhaldara tehsils) of Amravati district in Maharashtra show an altogether different type of political organization.A typical feature is the absence of any hierarchical structure, and also the absence of a tribal chief. Traditionally they have a horizontal pattern of power distribution somewhat federal without a central authority to control it.

The "kings" who ruled the Korkus were Rajput kings or chiefs. There were jagirs of Rajput chieftains at Susarda and Kot. The Korkus, particularly the Movasi sub-tribe, indulged in brigandage, raided the areas in the plains and paid a part of the booty to their Rajput chiefs as ransom. The Chavdi or panchayat was under their control. During the course of history these Rajput jagirs ceased to exist and now there are no traditional chieftains.

The only chiefs appear at the village level. The Patel functions as a village chief and gets priority on social occasions as well as rituals. The Bhumka and the Parihar wield supernatural powers which give them status and assures obedience to their authority. The Bhumka acts as priest and gets priority at ceremonies, festivals, etc. He is considered a traditional community leader and a socio-cultural guide. The

Parihar is visited with divine spirits as a mouthpiece.

The Patel, who is often a police Patel and the Bhumka yield authority on the village community in social, cultural and spiritual matters.

NOTES AND REFERENCES

1. Elwin, V., 1934: *The Baiga*, John Murrey, London.
2. Guha, B.S., 1935: The Korwas, *Census of India*, Vol.I, India, Part-III, Ethnographical, Simla.
3. Kabra, P.C., 1987: *Birhor, A Primitive Tribe*, Publication No. 53, Tribal Research Institute, Bhopal.
4. NCAER, 1963: *The Socio Economic Conditions of Primitive Tribes of Madhya Pradesh*, New Delhi.
5. Russell, R.V. and Hiralal, 1916: *Tribes and Castes of Central Provinces of India*, 4 Vols. Macmillan, Reprint Cosmos, New Delhi.
6. Tiwari, S.K., 1997: *Baigas of Central India*, Anmol, New Delhi.
7. Tiwari, S.K., 1994: *Encyclopaedia of Indian Tribals*, Rahul, New Delhi.

XIX

SAVARS AND THEIR REPRESENTATIVES IN M.P.

The Savars are the successors of the Sabara tribe, early history of which has been discussed in the preceding pages (Chapter XI. 21). Difference of opinion exists among scholars whether the Savars are Kolarians or Dravidians as far as their language is concerned. Colonel Dalton considers them as Dravidians while other authorities brand them as Kolarians which seems to be correct. In Central India, the Savars have lost their own language and speak Aryan Hindi or Uriya vernacular current around them.

DISTRIBUTION

Savar tribe is distributed in Orissa, Andhra Pradesh, West Bengal, Bihar, Maharashtra and Madhya Pradesh. In M.P. the Savars have been referred to more than once in the List of Scheduled Tribes as below:

1. They are Sonr and Sor
2. They are also Saur.

It seems that all the Kolarian tribes living in the valleys of the rivers Betwa, Ken, Dhasan are Savars. There is little doubt that the Savars are closely related to the Bhil group of tribals which includes Bhils, Bhilalas, Bhil-Mina and Mina. It seems that in their earlier distribution they were found from the coastal plains of Arabian Sea to the coast of Bay of Bengal.

Most of the tribals of this group had been warriors, plunderers and soldiers. Unlike other Kolarian tribes, they had grown up from the stage of hunting and gathering. This only means hunting and gathering became their secondary occupation long ago or when they could not get suitable opportunity for their chivalrous deeds.

It seems reasonable to include 'Saharias' with Savars. Saharias are now one of the prmitive tribes (PTG) of Madhya Pradesh.

SONR, SAUR, SOR

In the List of Scheduled Tribes, this tribe is found at three serial numbers referring them as Saur, Sonr and Sor along with Sahariya. In fact, the term Sonr (also referred to as Saunir) is just a nasal variation of Saur. It is with a nasal that the tribe refers to itself as Savar and not as Saur or Sor. The region of the tribe is southern parts of Tikamgarh and Chhatarpur districts, southwestern parts of Panna, northern areas of Sagar, Damoh and Raisen and western Vidisha. Their typical area is Hirapur-Shahgarh area of Sagar district and adjoining areas of Tikamgarh and Chhatarpur districts. Sonrs have escaped attention of anthropologists so far.

Since this tribe has been named twice in the ST list, its population has also been noted at two places. In 1981 the population of Sour (44) was given as 68,034 and the population of Sonr (46) as 4,8662. Thus their total population was 1,16,696 in 1981.

In the recent past, these tribals were extensively employed as Forget Guards by the erstwhile principalities of Bundelkhand. They were better known as 'Vanrakha' or the Keepers of the Forests.

In recent years Mishra (1986) has narrated the types and meanings of Sonr totemic septs. A description on the basis of his work is being given here.

Sonrs are said to have 28 Septs. Every Sept has a totem. These are follows:

Classification of Septs

A. Septs of High Social Order

1. Chandelia
2. Hardua

B. Septs of Middle Social Order

1. Siligile	9. Kenthoria	17. Konsarapa
2. Bagulia	10. Panrapa	18. Chhyolia
3. Surajmukhi	11. Jacheria	19. Vayas
4. Chakarya	12. Badele	20. Patele
5. Magarya	13. Sonorapa	21. Hiranya
6. Katharya	14. Banerapa	22. Bhatiya
7. Kathorya	15. Rajopalya	
8. Kurka	16. Ror	

C. Septs of Lower Order

1. Laraiya 2. Gilarya 3. Bandarya 4. Sungariya

I. Meaning of the Septs

In the following table meanings of some of the septs are given:

1. Hiranya	Deer	Worship the deer
2. Lahariya	Jackal	Worship the jackal
3. Gilariya	Squirrel	Worship the squirrel
4. sungariya	Pig	Worship the pig
5. Bandariya	Monkey	Worship the monkey
6. Kachorya	Tortoise	Worship the tortoise
7. Magarya	Crocodile	Worship the crocodile

II. Sept after a bird

1. Baguliya Cattle egret Worship the bird
2. Silgile Vulture Worship the bird

III. Sept after a tree or vegetable material

1. Ehandelia (Sandal-wood)
2. Hardua (Turmeric)
3. Chakarya (A twisted rope used to keep on head to put water-pots)
4. Surajmukhi (A flower)
5. Kurka (A tree)
6. Kethoriya (A Kaita tree)
7. Jacheriya (Vacher tree)
8. Badel (Wood)

9. Sanoriya (San bush)
10. Baneriya (Baner tree)
11. Rajolya (Rajgir bush)
12. Ror (Ror tree)
13. Kansoriya (Kans grass)
14. Chhyoliga (Chhyola bush)
15. Kayas (Kayas tree)
16. Patele (Small wooden stool)
17. Bhatia (Brinjal)
18. Kathariya (Mattress)
19. Ponrpa (Verandah)

Some Tribal Legends Related to Septs

1.	Surajmukhi	An ancestor of Sonr loved the flowers of Surajmukhi. The children of this Sonr adopted the totem of Surajmukhi.
2.	Kathorai	A Sonr while plucking a 'Kentha' fell down from the Kentha tree, but did not get any injury. In fact, the tree in the form of a man had caught him before he could fell on ground. The Sonrs of this totem never climb this tree. They also worship the tree.
3.	Sansoria	A Sonr was attacked by a bear, he was fatally wounded but somehow he ran away and took shelter in a 'San' bush. The bear did not reach it and the Sonr took it as a totem.
4.	Ror	An unmarried woman gave birth to a child under 'Rorbush'. An old woman heard the cries of this infant and brought her home. Later on the children of this boy accepted this totem.
5.	Silgile	The bird saved the ancestor when a teenager was stranded in a forest, provided food and shelter. During marriage an image of the bird is made of flower and honoured. A hen is sacrificed.

6.	Bagulya	The ancestors stranded in the forest were very thirsty, when the birds were flying in the sky and thus they reached the water to drink. In major festival an image of bird is made of flour and honoured.
7.	Kachhorya	An ancestor was fishing in a river, but he slipped and was drowned but there he found a big tortoise. He caught it and saved himself from the water.
8.	Magarya	A Sonr woman, while going to a river bank to take water, saw a crocodile, but the crocodile slipped in the water without harming her.The sons of that woman were called Magarya.
9.	Jacheriya	A Sonr family was living under a 'Jacher' tree. The family became prosperous and happy thus they accepted the 'Jacher' tree as their totem.
10.	Chheolia	A Sonr woman while plucking the leaves of Chhrda tree found that she was pregnant. Since she for the first time knew this fact under that tree, her child and later his pregnancy belonged to the 'Chheolia' sept.

Lowest Totems of Sonrs

The sonrs regard the persons of four totems as belonging to the lowest social orders. They are the persons having totems of a jackal, monkey, pig and a squirrel.

The story behind is that in early days, four close friends indulged in eating the meat of these four animals. Each one of them had special taste of one of these animals. The larger Sonr society did not permit the meat of these animals hence they and their children were socially punished. They had to accept the four animals as their totems.

Highest Totems of Sonrs

Chandelia and Herdua

The story relates that once sages came to the villages of Sonrs, where they asked for alms. One of the elder Sonrs gave Chironji in alms. The sages honoured him by putting a tilak of sandal-wood on his forehead. The children of this family were called Chandelia. Another elder Sonor gave 'Mahua' to the sages. The sages honoured him by putting a turmeric tilak on his forehead and his children were then called Hardua.

SAUNTA, SAONTA

The Saunta (Saonta) are found principally in Surguja and Bilaspur districts (about 65 per cent in Surguja, 15 per cent in Bilaspur, 15 per cent in Raipur and 5 per cent in Raigarh). Census figures being what they are, are useful to locate Sauntas in Raipur district. The Sauntas are also locally known as Turi and this is the name of their dialect also. They are bamboo-workers and forest-product collectors. The Sauntas sometime refer to themselves as Majhi or Kisan Majhi.

In 1981 Census their population was 3,173 or 0.03 per cent of the tribal population of the State.

According to legends, their ancestors served in the army of the king of Puri (Orissa). Then they belonged to 'Khandayat' community or the community which lived by the service of Khonda or 'Sword'. One of the soldiers of this community married a tribal woman. The offspring of this union were called Saunta.

They seem to have adopted the septs of the Gonds. These are Ghurwa, Pondwa, Markam, Sonwani, Telasi, Lavdarya, Sirathia, Bhainsa, Sua, Bagh, etc.

Sauntas have two branches—those living in Chhattisgarh are called 'Chhattisgarh Saunta', those living in Orissa are 'Oriya Saunta'.

SAHARIA

In Central India, the Sabaras, or Saharias as they are known here, were probably dispossessed and displaced by Rajput clans as a result of the pressure exerted on the latter by the Muslim invasions. The various rulers including Mauryas and the Guptas who held sway over these areas in various periods, more or less, did not interfere with the Saharias much. When these rulers showed signs of weakness, the Saharias strengthened their rule. This waxing and waning of the tribal influence continued for centuries till the rise of various Rajput clans. Venkatachar says, "We should rather look to the period of Rajput settlement for the disintegration of tribal areas, for the disappearance of certain aboriginal tribes and for the formation of Hinduized aboriginal castes".

For the displacement of the Saharias, we should look to the fortunes of the Kachhwahas who held Gwalior and Narwar and Parihars who held Bundelkhand before the Chandels. Subsequently, in the 15th century, the Bundelas held sway over this region having successfully defeated the Parihars and the Chandels. The Kachhwahas and Parihars must have carved out new states for themselves after dispossessing the Saharias.

The dispossession of the Saharias and the inundation of their language and culture by the immigrating Rajputs were facilitated by the easy terrain and topography of the northern lowlands. Venkatachar rightly says, "The nature of the north-Gwalior country could afford them no shelter as the Vindhyas have done for the other tribes".

Anthropologically, the Saharias are a Kolarian (or Munda) tribe. In Central India they have been so thoroughly submerged by the successive waves of Hindu migrations that they have now lost their language and speak the language of the area they inhabit. Even in Andhra where the Savaras are in large numbers their language has been heavily influenced by Telugu. But even then the Austric elements are clearly discernible.

The Saharia mother continues to work till the day of delivery. Delivery sometimes takes place in the forest where she goes to collect forest products for barter, or dead-fuel for domestic use. Other women attend to the delivery and bring the mother home. She takes rest for a day or two after which she resume her old routine.

The Saharias are generally of medium stature and constant use of liquor has taken away much of their charm of youth. Even a young Saharia does not look impressive.

Their skin colour varies from brown to dark. They have thick growth of hair on head but have scanty moustache and beard. In their youth, young women look impressive but since they get married at an early age and constant child bearing takes away much of their charm of youth, a woman of 20-25 does not look impressive at all. In no way, their bodies are well-built and undernourishment and semi-starvation are responsible for this. Their skin colour varies from brown to dark brown and even light black. Their hair is generally coarse, straight and black.

A Saharia feels at home only in his natural surroundings. He is fond of forests and can toil for long hours in forests extracting resin and collecting gum, honey, various tubers and edible roots. But his laziness is proverbial and he will never go out to work unless he reaches the state of starvation.

The Saharias are mainly located on the borders of Madhya Pradesh and Rajasthan. In Madhya Pradesh, they are known by phonetic variations and their dispersal has been recorded in 21 districts but their concentration is in Gwalior and Chambal divisions. In Rajasthan, their concentration is in Kota district.

It would be seen that their population in 1961 was confined to only 15 districts, while in 1971 they were enumerated in 21 districts. The number of persons in these six additional districts, however, is very small. The area of their concentration, therefore, remains unchanged.

TABLE-19.1

District-wise distribution of Saharias

S.No.	*District*	*Tribe Name*	*Population*	
			1961	*1971*
1.	Shivpuri	Saharia	54,060	56,075
2.	Guna	Do.	41,550	53,180
3.	Morena	Do.	39,965	44,933
4.	Gwalior	Do.	12,324	14,045
5.	Datia	Sahariya	2,016	4,984

S.No.	District	Tribe Name	Population 1961	Population 1971
6.	Tikamgarh	Sahariya	12	235
7.	Rewa	Sahariya	4	1
8.	Satna	Do.	-	-
9.	Bhind	Sahariya	172	401
10.	Indore	Do	40	249
11.	Ratlam	Do.	30	447
12.	Ujjain	Do.	-	29
13.	Dhar	Do.	0	2
14.	Dewas	Do.	102	184
15.	Khargone	Do.	-	8
16.	Rajgarh	Do.	9071,	683
17.	Shajapur	Do.	-	3
18.	Mandsaur	Do.	-	4
19.	Raisen	Sahariya, Sosia, Sor	3,256	4,169
20.	Sehore	Do.	1,703	21,142
21.	Vidisha	Saharia	1,215	22,614
		Total	**174,320**	**205,427**

Nothing is known about the early history and migration of this tribe. Even the older generation fails to give any account of their past history.

The Saharias treat the following gotras as incestuous: 1. Father, 2. Mother, 3. Nani, 4. Aajee, 5. Phupha. Even a 'Galiar' will have to avoid them. Same holds good for a 'Lagette'.

Dress

The dress of a Saharia is made very simple and he requires very few clothes. The man puts on a small dhoti, salooko (shirt), turban (safa). All these are purchased from the weekly markets as the Saharias have no knowledge of weaving. Use of shoes is rare.

The dress of a Saharia female also cannot by any means be said to be very elaborate. They put on ghagra, lugra and choli (bodice). Use of choli is not common to all. Women are also seen without blouse or bodice. The dress of a Sahariya woman is comparable to a Rajasthani woman, and in the way of dressing there is hardly any marked difference.

Ornaments

Among the Saharias both men and women put on a few ornaments as they are not in a position to save enough money to purchase ornaments. Those who are economically well off possess more ornaments.

Tatooing

Every woman should have tattoo marks upon her body. This is done by Saharia women themselves and by outsiders also. Pana Saharias of Bhojke village are very efficient in this art.

The Family

The family is a structural-functional unit of first degree for every Saharia man and woman. They call it 'Kutumb'. Mostly vertically extended families are popular with them. The separation generally takes place after marriage of the sons. The usual reason is bad relations between the women in the family. Sociologically, fatherhood is more important and in cases where women with living foetus get married their husbands do accept the issue as their own. Such a son enjoys the same status as any other and has the same claims everywhere. The line of descent passes from father to son.

Adoption is permissible but rarely practised. If there is no issue, the property goes to brothers and 'Kutumb kabila'. Sometimes they keep 'Ghar Jawai'. Sometimes, they adopt their wive's brother's son. But adoption does not change the Gotra of the adopted. Any form of marriage other than Biyah is known as Kari. When a widow is recruited in the family, she can bring her issues especially the one who is still sucking. These issues are known as 'Lgette'. Marriage, adoption and other methods, besides birth, help in recruitment in the family. On the other hand, death leads to reduction. Generally they prefer polygamous families and sometimes they have up to four wives.

Clan Organisation

The Saharias, like most of the tribes of Central India, are divided into a number of clans. A clan is known as 'Got' or 'Goti'. The tribe is endogamous and marriage outside the tribe is not approved. But territorial exogamy is not followed.

The following are the important clans of the tribe: 1. Samaria, 2. Daheria, 3. Gobaria, 4. Barelia, 5. Dubaria, 6. Chauha, 7. Masania, 8. Badrelia, 9. Pipari Baderia, 10. Mangria, 11. Jinihwar, 12. Barboolia, 13, Kudwas, 14. Dungaria, 15. Solakia, 16. Dhondia, 17. Bajulia, 18. Barondia, 19. Selia, 20. Karwaria, 21. Khadia, 22. Kadho, 23. Rawania, 24. Kellala, 25. Panwar, 26. Mohar, 27. Bagulia, 28. Nmria 29. Karondia, 30. Narbaria, 31. Jhilmilia, 32 Wogaia, 33. Abkaun.

Though the clan is very important functional sub-structure for them, the political structure is one important exception and is based on the organisation of the tribe as a whole. But the 'kinship system' is still the basic sub-stratum for them.

The landholding of this tribe is marginal and uneconomic. The average land held among landholders is about 1.5 ha. Only about 41 per cent of the Saharias possess land and the rest are landless. They do not have agriculture inputs like bullock, seed, fertilizer, etc. Sometimes, they leave the land unsown. The land utilisation feature of the area reveals that about 46 per cent of land is under cultivation, 49 per cent under forest and barren land is only 5 percent.

Besides cultivation, majority of the Saharias earn their livelihood through agriculture and other casual labour. About 22 per cent Saharias earn their livelihood through casual labour and other occupations. To work as labourer, they even migrate to neighbouring areas. They also migrate to the bordering States of Rajasthan and Uttar Pradesh during lean periods in search of labour. Such migrations cause them problems of housing and physical exploitation and thus disturb their whole family and the education of their children. These uncertainties make their life unsettled and miserable.

An analysis of the Table 19.2 reveals that the percentage of Saharia agricultural workers in all the five districts of M.P.

has come down to a great extent during the 1961-71 period. Datia is the only district in M.P. where more than 51% of the Saharia population are workers.

Another revealing fact is that during the period concerned their percentage of cultivation have also gone down in all the districts excepting Morena during the period and the percentage of agricultural labourers has gone up.

TABLE-19.2

Occupational Classification of the Saharias

Dist.	*Year*	*Popu-lation*	*Workers%*	*Cultivators*	*Agr. Labour*
Madhya Pradesh	1961	174,320	98, 182 (56.32)	42,08 (41.89)	33,932 (34.50)
	1971	205,427	88, 346 (43.01)	31,700 (43.01)	515.9 (58.35)
1. Shivpuri	1961	54,060	30,887 (57.13)	16,12 (51.19)	7,666 (24.82)
	1971	56,075	22,742 (40.56)	10,015 (44.04)	11,980 (52.08)
2. Guna	1961	41.550	23,959 (57.60)	9,769 (40.77)	10.716 (44.73)
	1971	53,180	25,016 (47.04)	8,061 (61.90)	4,199 (27.26)
3. Morena	1961	39,965	6,724 (54.56)	11,8353 (56.33)	4,687 (22.27)
	1971	44,933	15,401 (42.28)	9.533 (61.90)	4,199 (27.26)
4. Gwalior	1961	39,965	21,042 (54.56)	1,753 (26.07)	2,637 (39.22)
	1971	14,045	6,061 (42.15)	1,656 (25.67)	4,065 (67.07)
5. Datia	1961	2,016	1,196 (59.33)	270 (22.58)	165 (13.80)
	1971	4,984	2,575 (51.67)	296 (11.50)	2,038 (79.15)

Table 19.2 shows that as per 1971 Census, 61.70 per cent Saharias of Morena district are cultivators and in the rest of the districts, the figure is less than 50%. Datia is the only district which has lowest percentage (11.50%) of cultivators and highest percentage (79.15%) of agriculture labourers. Gwalior and Guna are other two districts where the proportion of agriculture labour is more than 60%. This shows the trend that Saharia cultivators are giving up their cultivation and working as an agricultural labourer and other forms of labour.

The Saharia community is mainly spread over in the northwest region of the State, surrounded by Uttar Pradesh in the northwest and Rajasthan State in the West. The western portion of the area is on the slopes of Vindhyachal, southern part in the plains of Malwa and the rest in the basin of river Chambal. The area is largely rocky with patches of lands wearing black cotton to sandy soils. River Parvati touches the southern finge of the area while Chambal is the main river flowing in the North. A number of seasonal rivulets and nalas flow through the area. The ground-water level in most of the areas is pretty low, in some cases even up to 60 metres below the ground.

The climate of the area is of an extreme type, being very cold in winter and hot in summer with scanty rainfall. The forest area in Shivpuri district is an exception to this, where the climate is comparatively moderate.

But for some patches of greenery in Shivpuri and Morena districts, there are hardly any forests left in the area. Even the remaining forests are poor in quality. All the trees are stunted in growth and unable to conserve soil and moisture in most of the areas. Salai, Khair, Tendu, Pals, Amla, Kulu and Siras are the main species found in these forests. The minor forest products available are gums of different varieties, resin, wax, etc.

Hunting

Hunting is one of the traditional occupations of the tribe. Since these people were exclusively dependent on forests at one time, hunting used to play an important role in their economy.

However, Saharias are not very reputed hunters. It is strange to know that they have no knowledge of bow and arrow which is the chief weapon used for hunting animals by most of the tribes in India. Their major weapon is axe which they always carry with them while going to work in the jungle.

When they go collectively for communal hunt, a party of six or eight persons tries to locate the part of the forest in which they are most likely to find animals. Others go in a team for quest. They yell at the top of their voice and make various peculiar sounds. From the sounds produced by the movements of the animal, they easily locate the direction in which it may be found.

Fishing

Fishing is another source of livelihood but it does not occupy important position in their economic pursuit. It is more a pastime than a profession. Men women and children all are equally interested in fishing in rainy season. They go to the nearby streams and nallas for fishing.

Surprisingly enough they do not have nets as used by other tribes for fishing. Theirs is a very crude and simple way of fishing. They go to a pond or stream and dam up a stream with stand. Then they spread the powder of chelha, golhar or bel on the surface of the water. This powder is a mild poison and fishes come up and run from one place to another in search of shelter. At this time, the Saharias beat them with sticks and take them. Another common method employed is to throw the water out of a little pool and catch the fish. This is more common in late winter and early summer when the water level of pool decreases. Yet another simple method is to spread a piece of long cloth on the bed of the stream or river. It is then taken out by catching the four corners carefully. This is not a very effective method and only small fishes are caught. Besides fish, tortoise is also eaten which is easily available in ponds and streams in late winter and early summer.

Society

Most of the houses of the Saharias are nothing but simple structure unfit for human dwelling. Each and everything is dumped in the same room which is used for cooking and sleeping purposes. Excepting a few houses of well-to-do families, all are ill-ventilated and provide a good place for breeding flies and mosquitoes. Cattle are also housed very near to human dwellings with the result that they pass urine and dung throughout the night making the surrounding dirty and unhygienic. Houses are broomed everyday in the morning and the floor is washed with cow-dung and clay once in a while. Most of the houses remain damp in the rainy season and ash is used to keep them dry.

Marriage

Marriage among the Saharias is very simple as compared to the Bhils and Bhilalas. The age of marriage is generally very early—10 t o14 years. As it usually happens in early marriages, the selection of the bride or the bridegroom is made by the parents. The selection of the partners is a very casual process. Sometimes unknown persons happen to meet on some road. They get acquainted and start talking. One has a marriageable girl and the other a marriageable boy. If they like each other and approve the details of their domestic circumstances, the marriage is fixed. Later, the details are settled and the marriage is performed.

Among the Saharias, the *dahej* is not an important consideration. It is the bride's father here who gives the *dahej* which is known as *var-dhan* or bridegroom's price. Poor people who are unable to give any *dahej* generally present their daughters with certain forests. The forest does not belong to him; what he endows is only the right of use of that forest. The father henceforth does not go to that forest for collecting minor produce.

More well-to-do Saharias use *palki* (palanquin) to carry the bridegroom to the bride's place. Ordinary people go on foot or in bullock-carts. The *barat* stays for a day and a night at the bride's place and after the ceremony is over, the party returns home the next day. Generally no band is employed for the marriage ceremonies. The usual custom is to beat copperplates (*thalis)* which make a sing-song noise.

The purohit or Hindu priest is called for performing the marriage. The marriage is largely Hinduized with usual fire as witness and seven circles round the nuptial fire.

Marriage is quite cheap. In case of the poverty of the bride's father, the whole village donates *rotis* or breads for feeding the bridegroom's party. The usual menu at marriage parties consists of *jowar roti* and *jowar karhi.*

Widow remarriage is common. Divorce is also prevalent.

Birth

The birth of a male child is heralded by the firing of guns and much merrymaking. Village women collect round the mother, sing songs and do the *tona-tutka* to drive the evil spirits away.

During the maternity period, the mother is fed on *gur* and *sonth, mahua-water* and *jowar dalia.*

The naming of the child is done by some old relative in the presence of friends and relatives. After the ceremony, *gur* is distributed to the relatives.

Death

The Saharias cremate their dead. The males are carried for cremation with the accompaniment of music. Women are cremated together with their ornaments. But if the ornaments are made of gold or silver, they are taken off before cremation.

No food is cooked in the house of the bereaved family for three days. This period is regarded as impure. The friends of the bereaved family bring food for the bereaved from their homes. On the fourth day there is bathing and washing of the house. Those who can afford it have a simple feast on this occasion.

Food

Only a few Saharias have two meals a day in view of their

pitiable economic condition. Those who cannot afford, simply eat mahua and such other forest products to satisfy their hunger while quite a few remain hungry. Jowar is the staple flood and is eaten in the form of chapatis. Along with bread, a little vegetable curry is also taken. Meat is not taken regularly as it is too expensive. The main food stuffs include: grains, jowars, bajra, mmaize and wheat, oil, mustard and gulli.

Vegetables

There is a lot of seasonal variation in the use of vegetables. Since the Saharias are mostly dependent on forests, they have a thorough knowledge of various green leaves suitable for consumption. They go to the forests, collect them, bring them back and eat after cooking.

Fruits, Roots and Tubers

These are also consumed in a large quantity and their use varies according to the season. The important ones are plums, mango, achar, tendu, jamun, guava, bel, khajur, etc.

Meat

Ordinarily, a Saharia cannot afford to purchase meat except on very important social occasions, but they go out for hunting in jungles to hunt small animals and various types of birds. Communal fishing is also organised from time to time.

Condiments include salt, various powders made of tamarind, mango and ber. Among the spices, haldi (turmeric), chillies, garlic and onions are common. The method of preparing food is very simple and the preliminaries are also not very elaborate. Chappaties are made of jowar and wheat is rarely used. Jowar flour is mixed with a little salt and is moistened and made into a dough which must be well mixed before it is rolled or patted into a pancake. This is baked on a hot frying-pan until well browned. It must often be turned in the process. Cheap varieties of rice are also consumed. Rice is simply boiled in large vessels.

NOTES AND REFERENCES

1. Atal, Yogesh (1965):*Adivasi Bharat* (Hindi), Rajkamal Prakashan, Delhi.
2. Bose, N.K. (1941): *Hindu Method of Tribal Absorption*, Proceedings of the Indian Science Congress, Reprinted in 1928, Calcutta.
3. Greigson, W.V. (1944): *The Aboriginal Problem in C.P. & Berar*, Nagpur.
4. Haimendorf, C.Von Furer (1982): *Tribes of India*, London.
5. Nadeem Hasnain (1996): *Tribal India*, Delhi.
6. Russell and Hiralal (1916): *Tribes and Castes of Central Provinces of India* (4 Vols.), MacMillan, London.
7. Tiwari, S.K. (1994): *Encyclopaedia of Indian Tribals*, Rahul, New Delhi.
8. Tiwari, S.K. (1982): *Madhya Pradesh Ke Adivasi*, Bhopal.
9. Tiwari, S.K. (1982): *Bharat Ki Janajatiyan*, Delhi.
10. Tiwari, S.K. (1997): *Antiquity of Indian Tribes*, Delhi.
11. Verma, R.C. (!995): *Indian Through the Ages*, New Delhi.

Pl. 15. A Kol woman

Pl. 16. Two Bhils

XX

BHILS AND THEIR NEAR RELATIVES IN MADHYA PRADESH

Bhils, Bhilalas and Minas form a major tribal group of western India. Authorities differ with regard to their anthropological relationship with the other peninsular tribes. It is said that they show close racial similarity with Kadar and Chenchu tribes. It is also said that they belong to Munda group of tribes. They also exhibit close similarities with Oraons. Their language is however, quite distinct to these tribes and it is closest to Indo-Aryan languages. Table 20.1 shows the Bhil population in India.

TABLE-20.1

Statewise Percentage Distribution of Bhil Population in India

State	*Percentage to Schedule Tribe Population*	*Percentage to Total Bhil population*
Madhya Pradesh	18.53	31.95
Gujarat	40.83	29.33
Rajasthan	38.58	23.70
Maharashtra	23.90	15.00
Karnataka	0.95	0.02
Andhra Pradesh	Negligible	Negligible
Tripura	Negligible	Negligible
India	12.83	100.00

Source: *Census of India,* 1971.

GROWTH OF BHIL POPULATION

During the decade 1951-61, the Bhil population increased from 2.3 million to 3.8 million, i.e. an increase of 64.50 per cent. Before 1961 Census, the population under tribal religions category had shown neither any marked stability nor any consistent changing trend. The irregularities in the decade variations of the population, in the past census, are much due to the confusions faced by the state authorities in the classification and naming of 'Tribals'.

TABLE-20.2

Growth of Bhil Population in India, 1911-61

Year	*Population*	*Growth Percentage*
1911	10,67,792	
1921	17,95,808	68.18
1931	20,13,177	12.10
1941	22,48,152	11.67
1951	23,30,278	3.65
1961	38,33,331	64.50

BHILS OF MADHYA PRADESH

In Madhya Pradesh, three tribes or tribal groups namely Bhil, Bhilala, Barela, and Patelia; the Mina and Bhil-Mina have been recognised as separate groups or individual tribes. In this way, the larger, the Bhil community has been placed at three places in the List of Scheduled Tribes. Obviously this has been done so that none of them are left unrecognised as Scheduled Tribes. A brief description of all the three is given below:

BHILALAS

Bhilalas are included in the Bhil group and are quite numerous, next only to the Bhils.

Bhilalas claim to be Rajputs and do not intermarry and inter-dine with the Bhils whom they consider to be of low status. Luard suggests that they are a mixed caste as a result of Rajput men marrying Bhil women of Central India. Russell confirms this view and further suggests that Bhilala is a corruption of Bhilwala, a term that might have been applied to those Rajput immigrants who came to Central India and in order to acquire estates here took the short-cut of marrying the daughters of Bhil chieftains who then possessed these lands. Luard suggests a different origin of the term. He is of the opinion that the term Bhilala is derived from Bhilara meaning a Bhil by mistake. Fuchs, who conducted anthropometric measurements of Bhils and Bhilalas, however, holds a very different view. He regards them, "racially more or less pure Bhils", and suggests, that "having acquired a better social and economic status, they have segregated from the ordinary Bhil tribal".

The Bhilalas consist of two main groups, the *Bade* and the *Chhote.* There is no intermarriage between these groups. But there is no prohibition of a Bhilala of *bade* (superior) caste taking water from the hands of another of the *chhote* (inferior) caste. Both these castes are further split up into numerous exogamous septs. In their customs and beliefs, Bhilalas are hardly distinguishable from Bhils. Perhaps the most important distinction lies in the fact that Bhilalas do not eat beef, whereas the Bhils do.

Malcolm has written very contemptuously of the Bhilalas. He has reflected the turbulent and unsettled condition then prevailing in Central India. And, none was more actively taking advantage of the existing chaos and anarchy than the Bhilala chiefs of Nimar and Rath. A very notable example of this type was the Bhilala, Nadirshah, who made his capital in the small village of Jamnia near Mandu. At one time, he had 200 horses and 700 soldiers. He was subsequently captured by the English and banished to Allahabad.

Their religious beliefs and social customs are like those of the Bhils with the only difference that the degree of acculturation due to Hindu influence is greater. Because of their historical association with the Rajputs, they have better land and economically they are better off.

BHIL, BHILALA, BARELA AND PATELIA OF MADHYA PRADESH

Numerically the second largest tribe of Madhya Pradesh and one of the largest in India, the Bhils inhabit a region comprising Ratlam, Dhar, Jhabua and Khargone districts. The tribe is migrant by nature and turn out in substantial number on road and construction works. The Bhils have earned a notoriety for high incidence of murder. Perhaps the most noteworthy feature of the Bhils is the *Bhagoria-hat* or the 'Market of elopement'. The markets fall immediately before the Holi festival. The typical Bhil area is Alirajpur, Sondhwa and Kathiwada region of Jhabua district. The Bhil habitat is a totally deforested area now and this deforestation is causing lots of problems to the people.

The Barelas appear to be a comparatively recent innovation and are, in all probability, an off-shoot of the Bhilalas. This tribe is mostly concentrated in the western part of Khargone district. Perhaps the first mention of them was made by C.S.Venkatachar in his Report of the Central India Agency (1931).

The Bhilalas are principally confined to four districts- Khargone and Dhar each having about 33 per cent of the Bhilala population, Jhabua having about 30 per cent and Sehore having 4 per cent of their total population. We do not desire to enter into any controversy whether or not a particular ethnic group should be treated as a Scheduled Tribe. However, the Bhilalas seem to have been largely acculturated with the Rajput clan names like Solanki. There is hardly any doubt that the Bhilalas are of mixed origin from the union of Rajputs and Bhils. The Bhilalas are substantial landholders and they usually carry the title of Rao or Rawat. The owner of the Omkareshwar temple at Omkar-Mandhata is a Bhilala. In physical appearance the Bhilalas are handsome people and do not show any trace of aboriginal descent.

C.S.Venkatachar, Superintendent of 1931 Census (Central India Agency) spelt the Patelia sub-tribe of the Bhils as Patiala, and he was correct. Be that as it may, the Patelias stand on the same footing as the Bhilalas are, next to the Bhilalas, the most important and most civilized section of the Bhils. In general appearance also, the Patelias are more akin to the Bhilalas than to the Bhils. The Patelias are found in Thandla and Patlawad tehsils of Jhabua district and in parts of Ratlam district. It is also likely that the tribe has got its name from Petlawas, its principal habitat. According to another interpretation, the term Patlya, Patlia or Patelia is derived from the Bhili term 'Bitle' meaning polluted owing to their intermixture with the Rajputs and other advanced castes. Nearly 123 of their sept names have Rajput appellations.

BHIL-MINAS OF MADHYA PRADESH

It is difficult to say who the Bhil-Minas are. In 1961, not a single member of this tribe was returned in the Census and in 1971 Census, there was return of 8 Bhil-Mina (6 males and 2 females) from Vidisha district. The Bhil-Minas are a tribe of Rajasthan where 16,453 of them were returned in 1971.

MINAS OF MADHYA PRADESH

It is a very small tribe of less than 1,500 population size and is found in Sironj subdivision of Vidisha district. It may also be noted that it is scheduled only in this limited area. The Minas are one of the ex-criminal tribes. They are divided into two groups—the Ujla and the Maile, the former approaching the Indo-Aryans type and the latter the Bhil type.

BHIL

Bhil and Bhil-Mina have little difference in their appearance. According to Hendley, a Bhil is generally very dark; with black hair, straight and long; smooth face, dark eyes with the apertures limited in size, making the eyes look small. The iris is grey, and chest has no hair. The face is large, wide and almost round, forehead of fair height, rather more square; vertex of skull, flatter. In some cases however, the roof of the skull seems to begin in the centre of the forehead. This rendering of the facial angle, measured in the ordinary way, appears large, and not affording a correct indication of carnal capacity. Eyelashes and eyebrows ample, bridge of nose broad and sunk, nostril dilated very round, nose slightly broad, clubbed at the tip.

Mouth large, lips thick, inexpressive, sensual, giving the impression that they were made merely to cover the teeth, which are large and coarse. Cheeks full. Molar bones flat and prominent. Ears large and prominent and very movable. Jaws evenly hung, massive lower square and large in proportion, angles square, large and widely separated. Expression amiable, but timid. They have dilated large nostril, the movable and prominent ear. To masticate hard and coarse food, their teeth are very large—the incisors are squares, broad, fixed vertically in the gums—but are generally flat instead of sharp at the edges, bearing marks like those of the horse, approaching the molar in appearance. Their teeth are very strong and attached to huge jaw which necessitates large muscles. These are accommodated in wide and projecting zygomatic arches.

Becon writes that the Bhils have dark skins, thick lips and broad noses. According to *Encyclopaedia Britannica*, the typical Bhil is small, dark, broad-nosed but well-knit.

Rowney writes that the Bhils are characterised by dark colour, diminutive size, prominent cheek-bones, large nostrils and great personal activity combined with an astonishing power of enduring fatigue.

Kurup narrates about the Bhils of western Madhya Pradesh. He writes, "They have a complexion varying from olive to copper, average Indian height".

According to Chakraborti and Mukherji, the colour of the skin varies from light brown to dark brown. The form of the hair is generally smooth and the colour black with occasional reddish tinge. Eye colour generally varies from dark brown to light brown, the common colour being dark brown. Mongolian fold is absent.

Bhils are noted for their playing of 'Nad' or musical instrument and keeping large moustaches. One 'Karna Bhil' had a world record for keeping longest moustaches.

ANTHROPOMETRIC DESCRIPTION

In 1944, Stepehn Fuchs measured 86 Bhils of the Jhabua

district and found them to be one of the most primitive groups. He observes that the average Bhils are of medium height. Of them 36 per cent are dolicho-cephalic, 59.3 per cent meso-cephalic, 3.5 per cent brachy-cephalic and most of them have round and oval faces. The chin is normally round or oval and slightly receding.

The forehead is straight retreating and super-orbital ridges are generally well-developed. The nasal measurements showed that 1.2 per cent are leptorrhine, 39.5 per cent mesorrhine, 53.5 per cent platyrrhine and 5.8 per cent hyper-platyrrhine.

Venkatachar measured Bhils of Satpura. He found that the Bhils are of the medium statured (mean stature 1649.52±9.23) with long head (the means cephalic index being 72.89±0.53). The vault of the cranium is moderately high (mean auricular height 120.48 ± 0.85) and the face short and narrow, the total facial length being only 110±1.01. The nose is broad at the root, the inter-orbital breadth being 30.30±0.27 and also very wide at the nostrils. It is moderately low as shown by the depth (mean nasal depth 21.11± 0.32) and given an almost chamaerrhine index (mean Nasal Index 8.138±0.95).

In order to evaluate the developmental sequence of all the bodies, Ranjana and Nath measured 285 male Bhils from the educational institutions of Udaipur in Rajasthan ranging between the age group 7 and 17 years. The variables were collected cross-sectionally and growth achieved by them is revealed in Table 20.3.

TABLE-20.3

Segmental Growth Rate of Different Parts of the Body of Bhils

Sl.No.	*Characters*	*Absolute gain (cms.)*
1.	Stature	45.8
2.	Sitting height	22.6
3.	Trunk height	19.0
4.	Head and neck length	3.7
5.	Total lower extremity length	31.2

Sl.No.	Characters	Absolute gain (cms.)
6.	Thigh length	14.6
7.	Calf length	15.6
8.	Foot length	7.6
9.	Total upper extremity length	25.3
10.	Upper arm length	11.9
11.	Fore arm length	9.1
12.	Hand length	5.7

RACIAL SIMILARITIES WITH OTHER ABORIGINAL TRIBES

To establish interrelationship with aboriginal tribes, Guha studied Bhils of western ranges of the Vindhya Hill, Munda and Oraon of Chottanagpur, Chenchu, Guntur district of Madras Presidency and Kadar and Nattu Malayan of the upper and lower parts of the hills of Cochin. The study is based on the data collected by P.C.Basu on Munda and Oraon and his own measurement of 50 Bhils of the Tadvi division of pure blood, 213 male Chencu, 44 Nattu Malayan and 12 male and 31 male Kadars. On comparing the data, he finds close racial similarities among the Bhils, the Chencu and the Kadar.

Considering auricular height, bignoial breadth, etc., the derived coefficient (6.11+0.59) shows close affinities with Chenchu. On the other hand, derived reduced coefficient (18.98+0.27) of Kadar has also shown close racial likeness. The findings by Guha are placed in Tables 20.4 and 20.5.

TABLE-20.4

Reduced Coefficient of Racial Likeness

Tribes	Kadar	(Based on 26 Characters) Bhil	Chenchu
Kadar	-	18.98 + 0.27	10.30 + 0.49
Bhil	18.98 + 0.27	-	6.11 + 0.59
Chenchu	10.30 + 0.49	6.11 + 0.59	-

TABLE-20.5

Crude Coefficient of Racial Likeness

		(Based on 26 Characters)	
Tribes	*Kadar*	*Bhil*	*Chenchu*
Kadar	-	19.09 + 0.19	3.97 + 0.19
Bhil	13.09 + 0.19	-	1.94 + 0.19
Chenchu	3.97 + 0.19	1.94 + 0.19-	

On the basis of the data, Dr. Guha concluded that the aboriginal population of India shows a short, long and moderately high-headed strain with often marked brow-ridges, broad short faces, the mouth slightly inclined forward and small flat nose with the alse extended. The hair varies from wavy to curly and the skin colour is a shade of dark chocolate-brown approaching black. This type of aboriginal tribes is found in Central and southern India. He, thus, considers Bhils, Chenchu and Kadar of the same group. It has, however, been disapproved by Majumdar on the basis that the view has been taken out from inadequate samples, i.e. 50 samples only.

Gulati and Srinivasan collected 110 blood samples of both sexes of the Bhils of West Khandesh in 1969. The sample represented 45.95 per cent O, 29.09 per cent B, 19.09 per cent A and 6.37 per cent AB.

Majumdar collected 369 blood samples from Panchmahals district of Gujarat of both sexes in December 1941 and found 37.5 per cent O, 27.5 per cent A, 26.0 per cent B and 9.0 per cent AB. Again in 1943 he tested 156 samples from Rajpipla Bhils of Balsamol plateau of Satpura hills (Gujarat). Majumdar found less of A and more of B among the Rajpipla Bhils compared to those of the Panchmahals district but both data are significantly different from those collected by Macfarlane. He disagrees with Macfarlane's estimate of B concentration in Bhils and says that "We have to seek for reservoir of group B elsewhere than among the Bhils". The blood-groups of Bhils collected by Uma Basu also depict a percentage analogous to that obtained by Majumdar. The blood group evidence shows that the Bhils might have originally belonged to the original racial stock. There are indications that they have been thoroughly hybridised by contacts with alien races.

ORIGIN AND ANTIQUITY

The origin of the word 'Bhil' is still clothed with uncertainty and various explanations put forward to unreveal the mystery of the appellation are well within the realm of conjecture. It is commonly believed that " the word Bhillis is derived from a Dravidian word for a bow which is the characteristic weapon of the tribe". The term 'Bhil' seems to have occurred for the first time in about A.D. 600.

Venkatachar mentions that the ancient Tamil poets termed certain savages of the pre-Dravidian blood as *Villaour* (Bhowman), and he suggests that possibly the modern Bhils are the tribe designated by the later term. According to this school of thought, Bhil is not a tribe name at all. Venkatachar is of the opinion that Bhils are a pre-Dravidian race, probably proto-Mediterranean, who spread "far and wide when a climatic crisis occurred in the grass steppes of Sahara, and it is this race which is responsible for the industry associated with Final Capsian culture in the Vindhyas". The Bhils are held to have occupied the Aravali hills and the western Vindhyas between the Banas and Mahi rivers. The Dravidians, a Mediterranean race, entered India through southwest and moved towards the south. "And it would be reasonable to suppose that Gujarat was on the way of the immigrant Dravidians in their march towards the Deccan and the South". It must have been here that the first contact and clash of cultures took place and earned the Bhils their present name.

It is commonly held that the Bhils are identical with the pygmies mentioned by Ktesias (400 B.C.) and the Phyllitae of Ptolemy (A.D. 150). Sometimes the word Nishad which occurs in the *Samhitas* and the *Brahmanas*, is held to mean Bhillas or Bhil. But Nishad meant one who sat low = (Ni+shad) and such could not be taken to mean any specific tribe. It is rightly held to be a generic name applied to non-Aryans who had accepted low positions in the Vedic society. Bose,

Pl. 17. A Sulphi tree

Pl. 18. Contemporary tribal art depicting Sulphi tree

basing his view on the *Arthasastra* and the *Dharmasastras,* is of the opinion that Nishad meant the offspring of a Brahman to a Sudra woman.

Still other identify it with the Pulinda tribe mentioned in the *Aitareya Brahmana* and the edicts of Ashoka. Venkatachar quotes Enthoven to the effect that the word Bhil occurs for the first time in the Kathasaritsagar wherein mention is also made of a Bhil chief opposing the progress of another king through the Vindhyas.

It may be safe to suggest that Rajasthan was the real home of the Bhils. When the Muslim invasion of India began in the 11th century, the Rajputs were pressed to leave the Indo-Gangetic plain and migrated to Rajasthan, in turn expelling the Bhils from there. Thus, there was a contact between Bhils and the proud Rajputs who were not averse to accepting Bhil maidens as brides. The unions resulted into splitting the Bhils into tribes such as Bhilalas, Pateilas, etc. The introduction of Rajput blood led to further distinctions among the Bhils: The *Ujle* (pure) and *Maile* (impure) Bhils which do not intermarry.

This view is strengthened by the tradition among the Rajputs to recognize the Bhil as the former residents and masters of the land by the fact that some Rajput chiefs could not assume the throne until they were marked on the forehead with a Bhil's blood. The alliance between the Bhils and the Rajputs resulting in marriages and other forms of social intercourse, however, were short-lived. Hinduism became more orthodox in Rajasthan and because of their habits of beef eating, the Bhils slowly started losing the position of equality and began to be treated with contempt. This change again forced them to migrate to the Central highlands where they had perforce to wander in the most inaccessible, remote and difficult regions on the hills, where, subsequently they had to make their homes.

LANGUAGE

Their dialect is called Bhilli. It is a mixture of words appearing from the Mundari (Munda group) and Dravidian languages. However, it is mainly derived from Gujarat and is influenced by Marwari, and Marathi in the Maharashtra area.

Hutton regards Bhilli as an Indo-Aryan tongue and perhaps a Kolarian language before that. At present it is found overladen with Gujarati and to some extent Marathi.

PROFESSION OF LAWLESSNESS

However, exaggerated and naive be the description, it does underline heavily the predatory and lawless habits of the Bhils during nearly two centuries of their recent past. The transformation of these former masters of Rajasthan into freebooters and unabashed savages can be traced to the Maratha invasion of Central India in the seventeenth century. Marathas treated the Bhils in a most cruel and merciless manner. If they found a Bhil in the disturbed part of the country, he was, without any enquiry, flogged and hanged. Hundreds were thrown over high cliffs, and large bodies of them, assembled under promise of pardon, were beheaded or blown from guns. Their women were mutilated or smothered by smoke, and their children smashed to death against stones.

Writing of the conditions in the Nimar district in the middle of the eighteenth century, Luard has also described the destruction heaped on the Bhils. Describing the campaigns of extermination against the Bhils, he writes, "These people were brought into Khargone and were required to give security for good behaviour. On doing so they were presented with a special collar to wear. All Bhils who did not give in were caught and beheaded at the chabutra in Khargone. The pillar to which the victims were bound for execution is still extant as also the axe used".

Forsyth also has given a very graphic description of the unsettled conditions then prevailing in the whole of Central India. Says he, "The hill tribes, Pindari plunderers and lawless Maratha soldiery with their daggers at each other's throats, were unanimous in robbing the husbandmen who ploughed their fields by night with swords and matchlocks tied to the rafts of their ploughs or purchased peace by heavy payments of blackmail".

It is evident that the tribal people were forced to a

profession of lawlessness and savagery as a consequence of being chased from pillar to the post by a succession of invaders. First came Rajputs who deprived them of their legitimate lands in the Rajasthan plains and pursued them to the most inaccessible parts of the hills. Then came the Marathas to whom the tribal life was no more precious than a common fly. Deprived of land to cultivate and opportunity to live at peace, the struggle for existence forced upon them a mode of guerilla warfare. Unbiased towards the tribal people, Forsyth readily admits that they were greatly maligned in being described as 'savage and intractable'. Malcolm also admits that "believing themselves doomed to be thieves and plunderers they have been confirmed in their destiny by the oppression and cruelty of neighbouring governments, increased by an avowed contempt for them as outcasts. The common answer of a Bhil when charged with theft and robbery is, "I am not to blame; I am the Mahadeva's thief". This fatalism, outcome as it was of the anarchy of the times and the historical development of centuries preceding it, had, however, not changed the nature and the basic character of the tribal folks. When once the conditions settled down and they found their necks safe from the knives of the marauders, they took to more peaceful professions". Forsyth, paying them the tribute of an administrator who had known them well as Settlement Officer, says, "They have long since gained the character of being a remarkably submissive and law-abiding people".

But the lands they lost to the Rajputs and other castes ranging high in the Hindu hierarchy were never restored to them, and to this day they cultivate the most unsuitable lands. Their overwhelming dependence on forests is also to be traced to the same facts of history.

MARRIAGE

The Bhils are divided into two *hagas*, which include brothers, cousins, clansmen and the wider circle of the *hagas* on the paternal side, and hagadadia, i.e. marriageable relatives. Marriages between two hagas is not permissible, i.e. there is endogamy at the haga level. Polygamy is common.

Thus, the tribe is endogamous, while the sept is exogamous. No one can marry in the same sept in which he has already married for at last three generations. The same prohibition applies to marriage in the sept to which his mother belonged. There is no prohibition of a man marrying two sisters.

The marriage is generally adult. But the Hindu influence has slowly effected a marked change in this respect. Child marriage is considered more respectable and fashionable today than it ever was in the past. Even then adult marriage is the rule. Several types of marriages are prevalent among the Bhils. They are:

(i) *Lagan mandwa* (Hinduised form of religious marriage).
(ii) *Lugda-ladi* (an abbreviated form of the conventional marriage).
(iii) *Aa bharana ar uchal jana* (marriage by intrusion).
(iv) *Ghees kar le jan* (marriage by abduction).
(v) *Ghar jamai* (matrilocal marriage).

WIDOWS

There is no prohibition against the remarriage of the widows. They can marry any person they like. Widow remarriage is known as *Natra*. The bride-price in case of widows is generally very low. The common practice is for the widow to marry her *devar* (husband's younger brother) if he is unmarried. This is known as *devar-batta* (levirate). The widows are, as a rule, not permitted to take the children along with them to the house of the new husband.

DIVORCE

Divorce is common among the Bhils. There is no formal procedure gone through for effecting a divorce. The woman just leaves the husband and enters the household of a man with whom she has had a prior understanding. This would be simply *Aa bharana*. In such an event, the former husband will demand the refund of bride-price and the expenses he had incurred over the present woman. A *jhagra-todna* panchayat would be held and the sum settled. Sometimes the divorce is settled through the panchayat, in which case the break of the relationship is signified by breaking a twinge or tearing a piece of cloth.

In cases of the existence of bad blood between the former and the new husbands or a refusal by the new husband to pay the damages, a bloody feud ensues, resulting in murders and arson running a lone course of destruction in the families concerned and passing on from one generation to another as a sacred behest.

POLYGAMY

It is prevalent in the tribe, but the practice is not very common. The reason is largely economic. As we have seen, the Bhil marriage is a costly affair and those who can afford it are few. The explanation generally given by a Bhil for taking another wife is invariably economic. She would share the work in the field and the house. Polyandry is altogether unknown.

DEATH

The Bhils cremate their dead. Only young babies and victims of leprosy and smallpox and snake-bite are buried. The corpse is laid on a bier, feet pointing South and head towards the north. After the body is consumed the unburnt bones are collected and placed in an earthen vessel and buried near the house. Sometimes the bones are deposited in some stream nearby. On the twelth day at the spot of burial of the ashes a ceremony is held.

Bhils give expensive feasts to pacify the dead. These feasts are known as *Nukta*. Mutton, liquor, rice, *makki roti* and *gur*, etc. are served in these feasts. This feast is an elaborate affair and several villagers join these feasts for which no formal invitation is deemed essential. If the deceased came of a poor family and his family was not in a position to bear the expenses, the friends and relatives coming for the *Nukta* bring goats, grains, gur, etc. with them as presents.

SOCIAL CUSTOMS

Bhils are very fond of tattooing and get various designs made on the cheeks, forehead, arms, chest and legs. In inaccessible areas the tattooting is done by the village people with *Babul* thorns and colour obtained from *Balor* and *Bijan*. Since the opening up of the areas, we can see the tattooing machines in operation in the village *hats* in the tribal areas. The tattoo operator has a very busy time, particularly with the tribal belles who flock to his shop in great numbers.

ORNAMENTS

Bhils are equally fond of ornaments and spend a good deal of money on this form of decoration. Even men like to wear ornaments in their ears and neck. The ornaments are generally made of silver and bronze.

DRESS

Men generally wear a *langoti* (loincloth) which just covers the organs leaving the major parts of the buttocks exposed. Even the most sophisticated Bhil prefers this *langoti* when at home or working in the fields and forests. It is only when he visits the market that he wraps a *picholi* (a piece of long cloth) round his waist, and sometimes puts on a colourful waistcoat known as *juldi* and a short turban known as *pagdi*. The *pagdi* invariably carries a short comb tucked inside.

Women wear a skirt known as *ghagra* with red or black prints. The *ghagra* is not strictly a skirt, for it is not stitched round. It is more like a long piece of cloth with the top carrying a *nara* to tie it round the waist. The *ghagra* is folded in front and passed between the legs and fixed at the back in the fashion of male *dhotis*, leaving a major part of the thighs exposed. The breasts are covered with a short *kanchli* with open back. An *orhni* on the head, also of a red or black print, completes the female dress. The *orhni* is generally worn by married girls. The children up to the age of 5-6 years go about naked. All their clothes are sold ready-made at the village hats. The art of the needle is almost unknown.

Pl. 19. Contemporary tribal art depicting Ganesha

Pl. 20. Burial Pillar (Bastar)

Pl. 21. Tribal mask

Pl. 22. Model of a traditional tribal house from Surguja

Men sometimes wear shoes which are called *Khada* in the Bhilli. Women generally go bare-footed.

FOOD

The staple food of the Bhils is makka (*Zea mays*) and jowar (*Sorghums vulgate*) and bajra (*Pencillaria spicata*) and other small millets. Makki is used for bread (finely ground) and thuli (coarsely ground) which they call as *rabdi.* The bread or roti is taken with salt and chillies. Chutney of kaitha (*Feronia elephantum*) and other fruits are is used with roti. Among the dals, their preference is for urad (*Phaseolus radiatus*) and tuar (*Cajanus indicus*), specially the latter. Rabdi is commonly taken with butter-milk. Generally vegetables are not used except those that grow wild. A very popular dish is thick and small makki bread covered with palas leaves and baked in slow fire. This is known as pania. Gur is highly relished. Rice is rarely eaten.

The cooking is done in earthernwares and not more than a karhai (deep frying pan made of iron) or lota (of brass or copper) and a thali (copperplate) would be found in most of the Bhil houses. For drinking water they use dried and hollowed gourds. Oil (sesamum and ground-nut) is commonly used for cooking. Milk and ghee are not used by the householders. They are reserved for the weekly markets where they are sold for purchasing weekly provision of oil, chilis, haldi, salt, gur and kerosene, etc. They take meat whenever they can get it.

In time of distress, they boil leaves, roots and wild tubers and eat them.

HOUSE

Bhils live in thatched huts. Each hut is situated on a high point separated from other huts. The hut is a simple and temporary affair. For long Bhils were a wandering tribe, going from one place to another in search of land and food. It is only in the last fifty years that they have settled down. The temporary nature of their hamlets is partly explained by the unsettled past and partly the explanation lies in their superstitious beliefs. If there is a sudden death in the family, they change their residence in the hope, perhaps, of throwing off the bad spirits.

The house is a katcha affair. The walls are generally made of mud and stones or bamboo or wattle and daub.

VILLAGE

The Bhil villages are usually on mountain slopes and are known as Pal. Each Pal has many huts and the headman is called Gameti (a distorted form of Grampati). In some areas he is also called *Vasavo*. This is a hereditary post and he is obeyed by all. He settles disputes and propitiates God. Caste panchayats are still active and consulted in settling disputes, marriages, cases of divorce, adultery, etc. Vartanio or Kotwal is an important functionary who performs rituals connected with death in the presence of the Bhils from the village and this assembly of villagers is called *Kol Padshah Mandal.*

OCCUPATION

Traditionally, the Bhils were food-gatherers and practised shifting cultivation. Large grazing lands are owned by their village community. They live a community life and help each other. Cattle-farming and agriculture are common occupations. They also work on farms as farm labourers and on other works. Bonded labour is also common. They are liquor addicts and drink mahua.

RELIGION

The religion of the Bhils is generally described as animistic. But a long contact with Hindus has resulted in the adoption of many of the Hindu gods and goddesses by them. The feeling of caste, also a result of Hindu contact, spurs their desires to be considered high in the social esteem. And, as a result, the Bhils living in contact with the Hindus, like to be regarded as Hindus. Particularly Mahadeva, Ganesh and Kali Mata, they have made their own. Instances are not rare where they worship Vishnu (Rama and Krishna avataras). As a matter of fact, Hindu religion itself is not a religion in the strict sense of the term but an agglomeration of religions not infrequently widely divergent and markedly antithetical to each other. It has been described by some as a vast canopy under which are collected all sorts of gods and goddesses. Many practices of caste Hindus are purely animistic in origin, concept and observance. To describe animistic, purely as that category of faith which includes all "pre-Hindu religions of India", would not be quite accurate in the light of the modern theories and views. Hinduism not only absorbed all faiths existing in India before the Aryans came, but also developed and evolved them in higher forms. Mahadeva, for instance, definitely a god of the Austric proto-Australoids, in the post-Aryan era, became altogether different.

The most important of the Bhil gods is the *Baba deo* or *Bara deo* who is the village tutelary deity. Every village has a separate piece of land allotted to *Baba deo*. It is marked either by a tree or pegs or sagi wood. The piece of land is held sacred and the forest on the land is never cut. Offerings of earthenwares, clay horses and toy swings are made to *Baba deo*. He is specially worshipped in the month of Shravan (July-August). On the day fixed for worship, the whole of the Bhil community collects round the 'Baba deo' and after making offering spends the day in drinking and singing. In cases of ailments, *Baba deo* is offered goats, cocks and other things to pacify his wrath.

TOTEMIC SEPTS

Bhils have totemic septs. The number of septs reported ranges from 27 to 36. Examples are: *Jamunia* (Jamun tree), Rohni (Rohan tree), Avalia (Amla tree), *Mori* (Peacock), *Solia* (sun), Sanyan (Cat), Ghodmarya (Horse killer), etc. In Rajasthan (Banswara district), 54 clans (Jati) have been identified which are exogamous. Some are reported to have 150-162 sun-clans.

HISTORY

As already noted above, the Sanskrit term Bhilla is said to have been derived from the Dravidian term for bow. The Bhils seem to be the 'Pygmies' of Ctesia (400 B.C.), and the Poulidnai and Phylitae of Ptolemy (A.D. 150); but the name by which they are at present known cannot be traced far back in Sanskrit literature. The Pulinda tribe is mentioned in the *Aitareya Brahmana* and the edicts of Ashoka. The Bhils are often mentioned as foes or allies in the history of Anahilvada. In *Kathasaritsagara,* reference has been made to a Bhil chief oppressing the progress of another king through the Vindhyas.

We have references of Bhils in the epics also. The noted author of the Ramayana, Valmiki, started life as a Bhil bandit named Walia. Later, he became a sage through the blessings of goddess Saraswati, and his extreme grief over his dark past turned into poetry.

Another reference has been made to a Bhil woman, Sabri, making presents of plums (Ber) to the hero of the Ramayana, Rama, during the exile.

The *Mahabharata* tells us about the famous archer Ekalavya, who was a Bhil. Ekalavya approached Dronacharya, the preceptor of the Pandavas, to learn the art of archery but his candidature could not be accepted. Later, he made an idol of Dronacharya and treating it as his Guru, practised the art of archery. He became a prominent archer. Knowing this, Dronacharya came to him and asked for forefinger of his right hand as Guru Dakshina, which he gladly offered.

Another tragic event occurred with the Bhils in the *Mahabharata.* By mistake Jaratha, a Bhil hit an arrow to Krishna fatally, though he had taken aim to shoot a deer. A curse is said to have thereafter descended on the Bhils so that they are not able to handle the bow with the forefinger of their hand.

Major Hendley interpreted this story in a different way. In fighting against Krishna, the Bhils were condemned to lose the forefinger of their right hand so that they might never enter into conflict with the friends of the hero. Hence, it is said, they never used the forefinger in drawing the bow.

About 1400 B.C. Krishna is supposed to have founded a kingdom in Gujarat after a fierce struggle with its inhabitants, many of whom were probably the Bhils. In fact, Viratnagar, a town in Gujarat, was at that time governed by Shridoshra, a Bhil queen, according to the local traditions.

Aboriginals had their relations with Lord Krishna and his kinsmen. It is believed in the local lore that a Bhil's arrow ultimately killed the lord and they were the people who had snatched the ladies of the royal family of the Yadavas while being escorted to Mathura by Arjuna, the Pandava, in spite of his famous bow Gandiva.

The Bhil kings have been mentioned in the *Mahabharata* as rulers of Rajputana, Malwa and Central India. From the time of the *Mahabharata* to 325 B.C. when Alexander invaded India, historic records mention nothing about any part of Rajasthan. In 200 B.C. Menander, a Greek invader, attacked Madhyamika Nagari, a town in the middle of Mathura and Ujjain. This town located around Chittor (known as Shivi Janapada) was well-known for its riches. The Shivi Janpada was under the Bhils' domination. Near the small village Nagari, at a distance of 9 km from Chittorgarh, finely dressed stones bearing exquisite carvings lie strewn over a large area to tell the glory of its past. But nothing can be said about the life led by the people living in vast expanses of the forest in the surrounding region.

The First Phase of Bhil-Rajput Co-operation (7th to 13th century A.D.)

About A.D. 626 Nagaditya, the ruler of Edur and the fourth in the dynasty of Guhilots, founded Nagda (near Eklingli) in Udaipur district with the co-operation of Bhils. At that time, Edur was governed by a chief of a savage race. His name was Mandalica. Somehow, getting tired of their snobbery or ostentation superiority, the Bhils assailed Nagaditya while hunting and deprived him of his life. Shiladitya, the successor of the assassinated ruler retired to Nagda and in order to improve the prosperity in his domain and his relations with the Bhils' he developed certain salt mines in his region. Among the early Guhilots in this region, Bappa Rawal has been most important and well-known. Bappa Rawal is a corrupt form of Vap-raj-kul (father of royal dynasty). The local legend and the Bhil lore state that Bappa was bred and brought up among the Bhils. Becoming their leader at a very early age he was given *Tika* of blood from the thumb by the Bhil chief of Ogana. Since then, the tradition of *Tika* has been continuing for the coronation of Rajput rulers.

The region around Chittorgarh was by this time appropriated by Mauryas of unknown origin who originally constructed the fort of Chittorgarh at the capital. During A.D. 725-38 Arabs, under the leadership of Junaid ravaged this region, and Man Maurya succumbed against them. But Bappa with the co-operation of the Bhils, was at last successful in driving the foreigners out and gain hold over Chittorgarh. There is little in the historical accounts about life and social status of the Bhils and their relations with other segments of the society during the next six centuries. But it is certain that the Bhils were in no way despised. They had their chiefs ruling over certain areas like other Rajputs and intermarriages were frequent. Instances occasionally occurred in which the children of a Rajput by a Bhil wife were recognised as Rajputs.

In A.D. 951 the capital of Maiwar was shifted from Nagda to Ahar, and the latter continued to be the capital of Maiwar in spite of being invested by Vakpatiraj Munja, the Paramara king of Malwa sometime between A.D. 974 and 933. The region around Chittorgarh including the fort was lost not to be regained from the hold of the Paramaras and latter from the Chalukyas of Gujarat for another two centuries. In A.D. 1174 Rawal Samant Singh revolted against the Chalukya authority, but the Gujarat forces in turn uprooted him altogether. The fugitive ruler, like his ancestor 540 years before, again sought shelter and co-operation of the Bhils. After killing Chaurasimal, the oppressor of the Bhils, he founded the kingdom of Wagar with its capital at Baroda, later shifted to Dungarpur.

In Maiwar, Kirtipal Chauhan of Nadaul (in Pali district) taking advantage of the unsettled political conditions, spread his sway. But Rawal Kumar Singh the younger brother of Samant Singh, husbanded the local co-operation and could easily reinstall Guhilot authority in the region.

In the eleventh century, Maiwar was held by the hillmen. The chief's name was Ashawhom Karan, the Gujarati king, defeated and slew at Ashawal, the site of the present city of Ahmedabad.

From the history of Udaipur it appears that in the eleventh century, a great part of Maiwar and the northwest parts of Central India was under the Bhils. In A.D. 1134 The king of Udaipur invaded their country and annexed part of their territory. Some of the predatory Rajput chiefs, too, bent on plunder and territorial expansion, entered the hills with the purpose of subduing the inhabitants. To this end they are said to have broken their caste rules by taking in marriage Bhil women. The intermarriage explains Rajput features so marked in many of the present-day Bhils. The intermixture of the Rajputs and Bhils has produced new castes, such as the Garasias, Bhilalas, etc., who claim to be socially superior to the hill Bhils.

About A.D. 1190 the king of Abu, Jethsi Parmar had a daughter Ichani Kumari. The Gujarat king, Bhimdeo II, wished to marry this princess and sent an ambassador to the Abu king with a request for this daughter's hand. Jethsi Parmar could not, however, entertain the proposal, as his daughter had been already betrothed to the son of the Ajmer king. Bhimdev, greatly annoyed, declared war against Abu and took the fort on the summit of the hill. It may be mentioned here that, at present, Parmar is a name of Bhil clan in Maiwar.

The Age of Marathas (18th to 19th century A.D.)

The age of Mughal invasions was over. After the death of Aurangzeb in A.D. 1707 the authority at Delhi was too feeble to launch any organised military operation on any part of Rajasthan.

Ahilya Bai, the widow of the king of Malwa was queen in A.D. 1767 in an area which formerly belonged to Dhanji. She continued to allow Bhils their claim to levy a small duty on goods passing through the hills.

Bhil Revolts in the British Period

Marathas ceded the province of Ajmer to the British in January

1818. The Marathas also agreed to give up their rights from all the States of Rajasthan. Thus, the British got opportunities of expansion of their empire in Rajasthan. Through treaties, the British paramountcy was established in Rajasthan by the end of 1818 and excepting the Sirohi State, all the States of Rajasthan concluded treaties while the Sirohi State concluded treaty in 1823. The early British policies in Mewar and Ajmer compelled the tribal people to revolt against the new order. Beginning from 1818, the tribals remained in constant revolt up to the end of the 19th century.

The Bhil and Mer revolts began coincidentally in the year 1818. The Mer revolt was short-lived while the Bhil revolts continued for a long time.

The anti-British feelings among the Bhils was also a cause of Bhil unrest. In fact, their freedom was snatched by the British and they were put under strict authority of administration for the first time. The new order in which a large number of parasitic classes and persons penetrated in the Bhil tract was also the result of the British policy who made their life painful. During 1818-60, the Bhils were crushed ruthlessly by the British which also generated hatred towards British among the Bhils. During the negotiation with Shyamaldas in 1881 the Bhils categorically mentioned that "If the Darbar does not kill us we can throw out the firangies from the country".

Attacks on the traditions and autonomy of the Bhils was another important cause of Bhil revolt. Under the new arrangements, the socio-politico organisations of the Bhils became defunct which was an essential part of their life. The Gametis and other Bhil chief used to settle all the disputes between the Bhils but after formation of Magra district the jurisdiction of civil officers was established. This caused inhuman and unprecedented subordination of Bhils. The tribal socio-political bodies also maintained social equilibrium, which became disturbed due to ineffectiveness of traditional socio-politico tribal bodies. Moreover, the new arrangements were considered by the Bhils as interference in their social life. Thus to protect it the Bhils resorted, to revolts.

The police atrocities upon the Bhils ignited the spark of Bhil revolts in 1881. In the first week of March 1881, a problem arose in the village Padona on the Udaipur-Kherwar road which gave rise to Bhil revolts. The Gameties Rupa and Kuvera of this village were summoned by the Thanedar sundar Lal of Barapal to appear as witness in some land dispute. Thanedar of Barapal sent a Savar (constable) Akbar Husain to summon the Gametis who refused to comply. When the Thanedar reached with force it excited the Bhils, and they attacked the Thanedar.

The Bhils feared the possibility of attack by the State troops. The Bhils made necessary arrangements to fight the State troops. On 26th March, the Bhils of Barapal, Tidi and Padona attacked the police station and the police post of Barapal and killed the Thandedar and all the constables. The Bhils became violent and on the 30th March a real war ensued between the revolting Bhils and the State forces. After four days of war, the forces could not succeed in rounding up the Bhils due to operational difficulties in the dense forest, hills and narrow valleys.

The Bhils blocked the advance of State forces by interrupting the communications. The desperate State troops and commanders encamped at Rikhabdeo and took defensive position. Here they were encircled by about eight thousand Bhils. The main leaders of the upsurge were Neema Gameti of Bilak Pal, Khema of Pipli and Joyta of Sagatri. The State commanders tried to bring the Bhils to peaceful agreement but could not succeed. The Maharana's personal secretary Shyamaldas who was accompanying the troops entered into negotiation with Bhil leaders through Khemraj Bhandari, the priest of Rikahbdeo temple.

On 10th April 1881, the Bhils put forward the following demands on which negotiation was to be conducted:

1. Bhils and their houses are not to be counted in future.
2. Bhil men and women are not to be weighed.
3. Muslims may not be allowed to live in Rikhabdeo.
4. The murder of the Thanedar and sepoys in Padona

and Barpal is regarded as a great offence; but it is to be pardoned. However, any person who commits such offence in future is liable to be punished.

5. Land of the Bhils is not to be measured..
6. The rate of Barar (tribute) is to be reduced to half.
7. Arrangements are to be made for not allowing the Kamdars (petty revenue officials) to give trouble to the Bhils at the time of Koonta (assessment of revenue), but there would be no refusal on the part of the Bhils in paying the proper demand of revenue.
8. The Koonta (share of produce as revenue) is not to be charged on Kodra (junglee grain) from the Bhils.
9. Tax is not to be levied on collection of mangoes and mahuwa leaves.
10. Custom duty is not to be charged on mahuwa which the Bhils collect for their own use.
11. In the Bhil areas, the Thanas are not to be increased in a number.
12. The Sawars (soldiers) of Patiya had till now taken the sum of 12 annas from the Bhils of that village for the choki of Poonam. In future, this sum is not to be charged.
13. Taxes on fetching grass and wood by the Bhils for their personal use may not be charged.
14. The amount received by the pals of Beeluk and Peepli from the treasury of Rikhabdeo is not to be paid to them.
15. Contracts for opium, salt, and tobacco are not to be given.
16. Contract for grass and wood is not to be given in the hills.
17. During the past three years, those Bhils who were imprisoned are to be set free.
18. The dak-hurkaras (postal points and carriers of postal materials) are to be removed from the respective pals.
19. The Sawars (soldiers) would not be kept on Chowkis (police or army posts) on which they are now posted

for safety of roads so long as the Bhils continued to be responsible for the safety of the road.

20. From pilgrims going to and from the shrine of Rikhabdeo and Shri Nathji, bolai tax is to be charged by the Bhils according to ancient customs.
21. In the villages of the Bhils, koonta (share of produce) may not be charged from the jogis and dhobis which they never paid.
22. Distilling of Mavri (tribal liquor) may be allowed to the Bhils for their personal use without tax.
23. There should be no interference in the social customs of the Bhils including internal feuds of the Bhils.
24. All the Bhils who had taken part in this uprising are to be pardoned.

The Bhils put 24 demands and asked not to interfere in their social and religious matters, stop Census work, withdraw Barar (tribute) tax, withdraw the State forces and give pardon to them. Finally, on 25th April 1881 an agreement was concluded with the Bhils. The State officials agreed to remit half the Barar (tribute) tax, not to trouble the Bhils by Census operations and give pardon to the revolting Bhils. The Bhils agreed to abide by the State rules and not to indulge in lawless activities.

The above agreement did not bring out complete peace. In March 1882, the Bhils of Bhorai and Nathara Pals again revolted. The revolt was crushed by the combined forces of State and Britishers.

For sometime, the Bhils did not resort to any revolt. But there was severe famine during 1899-1900. Hilly areas inhabited by the Bhils were more affected as they were not getting proper relief from the State. The tribals including Bhils, Minas and Grassias remained in unrest during the whole famine period. The desperate tribals to save their lives indulged everywhere in loot and plunder. Thus, the tribal revolts continued from 1818 to 1900 during the 19th century and were linked with the tribal revolts of 20th century.

The Bhils of the Udaipur State never accepted such conditions and did not submit before the British and the State.

In January 1826 Girasia Bhil chiefs Daulat Singh and Govindra revolted against the British in the Udaipur State. They collected a force of Bhils to resist. They attacked the police thanas and killed hundreds of soldiers. All the British efforts including army operations failed in rounding up the rebels. Thus, again in 1826, Bhil uprisings arose all over the Udaipur State under the influence of this rash revolt. It was only by the end of 1828 when Daulat Singh surrendered after a long negotiations. He was given a village named Bawulwara for his maintenance along with a liberal grant. Not only this but the Bhil estate of Jawas was restored which was confiscated in 1823. The Bhils were also allowed to collect bolai tax and the British and the Udaipur State followed a liberal policy towards the Bhils up to 1838 as the oppressive military attacks could not yield desired results.

Govind Giri

Another movement (1900-1912) occurred amongst the Bhils under the leadership of Govindgiri. He hailed from Bedsa village of Dungarpur district and belonged to semi-nomadic Banjara community. He was born on 30th December, 1858. He did not have much formal education.

It was a religious movement flared up with the objective of converting the tribals to Hinduism. Govind Giri's religious sermons were quite simple. He told his followers to worship Rama, adorn Rudraksha mala, perform havan and lead a moral life, speak truth, avoid sexuality, and not to steal. They should abstain from meat and wine and should take daily bath and wear clean clothes. Through this process he wanted to sanskritise the Bhils and bring them at level with other sections of the Hindu society. The followers of the movement were described as Bhagats.

By the year 1903, the movement reached its zenith, when Govind Giri went to Mangarh hill and performed a big havan and hoisted religious banner. Thereafter this ritual continued uninterrupted till 1907.

The rapid rise of the influence of Govind Giri seems to have turned the history of Bhils. When Giri reached Mangarh in the first week of December 1908, for his annual ritual, he started collecting armed Bhils. It is alleged that he began to plot nothing less than a Bhil state of which he would be the head. The present-day followers of Govind Giri deny this charge. They, however, admit that Govind Giri exhorted the people not to render forced labour, not to pay exorbitant land revenue and other levies. From the point of view of colonial administration and princely states, it was a political movement. The rulers of native states of Banswara, Sant Rampur, Devgarh Baria and Dungarpur approached the Political Agent to dispatch the Maiwar Bhil Corps to deal with the situation. The Bhil Corps were moved to Mangarh hills with machine guns and artillery under the command of Colonel Sherton to help the native troops. It is said that nearly one and half lakh Bhils had gathered on Mangarh hills.

Events were moving quite fast in a fluid situation. Some Bhils raided the Police outposts of Mogagadda and Khedpa Gaddi Station of Sant Rampur, killed one Inspector and took many policemen as hostages. On the way to Mangarh hills, the Bhils established outposts at various points and nobody was allowed to escape.

Now the Bhils and the native troops were poised against each other. The native troops and Maiwar Bhil Corps were on the eastern side and the Bhils were on the western side. A small valley divided the two sides. Soon after camps were established. Colonel Sherton started negotiations with the aides of Govind Giri with a view to persuade the Bhils to withdraw peacefully from the hills. He offered on behalf of the native rulers to reduce land revenue and also not to subject the Bhils to forced labour and other levies. But Govind Giri did not accept any settlement. Even warning by Colonel Sherton of dire consequences had no effect. This led to skirmishes between the two sides. Colonel Sherton ordered to fire warning shots in the air. Naturally it did not hit anybody and Bhils in retaliation started shooting arrows and gunfire on the native troops. Finally, Colonel Sherton ordered machine guns and artillery fire. The ill-equipped Bhils were no match to superior fire-power of the native troops and in a few minutes nearly one and half thousand people were indiscriminately shot down on December 7, 1908. But the shrewd potent Bhils escaped unhurt and hid in a cave. Their followers fled ahead towards the southwest. They were not chased by the native troops.

Govind Giri was put on trial and sentenced to death. But this was converted into life imprisonment, part of which he served in Ahmedabad jail. After the victory of allied forces in the First World War, he was released on parole. He settled in Idar for sometime and then was again imprisoned to serve the remaining period of the sentence for his alleged involvement in the Home Rule Movement. He remained in jail for three years. On his release, he worked with Thakkar Bappa at Dohad but soon left him. In prison he had become addicted to hemp smoking. He died in Kmoi village near Jhalod as a forlorn man. However, his religious mission still survives.

Revolts of Minas

The Minas constituted the largest tribal group of Rajasthan. As the Bhils were concentrated mainly in the South and southeast while the Minas were distributed in all the parts of the province, it can be said safely that the Minas are among the earliest inhabitants of Rajasthan and were formerly the rulers of much of the province. The Bhils and the Minas originally belonged to one tribal group but during a long span of time these became two distinct tribes due to different professions, habitations in different geographical conditions and social interaction with non-tribal social groups. The Mers and Meos were the members of Mina family of tribes.

By the end of 1818, the Mers revolted against the British. In March 1819, a British force under F. Wilder (the Superintendent of Ajmer) attacked the Merwara tracts. The revolting Mers were punished and police outposts were established. Such repressive measures gave birth to a widespread and formidable revolt of the Mers. In November 1820, massacre of the British police at Jhak (a village in Nerwara) alarmed the British as well as the States of Mewar and Marwar as the Merwara was under these three parties.

By the end of January 1821, the British, the Newar and the Marwar forces succeeded in suppressing the Mer revolt.

The tribal people did not relish with the new political and administrative arrangements made by the British. In 1851, the Mina tribe of Jahajpur Pargana in the Udaipur State revolted against the British to show their anger and resentment towards new order. The Mina revolt was so strong that the British and the State armies could suppress this by the end of January 1855. In February 1855, a cantonment was established at Deoly to combat with the Mina troubles in future. And also to keep a regular watch upon the Minas of Jahajpur certain police stations were also established. Again the Minas in 1860 mutinied but the forces crushed this mercilessly and up to 1947, the Minas could not rise again.

The movement of the Mina tribe took a different path during the first half of the 20th century. For a long time after 1860, there was no movement among the Minas. In 1871, the Criminal Tribes Act came into being and Mina tribe was put under that. But in 1924 the ammended Criminal Tribes Act provoked the Minas to fight against the injustice imposed upon them. With the establishment of Mina Jati Sudhar Samiti itself in 1924, the social and political movements of the Minas began on moderate lines. In 1942, an organisation known as Akhil Bhartiya Mina Kshatriya Mahasabha was established. During 1942-47, many other organisations of the Mina tribe came into being. These organisations organised demonstrations, rallys and conferences and by 1947 they succeeded in getting their grievances solved to some extent. Thus, during 1942-47 these movements gained momentum and during 1949-56 the Minas succeeded in getting social, economic and political justice to a large extent. In 1952, the Criminal Tribes Act was replaced by the Habitual Offenders Act, which is applicable equally to all habitual offenders of law, irrespective of their caste and creed. In 1950, the Minas were not included among the Scheduled Tribes. The Mina social workers and political activists represented before the Government of India and demanded the inclusion of Minas in the List of Scheduled Tribes. Thus, in 1956, the Mina tribe was recognised as a Scheduled Tribe.

NOTES AND REFERENCES

1. Anderson, J.D. (1982): *'Bhil' People of India,* Cambridge, 1913 Reprint, New Delhi.
2. Bachhan Kumar (1997): *The Bhils: An Ethno-Historic Analysis,* Sharada Publishing House, Delhi.
3. Barnes, E. (1906): The Bhils of western India, *Journal of the Society of Arts,* Vol. LV, 1906-07.
4. Biswa, P.C. and Bhattacharya, D.K. (1964): Anthropometric study of Bhils, *The Anthropologist,* Vol. XI, 1964.
5. Fuchs, Stephen (1973): Bhil, *Tribes in the Central India (Chapter-V), Aboriginal Tribe of India,* New Delhi.
5. Fuchs, Stephen (1973): Bhil, *Tribes in the Central India (Chapter-V), Aboriginal Tribe of India,* New Delhi.
6. Jain, S. K. (1981): *Adiwasi Bhil-Mina* (Hindi), Jaipur.
7. Karve, Irawati (1968): *Kinship Organisation in India* [Reprint], Calcutta.
8. Majumdar, M.P. (1972): The Bhils of Gujarat, *Modern Review,* Vol. XLI, No.3
9. Nath, Y.V.S. (1970): *Bhils of Ratanmal,* The M.S. University of Baroda.
10. Netram, J.W. (1940): *The Bhils,* Jabalpur Mission Press, Jabalpur
11. Pande, Ram (1984): *Tribal Movements* (edited), Jaipur.

XXI

DRAVIDIAN TRIBES OF MADHYA PRADESH

Dravidian group of tribes form the most important tribal group of India. In Madhya Pradesh, their number is highest although they are also found in neighbouring states. Gonds are the most important tribal group of the Dravidian group of tribes. Gonds are classified in many ways, i.e. by geographical distribution, by the number of gods they propitiate and by cultural strata.

The Dravidian tribes of M.P., of which the Gonds are most important, may be studied under following heads:

1. Gond tribes of Central India
2. Gond population
3. Gond tribes of Bastar
4. Dravidian tribes of Bastar
5. Dravidian tribes of Chhattisgarh, Oraon and Kamar
6. Bharias of Narmada valley and Chhattisgarh
7. Other Dravidian tribes of Madhya Pradesh

1. GOND TRIBES OF CENTRAL INDIA

The Gonds are the most widespread tribe of Madhya Pradesh and also most numerous. Though they are found in sizeable strength of more than 1,000 in more than 20 districts of the State, their largest population is in Mandla district. The typical Gond areas in Madhya Pradesh are located in the districts of Jabalpur, Mandla, Seoni, Chhindwara and Betul where, during the 15th-16th centuries were situated prosperous kingdoms of Garha-Mandla, Deogarh and Kherla.

The problems related to origin, antiquity and early history of the Gonds have already been discussed in the preceding pages (Chapter XIV). In the present context we are concerned only with that group which represents the three different habitats of the vast Gond society including (a) the Bastar group (b) the Orissa group and (c) the Satpura group in the Chotanagpur and Madhya Pradesh region excluding Bastar. The entire region, historically known as Gondwana, comprises the northern bank of the Godavari river, the Mahanadi and its tributaries, the Narmada, the Wardha and the Wainganga, the Eastern Ghats and Satpura ranges including the Maikal range. The ancestors of the present-day Gonds might have lived in some of these areas even two million years ago. They must have lived as small clans in isolated forests and hilly regions as gatherers, fishermen and hunters. Due to absence of roads and communications, the earliest migrations must have taken place during more than one thousand years, and these could have been due to compelling reasons of survival in times of disease, calamity, war, food shortage and search for females.

The task before Grierson who took up the Linguistic Survey of India, was difficult because even before the beginning of this century, the Gonds of Orissa, Chhattisgarh and Bundelkhand were speaking Oriya, or Chhattisgarhi or Bundelkhandi. The Gonds of Andhra speak Telugu as well as Gondi. Probably the Gonds of Berar and Nimar were speaking Marathi for many centuries.

Grierson has given a careful study of Gondi, which he has considered to be the fifth Dravidian language, though without a script, born out of an original Andhra-Dravida language of South India. This theory does not take into account the usual origin and growth of primitive dialects, and their acculturation and eventual assimilation with more advanced languages. In his volume on Dravidian languages, Grierson devoted more space to Gondi than to the other Dravidian languages. He has carefully compared the Dravidian with the Kolarian dialects. He was able to conclude that Kherwari was a kind of parent dialect of all the Kolarian dialects; and yet he was not able to reach such a conclusion about Mari, Koi, Kui or Kandh which are probably the oldest of the dialects spoken by the Gonds, prior to the emergence of what has been called Gondi. As the Gonds are not a tribe, but a larger social complex, Gondi cannot be regarded as a tribal dialect. At the same time, in absence of a script, literature and grammar, it is only on the way to become a language. It does not stand comparison with the major Dravidian languages.

Though there are cultural variations in the Gonds found in all these areas, they speak Gondi or deviation of Gondi dialect and consider themselves as Koitur, the universal equivalent of that name in all Gondi dialect. In the Telugu area they speak Koya while in Madhya Pradesh their dialect is mixed with Hindi. Gondi with its local dialects is a Dravidian language akin to Tamil and Kannada and to Telugu.

The different regional groups among the Gonds are identified with different names which appear like the sub-groups of the great Gond tribe. The Raj-Gonds, Koitur/ Koya, the Naik-pods, the Dhurve, the Khatulwar Gonds, the Madia Gonds, the Muria, the Hill-Marias, the Bison-Horn Marias, the Parajas, etc. are all Gondi-speaking sub-groups of the Gonds. In fact, ethnically, culturally and even linguistically, the tribal group recognized as Pardhan is also a castaway ethnic group of the Gonds and is given a lower status below the Gonds. The Maria, the Muria and Bison-Horn Maria are at low levels of acculturation and are classified as 'primitive' in some parts.

The Gonds have varieties of clans which are based on the number of gods worshipped. There are Four-God, Five-God, Six-God, Seven-God groups called Yerwen, Sarven, Saiven, Nalven respectively. Rarely a Twelve-God group (called Torey) is found. These are all exogamous groups. There is endogamy at clan level. Clan names are totemic, though totem is not practised by the Gonds.

Superstitions are common. Magic is also practised for warding off evils or black magic against the enemy. The class of priests called Pujari, Perma or Bhagat is common. They perform rituals, propitiate gods and spirits of the dead and may also offer magical cures. Some Permas have good knowledge of herbal medicines.

Seasonal ceremonies and offerings are common. Before sowing seeds, at the time of harvesting and while eating the first produce, etc., poojas are offered which are mostly on a community basis. Feasts with liquor, mostly toddy or mahua are common on such occasions. The festivals observed include Dusshera, Diwali and Holi. Respect and offerings are presented to their traditional Maharajas on the Dusshera day which shows their link with the erstwhile feudal kings of the Gonds.

The main occupation of the Gonds includes agriculture, picking up of minor forest produce, working as labourers on farms or in forests, and minor occupations like smithy, metal work, goat-keeping, piggery, etc.

2. GOND POPULATION AND THEIR SUB-GROUPS

The Central Indian Gonds are said to have migrated to the northern parganas of Bastar, and there was intermarriage between the Kanker Gonds and the Bastar Murais. The Murais of East Kondagaon represent the true Bastar autochthon. A confusion is created as some claim to have come from Langi Dhamda in the North. W. Greigson likewise made a distinction between the Jagadalpuri Murias, the Jhoria Murais, and the aboriginal Murias of Kondagaon. In 1931, 80,803 Gonds were returned from the Gond State of Kanker alone though they could be identified with the Murias of North Bastar. Greigson calculated the population of Hill Marias of Bastar to be 12,000 though there had been an emigration due to their persecution by the Patalkot zamindar.

In 1931, the Census gave the number of Gonds in Bastar to be 24,407 whilst the Marias numbered 1,46,070, the Murias 1,24,993, the Bhattras 36,611, the Parjas 17,568 and the Koyas 9,988. The Dorika Koitors were included amongst the Gonds.

In 1941, 39,553 Marias and 5,179 Murias were recorded in Central Province and Berar.

The Pardhans, though members of the Gond society, have been enumerated separately in Central Province and Berar. In 1911, they were 1,14,877. The number varied to 96,921 in 1921; 1,15,813 in 1931, and 1,21,494 in 1941.

W. Greigson then wrote that "Even now, the classification has been over-simplified, and is of little use of scientific purposes". The Census Officers had asked the Dorelas to call themselves Koyias, but they refused and got themselves enumerated as Gonds. 4,981 Dorelas of Lingiri called themselves Hindu Gonds. According to Russell, the Mannewars, who take their name from the Telugu meaning forest, 'war', being the plural termination 'appear' to be the inferior branch of the Koya Gond".

Among the tribes of the State, the Gonds are one of the elite ethnic groups. In many areas, as in Mandla, they are alternatively referred to as kisan, i.e., cultivators. In Madhya Pradesh, if a line is drawn from the southern boundary of Tikamgarh district, to the middle of Dhar district, the Gond belt could be said to lie South and East of this line.

In the List of the Scheduled Tribes of Madhya Pradesh, the Gonds include 51 other names within it. Some of the 51 other names refer to distinct ethnic groups like Dhobas, Dhurwas, Nagwanshis, etc. and are separately described. Others are perhaps referable to Gond sub-tribes. These may be briefly referred to in the following:

(A) Bhuta, Koilabhuta, Koilabhuti

All the three refer to the same ethnic group. These are the professional dancers and entertainers, the women of the groups working as dancing girls and sometime earn a rather bad reputation. They are found in very small number in Mandla district.

(B) Bhar

The Bhars are actually allied to Kol and the Chero tribe and not to the Gonds. Be that as it may, the Bhar are not found in Madhya Pradesh.

(C) Dhulia

The term Dhulia has origin in Dhol meaning drum. They are more commonly known as Dholia or Dholi and are the musicians of the Gonds. They also make big baskets known as Dholi used for storing grain. They are found in small numbers in Mandla, Seoni and Chhindwara districts.

(D) GAIKI

Russell and Hiralal describe sub-tribe of Gonds in Betul district but they do not appear to be found in Betul now and the likelihood is that they refer to themselves as Gond.

(E) GAITA

The Gaitas as a sub-tribe of Gonds are found in Chandrapur district of Maharashtra and not in Madhya Pradesh.

(F) GATTA, GATTI

In all probability, the names Gatta and Gatti, are incorrectly spelt in the list and the correct name is Gotte or Gattu. The Gotte or Gottu are the hill Gonds of Chandrapur in Maharashtra. They are not found in Madhya Pradesh.

(G) GOND-GOWARI

This is a small tribe formed out of the union of Gonds and Gowari, the latter being cowherds. This sub-tribe of the Gonds is found in Seoni and Balaghat districts.

(H) KALANGA

Though the Kalangas are shown to be a sub-tribe of the Gonds, there is some reason to believe that they are more akin to the Kawar and Chero tribes than to the Gonds. For example, in the erstwhile Phuljhar zamindari of Raipur district, the Kalanga have three subdivisions, viz., Kalingia Kalanga, Kawar Kalanga and Chero Kalanga. The Kalangas are found in Raigarh and Raipur districts in areas adjoining Orissa. It is noteworthy that Russell and Hiralal devoted an independent article on them instead of describing them under Gonds.

(I) KANDRA

Though Kandras are shown as a Gond sub-tribe in Madhya Pradesh, it is only in Bhandara district of Maharashtra where the Gonds have a bamboo-working sub-tribe with this name. It is not known if the Kandras are found in M.P. also.

(J) KHATOLA

The Khatolas are one of the two aristocratic subdivisions of the Gonds, the other being Raj-Gond. Their name is derived from Khatola, a former estate said to have been governed by the Gonds. The Khatola Gonds are found in Sagar, Narsimhapur and Chhindwara districts but they usually return themselves as Gond. They also wear the sacred thread.

(K) KHIRWAR, KHIRARA

It is not clear as to which tribe or sub-tribe is referred to by this name in the List of Scheduled Tribes. No reference is found in any earlier work nor are they found in any district.

(L) MANA

The Manas are found in Chandrapur district of Maharashtra and not in Madhya Pradesh. As far back as the second decade of the 20th century, Russell and Hiralal had thought that owing to their general adoption of Maratha customs the Manas were regarded as a caste and not as tribe. In any case, the Manas are not found in M.P.

(M) MANNAWAR

Like the Mana, the Mannawars are also found in Chandrapur district of Maharashtra and not in Madhya Pradesh. In Chandrapur (Maharashtra) they are found in the Telugu-speaking areas adjoining Andhra Pradesh.

(N) MOGHYA, MOGIA, MONGHYA

The Mogai (Moghya, Monghya) are shown in the List as sub-tribe of the Gond and they are found in Sehore, Raisen and Bhopal districts. But till research findings based on fieldwork are available, it is difficult to say that they belong to Gond stock. Russell and Hiralal give 'Moghia' as a synonym of Pardhi. In 'A Guide to Criminal Tribes', the Mogias are bracketed with Badak and C.S. Venkatachar in his Report of 1931 Census (Central India Agnecy) equates Mogia with the Bagri, then a well-known tribe of thieves and robbers.

(O) NAGARCHI

The Nagarchi are a subdivision of the Dhotia (Dhulia of the list) already described at (c) above. They are also sometimes known as Chherkya. The tribe is the traditional drummer section of the Gonds found in Seoni, Chhindwara, Mandla and Balaghat districts.

(P) OJHA

The Ojhas were the traditional bards of the Gonds as well as the Kurkus. Their women also act as professional tattoers of tribal women. The Ojhas are found in Mandla, Seoni, Balaghat and Betul districts.

(Q) RAJ

There is no reference about this sub-tribe of the Gond in any literature and therefore it is not possible to say who they are and where they are found. However, advantage is taken of this name in the List by the Rajgonds, and aristocratic section of the Gonds. In all probabilty, the Raj are the tribal masons.

(R) SANJHARI-JHAREKA

The word 'Son-jhari' means gold dust and the word Jhareka means sorter or paner and the name Sonjhari-Jhareka refers to the ethnic group who pan out gold particles form the sands of some rivers like the Ib river in Jashpur. This tribe is found in Jashpur subdivision of Raigarh district and in Bilaspur district.

(S) THATIA, THOTYA

The Thatia (Thotya) are the wandering minstrels who sing in honour of the Goddess of small-pox (Mata). In former days, these Thatia used to be in great demand in tribal areas. Due to eradication of smallpox, the traditional occupation of the

Thatia has no business now and the Thatias have given up their name and have started referring to themselves simply as Gond. They also do bamboo-work and their women work as village quacks. It may be presumed that they are found in the Gond-preponderant areas of Mandla, Seoni, Balaghat, Chhindwara and Betul districts.

(T) DAROI

The term appears to be in local usage for Gonds in Raisen and Sehore districts. However, no individual belonging to this group was returned in 1961. The Scheduled Tribes List (Modification) Order, 1956 also tends to suggest that Daroi is an alternative term for Gond in erstwhile Bhopal State.

(U) KHOND, KONDH, KANDH

This tribe is nearly 8,000 strong and about 60 per cent of them are found in Raipur district and another 37 per cent or so are returned from Rajgarh district. In Raipur they inhabit Mahasamund tehsil and in Raigarh district, Sarangarh tehsil. The Kanda (Khond, Kondh) have two subdivisions like many other tribes—the Hill Kandh or the Kutia Kandh and the plains-dwelling Kandh. The dialect of the tribe is Kui.

(V) BHIMMA

The Bhimmas are the tribal dancers and musicians. They have taken dancing and singing as a profession. They are mostly found in Mandla district.

(W) BHATOLA

In all probability, this is an infructuous entry. There is no mention of this group in any literature. In the List of Scheduled Tribes, they are shown as a Gond sub-tribe.

3. GOND SUB-GROUPS OF BASTAR

MARIA

The List of Scheduled Tribes contains the following names which are all referred to the Maria tribe—Badi Maria, Bison-horn Maria, Chota Maria, Dandami Maria, Hill Maria, Kucha Maria, Kuchaki Maria, Mandal, Nade Maria and Vade Maria. Some of these terms which are evidently spurious are (Badi) Maria, Bada Maria, Wade Maria, Vade Maria, Chota Maria, while others (Kucha Maria, Kuchaki Maria) are obviously clan names.

The Maria tribe has been considered to be a Gond sub-tribe. It is not proposed to enter into any controversy, whether or not the Marias are Gonds. The tribe is mainly divided into two sub-tribes, viz., Bison-horn Maria and Hill Maria. The former are found in Dantewada, Bijapur, Konta and Jagdalpur tehsils of Bastar district, while the latter inhabit the difficult physiographic terrain known as Abujhmarh. The Abujhmarh covers an area of about 3,900 sq. km and is spread over three tehsils, Narainpur, Bijapur and Dantewada. The Hill Maria of Abujhmarh have been considered as one of the six primitive tribes of the state. The speech of the Maria tribe is known by the same name. The terms Bison-horn Maria and Hill Maria were devised by Greigson as anthropological makeshift, but these terms have persisted and have even found place in the List of Scheduled tribes.

MURIA, MUNDIA

In the List of Scheduled Tribes, the Muria (Mundia) have been shown as a sub-tribe of Gond, the classification being correct. However, like the Dhurwa and Maria, they are being described here separately. The Murias are a very colourful and lively tribe of Bastar district who have been immortalized by Elwin in his *The Muria and Their Ghotul*. The Murias are divided into three well-marked divisions—the Raja Muria, the Ghotul Muria and the Jhoria Muria. The Raja Murias are found around Jagdalpur. The Ghotul Muria are found in Kondagaon and Narainpur tehsils and are so-called because they have the combined dormitory or Ghotul for unmarried boys and girls of the village. The Johria Murias are perhaps the prettiest and most livelier of them all. The Johria Murias, commonly known as Johrias are found to the West of Bare Donger in Narainpur tehsil and are considered to have originated by the union of the Hill Maria and the Muria.

4. OTHER DRAVIDIAN TRIBES OF BASTAR

PRADHAN, PATHARI, SAROTI

The Pradhans are considered to be junior branch of the Gond tribe and their traditional occupation was to act as priests, bards and minstrels of the Gonds. They are mostly confined to Mandla, Seoni, Chhindwara and Balaghat, in which district nearly 80 per cent of them are found. The Patharis are also traditional bards, genealogists and minstrels of the Gonds. In fact, on the Satpura plateau and Chhattisgarh, the Pradhans are known as Pradhan Pathari. The Sarotis are actually speaking a sect of the Pradhan tribe.

HALBA, HALBI

The Halba tribe is found in Rajnandgaon, Durg, Raipur and Bastar districts and they have to be distinguished from the weaver caste known as Halba Koshti found in Chhindwara district. The Halbas are now all cultivators. They are divided into two endogamous subdivisions known as Purait halba and Nekha halba. The dialect of the tribe is known as Halbi, the tribe itself is nowhere referred to as Halbi but only as Halba. Russell and Hiralal have described Halbas as a caste and not as a tribe. The Kanker copperplate inscription of Pamparajadeva, dated A.D. 1213 (*El*, Vol. IX.) mentions Halba-Gaita for the first time.

BHATTRA

This tribe confined to Bastar district is found concentrated in Jagdalpur and Kondagaon tehsils. The dialect of the tribe is known as Bhatri. The tribe has three divisions viz. Pit Bhattras or the pure Bhattras who work as village priests in tribal Bastar, Amnait Bhattra and San Bhattra.

DHURWA, PARJA

The Dhurwas and Parjas are one and the same tribe. However, in the List of Scheduled Tribes, the Dhurwas are shown as a sub-tribe of Gonds whereas the Parjas are shown as an independent tribe. Formerly this tribe was known as Parja but this name being considered derogatory has slowly been given up for a seemingly more honorific name Dhurwa. The Dhurwas (Parjas) are all found in Bastar district. They are also found in Orissa where they are known as Poroja which is nothing but the Oriya equivalent of the word Parja. The List of Scheduled Tribes contains another entry—Dhuru as a sub-tribe of Gonds. However, there is no such tribe or sub-tribe though the Gonds have an endogamous division known as Dhur Gonds. It is not possible to say whether the Dhurus are the same as Dhur Gonds or whether they are the same as Durwa.

Dorla, Koya

In Madhya Pradesh, the Dorlas are all confined to Bastar and are found in the southern and southwestern parts thereof in Konta and Bhopalpatnam areas. The name Dorla appears for the first time in the Census of 1931 previous to which the tribe returned itself as Koya. Even today the Dorlas are locally known as Dora Koya.

Gadba

The Gadbas are actually a tribe of Vizagapatam district of Andhra Pradesh from where it spilled over to neighbouring parts of Orissa and Madhya Pradesh. They are found in Bastar district in some villages contiguous to Orissa.

Dhoba

Russell and Hiralal considered the Dhobas to be a caste rather than a tribe. However, they have been included in the list as a sub-tribe of the Gonds which connection the Dhobas strongly repudiate. The Dhobas live in association with the Baigas and are all confined to Mandla district. They are mostly cultivators but sometimes also act as priests to the Gonds.

5. DRAVIDIAN TRIBES OF CHHATTISGARH

Oraon, Dhanka, Dhangad

The Oraons are found in Raigarh and Surguja districts. This

tribe has largely come under the sway of Christianity and in the Census of 1971, more than 8 per cent of them had returned Christianity as their religion in Raigarh district. Because of this the Oraons are divided into two groups—the Christian Oraon and Sansaria Oraon (the non-Christian Oraon). Oraon could easily be said to be the most literate tribe of the State. The Oraon tribe has five synonymous groups, viz., Kurukh, Dhangad, Dhanka, Kunda and Kisan. Of these Dhangad and Dhanka are included in the List of Scheduled Tribes. The original name of the tribe is believed to be Kurukh and this is the name of the speech of the tribe. One characteristic feature of the Oraon tribe used to be the youth dormitory known as Dhumkuria, but this institution has disappeared in Madhya Pradesh.

In Madhya Pradesh, their population in 1981 was 88,817 or 0.74 per cent of the tribal population. The tribe has a high literacy percentage. In 1981, 22.61 per cent people of this community were literate. The percentage of male literacy was 30.86 and 14.58 that of female literacy. This was due to the efforts of Christian Missionaries.

The Oraons are an important tribe of Central Indian Tribal Zone, but their native place is Chotanagpur, now in Jharkhand State, a part of old Bihar, as shown in the below mentioned in Table 21.1.

TABLE-21.1

Oraon Population (1961)

S.No.	*State*	*Population*
1.	Bihar	7,35,025
2.	West Bengal	2.97,394
3.	Madhya Pradesh	2.83,073
4.	Orissa	1,29,061
5.	Tripura	2,871
6.	Maharashtra	1

The Oraons believe that their original home was in the

neighbourhood of Rohtas. For, in the district Shahabad in Bihar, they speak Dravidian language. The only other speakers of this family in Bihar are Maler and Mal Paharias of the Rajmahal Hills in Santal Parganas.

The family among the Oraon is patrilineal and patrilocal. Their worship largely comprises totemistic rituals for purposes of marriage. The tribe is divided into a number of exogamous totemistic clans. The initial step for searching a bride is taken by the boy's father. Bride price is a prevalent custom.

The Oraon practice of burying the dead is interesting. When a man dies, some cooked rice along with urad is put in the mouth of the corpse and oil is applied to the dead person by his sister, wife, mother or elder brother's wife, and then the corpse is carried to the burial ground. The dead body is placed in the grave, the head facing towards the North and feet facing towards the south.

By coming into contact with the civilization of the plains, they have adopted the Hindu deities like Vishnu, Parvati, Ganesh, Ram and Sita. Songs and dances form their chief winter-night entertainment; they assemble at village akhadas and sing and dance from evening to midnight. Their most popular dances are Jadur, Sarhal and Jatrakharia.

The Oraons have their own dialect called Kurukh, which is quite different form Gondi. The Oraons have no tradition of marital or ruling race, but have evolved democratic institutions like tribal council, called "Partha Panch".

The Oraons are stocky, well-built, muscular with pronounced Dravidian features. Their remarkable characteristic, as elsewhere, was expression of cheerfulness. They seem to be given to a life of gaiety, fun and frolic, and have an eye for the splendid moment during festivals, through their songs and dances. They are also fond of cutting jokes even between members of the family, including brother-in-law, sister-in-law, cousin sisters, etc. Their hair is jet black and look frizzy.

They insist on recognition of their ancestry from the mythical hero king Harakh because the name by which they are known to each other is 'Kurukh' which is also the name of their dialect. Whatever may be the ancestry of the Oraons, perhaps the word "Kurukh" in some obsolete Dravidian sense meant man, and it is likely that the mythical king Kurkukh imparted to the word its own meaning.

The Oraons show indifference to hygiene and that is why other tribes have nicknamed them as 'Ravan Bans' taking the euphony of the word Oraon to suggest Ravan. However, the Oraons are cheerful in disposition and 'eat, drink and be merry' is their characteristic style of living.

KAMAR

A very primitive tribe who principally inhabit Bindranawagarh, Dhamtari, and Mahasamund subdivisions of Raipur district and also adjoining areas of Orissa. However, they are not identified as a Scheduled Tribes in Orissa. The Kamars were originally shifting cultivators and this having been prohibited, they have not yet been able to take to settled cultivation. At present they are mainly bamboo-workers and collectors of minor forest products. The tribe is arbitrarily divided into two groups known as Paharpatiya and Bundharajya depending on whether they inhabit hilly terrain or the plain areas. It has been recognised as a primitive tribe of Madhya Pradesh. The dialect of the Kamars is known as Kamari.

In Madhya Pradesh, their population in 1981 was 17,500, which constituted 0.11 per cent of the tribal population of Madhya Pradesh.

The Kamars are generally of a medium stature, though tall individuals are not uncommon. Their bodies are well-built and limbs are well-proportioned. Constant use of axe, bow and arrows in the forest gives a good shape to their muscles. Specially, the muscles on their shoulders are very well-developed.

Their skin colour varies from light to dark brown and even light black. A few individuals are found to possess golden or wheat colour, but they do not represent the typical Kamar complexion. Their hair is generally coarse, straight and black or dark brown. Often wavy and curly hair is also met with. They have a very thick growth of hair on their heads, but generally have scanty moustache and beard and other bodily hair. The eyes are generally black or dark brown.

Young men look very impressive with shapely, strong and slim bodies. They retain some of the dignity of their bearing and appearance even when they grow old. In their youth the women are delicate, comely and beautiful. Strenuous work in the field and forest and constant childbearing, however, sap most of the charm of their youthful bodies and as they grow old, a dull coarseness replaces the freshness of the delicate features of their youth.

Certain traits about the Kamar character are very important for all those who are interested in their planning. The Kamar is an individualist by nature. He wanders alone in the jungle with his bows and arrows. It is because of this character that the tribe has not been able to retain and consolidate a central tribal authority. Another notable trait of Kamar character is his sense of dignity. He does not like waiting long in courts and offices and wants quick results.

There are a number of complex rules and regulations governing the interaction and intercourse of the Kamars with other tribes and castes, specially prohibiting them from eating food cooked by outsiders. Tribal law prescribes that Kamar women should not eat anything prepared or touched by a person of other caste or tribe. In the tribal code of the Kamars, getting beaten by a person of another caste or tribe is an offence. If a Kamar is beaten by a Muslim or a person of Scheduled Caste, he stand ostracized.

The Kamars are the autochthons of the area. According to their folk-legends, they were the masters of all they surveyed and they used to earn their livelihood by carrying out shifting cultivation which, according to them, was obtained by no less a person than Mahadeo himself. According to legend, their name at that time was not Kamars but Gauntias or 'masters of the land'. Later, when they saved the lives of Rama and Lakshmana from starvation, they were presented with bows and arrows by the princes from Ayodhya and it is since then that they came to be known as Kamars or the people who wield bows and arrows. Even today the Kamars earn their livelihood with the help of bows and arrows.

Perhaps the earliest reference to the Kamars in modern times is available in the note by John Ball in his 'Jungle in India'. This book by Ball contains the following reference to the tribe:-

> Proceeding along the bed of the valley I came upon two colonies of a wild race of people called Kamars by their neighbours. They were regular troglodytes in their habits, dwelling in caves and existing chiefly on roots and fish. It is singular to observe how little the people of these wild races do to protect themselves from the inclemency of the weather. In one of these caves I saw the sole protection from the air was a lean-to-thick layer of loosely placed branches. The people seemed to be very timid, hiding themselves on our approach. I did not, therefore, like to attempt an examination of their dwellings. After some calling on our part, one man was induced to make his appearance. He was a most wretched-looking object, having lost several fingers and toes. He could not give very definite explanation as to his means of subsistence. All he could say was that he lived by picking up odds and ends here and there. However, he seemed to afford himself the solace of tobacco. A few cocks and hens at one of the caves, and a goat at the other, were the only domestic animals which I saw.

It is significant to note that 'A Report on the Subha or Province of Chhattisgarh' written by Major P. Vans Agnew in 1820 does not say anything about the Kamars. The Census Reports have made stray references on the Kamars but they are too meagre and insufficient. It is also significant to note that the 'Report of the Ethnological Committee—1866', does not make any mention of the Kamars though they have included Bhunjias in their description.

In the Report on the Land Revenue Settlement of Raipur district, 1869, J.F.K. Hewit has recorded a very brief note on the Kamars. He states: "The Nahurs and Kamars utterly refuse to cultivate and generally live in the most remote jungles, supporting themselves on jungle fruits and small game". The Gazetteer of the Central Provinces of India, 1870, took these very words in describing the Kamars.

M.A. Sherring in his *Hindu Tribes and Castes* gives a very short description of the Kamars in just two sentences: "The

Kamars are found in the remote jungles of Raipur, where they lead a wild life, subsisting on game".

Population

The Kamars have very few villages of their own. The Kamars inhabit 201 villages (134 in Gariaband tehsil and 69 in Dhamtari tehsil) of Raipur district. Block-wise distribution of these villages is as below:-

Gariaband block	53
Chhura block	39
Mainpur block	41
Nagri block	86
Total	219

According to the survey conducted by Tribal Research and Development Institute, Bhopal, these 219 villages can be classified according to the number of households present as given in Table 21.2.

TABLE-21.2

Kamars Living in Villages

No. of Kamar Households	*Bindranawagarh Tehsil*		*Dhamtari Tehsil*	
	No. of Village	*%*	*No. of Village*	*%*
1-5	33	24.81	41	60.29
6-10	44	33.08	12	17.65
11-15	13	9.77	6	8.82
16-20	20	15.03	6	8.82
21-25	10	7.52	1	1.47
26-30	8	6.01	1	1.47
31-35	1	0.75	1	1.47
36-40	2	1.50	-	-
41-50	-	-	-	-
46-50	2	1.50	-	-
Total	133	99.97	68	99.99

The Kamars have few villages exclusively of their own. In general, they live in scattered and small settlements in groups of one to ten households each. About 58 per cent villages in Bindranawagarh tehsil and 78 per cent villages in Dhamtari tehsil are those where the Kamar households are one to ten in a number, i.e. about 50 in population.

The number of villages, the number of households and the approximate population of the Kamars in the four development blocks would be as given in Table 21.3.

TABLE-21.3

Households of the Kamars

Block	*Total Population house-holds*	*No.of Kamar Population to ST*	*Estimated Kamar to Total population*	*% of Popu-lation*	*% of Popu-lation*
Gariaband	4459	697	4238	17.11	9.57
Chhura	55092	466	2834	10.66	5.14
Manipur	57046	587	3569	12.54	6.26
Nagri	96177	470	2850	4.74	2.97
Total	25274	2220	13500	9.63	5.34

The Kamars are an economically backward people inhabiting the south eastern parts of Raipur district. The area which forms the Kamar habitat is situated in two tehsils-Bindranawagarh and Dhamtari, situated away from the standpoint of development blocks and the sub-plan projects. The Kamar habitat comes under ITDP Gariaband, comprising the blocks of Chhura, Gariaband, Mainpur and Nagri, the former three lying in Bindranawagarh tehsils and the last named being situated in Dhamtari tehsil. All the four blocks are contiguous and constitute a compact area.

They are found in about 200 villages in this area and nowhere else, though Census figures wrongly show the presence of Kamars outside this area also.

The distribution of Kamars in the *Census of India*, 1961 and 1971 was as given in Table 21.4.

TABLE-21.4

Kamar Population in Districts of M.P.

Area		*Population*	
		1961	*1971*
Raipur district	(R)	11,008	12,418
Bastar district	(R)	746	727
Raigarh district	(R)	22	22
	(U)	3	1
Surguja district	(U)	6	1
Bilaspur district	(R)	4	-
	(U)	1	-
Seoni district	(R)	4	-
Durg district	(U)	1	4
	(R)	-	6
Hoshangabad	(U)	-	6

R-Rural population U-Urban population

The Kamars, a tribe of nearly 13500 population, is a circumscribed tribe living in the fastness of hills and forests of southeastern part of Raipur district.

As a rule, the Kamars do not live in regular Chhattisgarh mixed up with the other tribes and castes. They always build their separate Kamar hamlet or settlement. This Kamar settlement is generally at a distance from the normal Chhattisgarhi village and is separated from it by a small patch of forest.

The larger and exclusive Kamar settlements are situated on the hilltops. Even where the Kamar settlement is near the road, as in Pantora, they will build their houses away from the road and inside the forest. In the comparatively wilder regions and hills of Mainpur tract, the Kamar villages and settlements are in the nature of scattered houses and do not present the picture of a corporate village. For example, in Kulharighat, the houses are scattered in the jungle in clusters of two or three houses, separated from one another by distance of about 100-200 metres. On the other hand, in Kamar settlements like Garbhantora and Chikkli, the picture is that of a corporate village. But such villages are few in a number.

In the matter of selection of house-sites for their settlements, both natural and supernatural considerations take part. Nearness to water supply like a river or a stream, availability of wild roots and tubers in the forests, a comparative degree of seclusion are the usual considerations. The Kamar settlements are not shifting in nature but are permanent. New settlements are not coming into existence and all these considerations that proved an important role in the selection of the village sites are no longer relevant now. For example, the streams that were perennial or were flowing for most of the year, are no longer perennial and the wild roots and tubers have become scarce because of decades of exploitation. The Kamar settlements thus face difficulty of water supply and edible roots and tubers now.

The Kamar habitat comes under the jurisdiction of two forest divisions—the East Raipur Forest Division and the South Raipur Forest Division. The former has jurisdiction over Gariaband, Chhura and Manipur blocks while the latter controls the forests of the Nagri block.

TABLE-21.5

Block-wise Area—Kamar Habitat

Block	*Total Area*	*Area under Forest*	*%age of Forest Area to Total Geographical Area*
Gariaband	660.73	372.86	56.43
Chhura	690.23	254.53	36.87
Manipur	615.93	228.39	37.08
Nagri	714.68	215.33	30.13
Total	2681.57	1071.11	39.94

The entire project area is predominantly Sal forest area. Sal (*Shorea robusta*) occurs with other species like Saja (*Terminalia tomantosa*), Bita (*Pterocarpus marsuplum*), Dhawara (*Anogeissus latifolia*) and Kauha (*Terminalia arjuna*). Teak plantations have been raised by the Forest Department. Bamboo is found in the eastern part of the area. Among the fruit bearing trees found in the forests, mention may be made of tendu (*Diospyros malanoxylon*), Char (*Buchanania latifolia*) and Mahua (*Bassia latifolia*). The fruits of these trees are used by the Kamars to supplement their otherwise meagre diet. Several varieties of thick shrubs and creepers also grow in the forests. A number of edible roots, tubers and leafy vegetables are found in the forests and are abundantly used by the Kamars as items of food.

Also found in the forests are a variety of grass. The grass known as Khadar or Khar is used by the Kamars to thatch their roofs. Another grass is the phoolbahari grass which is collected and good brooms are prepared of it for sale in the market.

TABLE-21.6

Some Population Characteristics of Kamars

1. Total population covered:		1000
Male	50.13%	
Female	49.87%	
2. No. of household studie		317
3. Average size of household		4.7
4. Sex ratio F/M ′ 1000		987
5. Age structure:		Percentage
	0-14	42.09
	15-59	53.19
	60+	4.72
6. Landholders (percentage)		43.53
7. Landless (percentage)		56.47
8. Average land size of sample household		2.71 acres
9. Educational Level:		
Literate	13.03%	M=9.2%
Illiterate	86.97%	F-3.8%

Demographic Characteristics of Kamar Tribe

Majority of households were nuclear (81%) and the average household size was 4.7 persons.

The sex ratio observed in the population was favourable for females (1037 females/ 1000 males).

The median age of the population is 21.4 years. It is slightly higher for males (21.7) than the females (21.06). The population is young.

Percentage of population below 15 years is 41.1 and above the age 60 years is 3.7. The percentage dependency rate is 84.9, i.e. out of 100 working persons, there are 85 non-working persons in the population.

The index of longevity is low. The lifespan seems to be shorter as compared to other population. The proportion of population aged 60+ years is higher for males than the females.

The percentage (7+ yrs.) in the population is 10.4. Males are more literate (15.5%) than the females (5.3%). The literacy has considerably improved over time, particularly among the females. It is 22 per cent for the cohort 1957-67 (0.3%) and prior (0.2%). The literacy among the males born during the same cohorts were 34.6%, 24.7%, 5.9%, 2.1% respectively.

The population is economically backward. Only 1% households have income more than Rs. 10,000 per year. The type of households is highly associated with the household income. High percentage of nuclear households is below poverty line. Average income per year for a nuclear household is Rs.3,896/- while it is Rs.4,723/- for joint households. There are only 19 per cent households which are of joint type.

More than 50 per cent population have occupation as labour. Only 0.1% are engaged in service.

About 47 per cent population is unmarried. Percentage of divorced/ widowed/ separated cases among the females is higher (6.8) as compared to males (3%).

Mean age at marriage for females is 15.8 years and for males 19.6 years.

Average number of children born to an eligible Kamar female is 2.59 births. The fertility is maximum in younger group (20<years) and then decreases with the increase in age of wife. The total fertility rate is 3.67 births. The fertility performance is lower as compared to the various other tribes.

Time taken for first birth after the marriage is on the average 2.1 years. The interval varies according to age at marriage. The interval for first birth is a function of age at marriage of wife. Interval for Ist birth = 4.14-0.13 (age at marriage of wife).

The education of husband has insignificant association with the fertility in their wives. The wives of illiterate husbands give births to 2.6 children on the average, while it is 2.4 births for wives of the literate husbands. Occupation of husband is associated with fertility of their wives. Husbands engaged in agriculture have high fertility (3.1 births) as compared to the wives with husbands engaged in labour (2.5). The difference is highly significant.

Society

Round their loins, boys put on a small rag. Similarly, young girls also tie a small piece of cloth round their waist.

Among the Kamars, both men and women put on very few ornaments. Some men put on bracelets on each wrist. They also put on rings in their fingers. But the bracelets and rings are by no mean universal among the Kamars. In rare cases, they may be of silver, but generally they are of aluminium or any other cheap metal. The ring may be even of copper or brass. In a few stray cases earrings are also put on by men. It is customary for them to put on metal chains or bead necklaces round their necks. Women also put on bracelets on their wrists. They use a number of bead necklaces. They tie their hair with woollen or ordinary cotton funda. In the ear, they put on flower or umbrella-shaped khilwas, the latter type being more popular. The khilwas are made either of light wood and lac, or of brass or silver. The wooden and brass khilwas are common; women put on silver khilwas. On their legs, the women put on pairi. Besides these, they also put on a number of glass bangles in their wrists. In the Mainpur circle, the Kamar women have now begun the practice of nose-boring and put on a small nose-pin. But perforation of nose and use of any ornament is prohibited in other tracts of the Kamar community.

The Kamars do not have any ceremonial or special dresses for dance. For the chherchhera dance, however, they put on gourd masks and cloaks of bear's skin.

For protection from rains, the menfolk put on Khumri and women use mora. These rain hats are made of split bamboo and leaves.

For keeping money, nearly all men, women and children have a gupti which hangs to a thread tied round their waist or neck. The menfolk have a leather bag in which they keep their tobacco, flint and steel. In the hollow of a small dried bel fruit, they keep some cotton semar. This bel is kept either separately or in a leather bag which constitutes the Kamar's complete outfit for smoking.

When young, the Kamars bestow considerable amount of care to their hair; but as they grow old they gradually become indifferent to it. They share the task of hairdressing and shaving among themselves as the utilisation of the services of a barber is prohibited by the tribal custom. Some Kamars allow their hair to grow unhampered; others shave off the front portion of crown. The long hair at the back is then tied into a bun. Some Kamars do not tie their hair; they simply comb and allow it to hang backwards. Some other completely shave their heads only leaving a small choti.

The women are tattooed either before or after marriage, the usual figures being a peacock on the shoulders, a scorpion on the back of hand and dots representing flies on the fingers. On other arms and legs, they have circular lines of dots representing the ornaments usually worn and they say that if they are destitute in the other world they will be able to sell these. This indicates that the more civilised of them, at any rate, now believe in a future life. They also have circular dotted lines round their knees which they say will help them to climb to heaven. Like the Gonds, the men sanctify their bodies by burning the outer skin of the forearm in three or four places with a small piece of burning cloth.

Dress and Decorations

The dress of the Kamars is very simple. They require very few clothes. Men often put on a patuka or a very small dhoti. Generally, they put on only a langoti, the broad flap of which hangs down in front. The patuka is at first put on like a langoti and then the remaining part of it is tied like a skirt round the waist. Above the waist, they do not generally put on any other cloth when they are at home. Some of them, when they go to court or weekly markets, put on a fatuhi or a salukha. A few of them now put on skirts also. Except the persons belonging to the Sori clan, no other Kamars wear shoes.

Social Divisions

In their description, Russell and Hiralal have stated that the Kamars have two subdivisions—the Bundhrajiya and the Makadia. In his monograph on the Kamars, Dube could not find any trace of the Makadia subdivision but instead found that there were two arbitrary divisions—the Paharpatiya, i.e. the dweller of the hills and the Bundhreajiya or dewellers of the plains. It is, however, found that there is yet another arbitrary division—the Kachharpatiya or the dwellers on the river banks.

The Kamar tribe is divided into a number of clans which are called got. Dube has given a list of seven clans but, in fact, there are only six. These clans are principally totemistic.

TABLE-21.7 — Totems of Kamars

Clans	*Totem/Titular Significance*
1. Jagat	Those who wandered all over the world
2. Netam	Tortoise
3. Markam	Tortoise
4. Sori:	
(a) Bagh Sori	Tiger
(b) Nag Sori	Gouha snake
5. Marai (titular)	Those who do not eat any animal that has died a natural death.
6. Chhedaiha	Those who are youngest

The Kanjam mentioned by Dube is not present among the Kamars. These clans are exogamous in nature. Apart from regularising marriages they do not seem to have any other function for they do not possess separate organisations of their own.

Adult marriage is the rule in the Kamar society. Because of difficulty in ascertaining the correct age, it is not very safe to rely on the Census statistics. As they are, the Census statistics show that in 1961, there were 0.6 per cent males and 2.6 per cent females in the age-group 0-14 years who were married. In 1971, the population of males and females of 0-14 years who were returned as married was 0.6 and 3.7 respectively.

TABLE-21.8

The Annual Economic Cycle of the Kamars

The Kamar Month	*Corresponding Period*	*Economic Activity*
Chait	March-April	Food gathering from forests, hunting, fishing, basket-making, forest labour.
Baisakh	April-May	Hunting, fishing, forest-labour, food gathering, basket-making.
Jeth	May-June	Field levelling and ploughing, etc., where Kamar households have land, collecting dry wood and fuel wood, repairing house, collection of grass, fishing in ponds and pools, hunting and gathering wild roots and fruits, basket-making, forest labour.
Asadh	June-July	Sowing maize, beans, pumkins, etc. in the bari, ploughing the field in case of cultivating household, collection of roots and vegetables from the forests, basket-making, forest labour.

The Kamar Month	*Corresponding Period*	*Economic Activity*
Sawan	July-August	Collection of roots and vegetables, collecting tender edible leaves and bamboo shoots, etc. from the forests, basket-making, weeding in case of cultivators, agricultural labour.
Bhadon	August-Sept.	Agriculture labour
Kuar	Sept.-Oct.	Harvesting rice and millets, agricultural labour.
Katik	Oct.-Nov.	Basket-making, forest labour, agricultural.
Aghan	Nov.-Dec.	Forest labour, collection of food from the forest, basket-making.
Pus	Dec.-Jan.	Labour in forests, Food gathering from forests, basket-making.
Magh	Jan.-Feb.	Labour in forests, hunting, fishing and food gathering from the forests, basket-making.
Fagun	Feb.-March	Labour in the forests, fishing, hunting and basket-making.

The economical cycle of the Kamars as shown above clarifies the statistics regarding their economic life. In spite of a higher participation rate, the Kamar economy is at a precarious stage. Basket-making and collection of food in the form of roots, leaves and tendrils is the perpetual economic activity; agricultural labour and forest labour is a seasonal economic activity and sustain the Kamar economy for only a part of the year.

Household Possessions

The Kamaras are very poor and do not have much of household possessions worth the name. They have only the barest equipment necessary for their primitive mode of life. A few utensils for cooking and eating their meals, bows and arrows of various types (i.e. for killing bigger and smaller animals, birds and fishes), comprising axes, sticks for digging wild roots (known as bongi), various types of fish traps and ground-water pits, special baskets for keeping fish, etc. (known as dhuti), bamboo mats for sleeping are perhaps all that may be seen in a Kamar house.

Some households have cots which are woven with the bark of a creeper (Bauhinia Vahilli) which is popularly known as mahul in some parts of the State. However, only the males sleep or sit on the cots; it is taboo for women to sleep on cots and they sleep on the ground on bamboo sleeping mats.

Food

The Kamar is an omnivorous tribe and eat almost anything that could be eaten. In the olden days Kamar staple food was *Eleusine coracana*, a variety of coarse millet and even today the Kamars feel sore and sorrowful that it was *madia* that used to keep them young and enable them stand the strains of hard and rough life in the wild, hilly areas.

It is indeed remarkable that the Hill Marias of Abujhmarh also have the same opinion about this crop and so have the Baigas of Baiga-chak. The Kamars say that with the absence of madia from their food and their dependence on paddy, the backbone gives way rather early and they grow old sooner. A serious research is urgently required about the food value of this crop and its immediate propagation if the results are positive.

Madia had three more advantages to the Kamars. First, it used to grow on poor soil and high-lying land. Second, it did not depend on the vagaries of monsoon and used to yield good harvest even in case of failure of monsoon. Third, being an early-ripening crop, it could yield them food as early as in August.

After the herbivorous wild animals vanished, the Kamar diet has become lacking in protein content, for, even field rats, birds and squirrels have become scarce. Catching and eating field and house rats is one of the most engaging foods of the Kamars. The entire settlement would spend the whole night trying to catch a rat. Squirrels are similarly caught or killed and eaten. The Kamars eat even snakes of non-poisonous varieties and they have a special liking for a snake known as dhaman.

However, the Kamars are not beef-eaters. Killing a cow or a bullock is a very serious offence. Apart from beef, the Kamars eat almost anything and it is difficult to prepare a list of their eatable items such as jungle fruits, peacocks, jungle birds, snakes, rats, squirrels, wild boars, deer, crabs, fishes, goats, etc. which are all eaten. A large number of roots and tubers and leaves are also eaten to supplement their diet and these, in fact, are the only food during the monsoon.

Rivers and hilly streams have a good supply of a variety of fishes. Among the jungle birds, green pigeons, jungle fowls and patridges are found and eaten by the Kamars and other tribes.

6. BHARIAS OF NARMADA VALLEY AND CHHATTISGARH

Bharias are found in the Narmada valley as well as in Chhattisgarh. They are found in Jabalpur, Mandla, Bilaspur, Shahdol, Surguja, Raigarh and Bilaspur. They have different local names like Bhuiyan, Bhuinhar and Pando.

In the year 1981, their population in Madhya Pradesh was found to be 1,95,490 or 1.63 per cent of the tribal population of the State. A small sub-group of this tribe living in Patalkot is included in the PTG list of M.P.

The Bharias relate many stories of their origin. One such story relates them to Arjuna, the Pandava prince. The story goes that in the Mahabharat war Arjuna used 'Bharru' grass against Kauravas, which, when he pressed, produced a host of warriors who fought in the battle. Its real meaning may be that the ancestral Bharias supplied 'Bharru' or other kinds of grasses which were used in manufacturing arrows or the other arms and in time of emergency during the war, some of them might have fought for Arjuna.

The Bharias in their folkores also speak about the Puranic Jambudvipa, Lakshadvipa, etc., which means that there have been by tradition close links with Kshatriya kings of the north, and they took shelter in Patalkot during relatively later period of history.

BHARIAS OF PATALKOT

Patalkot is a bowl-shaped formation under the Tamia block of Chhindwara district of M.P. The area of Patalkot is unique in its topography. This area is a deep depression in the hilly region of the Satpuras. The depression has saucer-like plain in the centre, surrounded by extremely vertical ridges, locally called 'Kanat'. Physiographically, the area is divided into two natural divisions—the hilly ridges and the valley. The highest contour of the area being 3,750′ (1209m), are noticeably on the South extending to North East and form the boundary of Patalkot. The hilly ridges inside the area have their altitude ranging between 887 and1050 m above the mean sea level. The outer ridge is like a straight wall, and it is, therefore, called as 'Kanal'. The lowest portion of the 'Kanal' is in the northwest, the site of the origin of river Dudhi. There are many perennial streams. Dadhi river is a tributary of the river Narmada.

The estimated total area of Patalkot is about 79 sq. km which is rich in forest resources. The forest is of the tropical dry deciduous type with teak (*Tactona grandis*) and sal (*Shorea robusta*) as the most important species. Bamboo mixed with teak and sal grows in almost the whole area.

Climate of Patalkot is pleasant. The maximum and minimum temperature of this area ranges between 46° to 18° C.This area receives most of its rain from July to September. Annual rainfall ranges between 1250 and 1550 cm.

The soil found in the area is generally 'Earra' and 'Motharra' which are of poor fertility for food crops. Sandy and limestone soils are poorer and usually support only poorer type of grasses. The soil is, however, good for the tree and bamboo plantations of various species. Patches of black soil are also found in the area which is good for food crops like wheat, gram, etc.

The area also has a considerable stock of harra (*Terminalta chabula*) tree. Besides these important species, the area also contains bija (*Pterocarpus marsupium*), dhawra (*Anogeissus latifolia*), tendu pakar (*Fcus infectoria*), palas (*Butea frondosa*), bel (*Aegle marmelos*), ber (*Zizyphus fujiba*), gular (*Ficus glomarata*) haldu (*Adinis cordifolia*), pipal (*Ficus religiosa*), salmalia malabarica, achar (*Buchanaria lanzer*), etc.

The valley has a rich potential of medicinal plants which can be explored and used for manufacturing Ayurvedic medicines. The National Botanical Research Institute, Lucknow, has recently conducted a survey in the area but their report is awaited.

The population of Bharias living in Patalkot is very small. Here the Bharias live with Gonds.

TABLES-21.9
Population of Patalkot

S.No.	*Census*	*Total*	*Population*	
			Male	*Female*
1.	1911	1,164	569	595
2.	1951	958	453	505
3.	1961	1,149	594	554
4.	1971	1,375	697	678
5.	1981	1,614	792	822

The population growth rate indicates that the male population growth rate was comparatively smaller than the females. The sex ratio in the area was 931 in 1961 which grew to 972 in 1971 and 1038 in 1981. The reasons may be:

1. Preferential immigration of families from outside areas of Patalkot.
2. Migration of male workers to areas outside Patalkot in search of livelihood. Tiwari (1984) states that the Bharias of Patalkot felt that their native place was rich, hence Bharias of other neighbouring places gave their daughters to the boys of Patalkot.

The total number of inhabited villages within Patalkot is 12. They are located at different altitudes. The classification of villages according to their size of population is tabulated given in Table 21.10.

TABLE-21.10

Population Size Numbering

100	50-150	100-200	150-250	200-300	250-	300 & above
No. of villages	3	2	1	4	1	1

The difficult terrain, hard life and almost negligible development have given rise to smaller size of the villages. The Table 21.10 shows that out of 12 villages, two have population of less than 50 person, the smaller being Jhiran with a population of 7 souls and the largest being Ghat Linga with population of 342 souls. Out of 12 villages, there are 10 villages which have population of less than 200 persons.

Patalkot is inhabited by Bharias and Gonds, Bharias being comparatively much larger in a number. The total population according to the 1981 Census was 1,614, as against 1375 in 1971, and 1,149 in 1961. The decennial growth works out to be 19.67% during 1961-71 and 17.38% during 1971-81 decades. These growth rates among males are less than that change during the past two decades. The sex ratio in the area was 931 during 1961 Census, which grew to 972 during 1971 Census and 1,038 during 1981 Census. The reasons may be preferential immigration of females through marriages from areas outside of Patalkot. It was reported by the Bharias of Patalkot during the field study that Bharias living outside Patalkot always prefer to give their daughters in marriage to the Bharia boys of Patalkot area, because they feel that the Patalkot was a safe place.

TABLE-21.11

Decadal Variation of Village-wise Population in Patalkot (1971-81)

Name of the Village	*1971*	*1981*
Gudhi Ghatri	131	173
Ghat Linga	226	342
Palani Gaildubta	114	167

Name of the Village	*1971*	*1981*
Ghat Saldhana Kodia	170	180
DhumiMalni Domno	38	17
Khamarpur Sahrpachgol	162	174
Jad madal Harakachar	151	145
Jhiran	6	7
Chimtipur	64	66
Sukhabhand harramau	58	76
Ghogri Gujjadongri	6	13
Kaream Rate	249	254
Total	1,375	1614

Economy

Out of the total families of the area, 185 possess land. The remaining 67 families subsist on collection of minor forest produce and other tubers, roots and fruits. They also work as farm servants or engaged as labourers by the Forest Department. This provides them employment for about 50 to 70 days in a year.

In the self-sufficient economy, where most of the production is consumption-oriented, there is either no indebtedness or else its incidence in low. This position exists amongst Bharias of Patalkot as well. The inaccessibility of the area and the difficult terrain make the marketable goods in surplus. The element of economic exploitation by the traders is also at a low key. With the increase in production and consequent marketing needs, the possibilities of their becoming a prey to the exploitative forces, will have to be watched by taking timely remedial measures.

The total number of cattles available in Patalkot is 1,076 which includes 335 bullocks, 464 cows, 66 buffaloes and 259 goats. The average distribution of cattle among 250 families of Patalkot comes to about 4.5 cattle (say 5) per family. The average number of cattles per family apparently appears to be satisfactory but looking to the quality of cattle, the number has little value.

Cows are generally reared for bullocks needed for

cultivation while buffaloes are reared for the milk produce. For tribals of Patalkot, milk is a subsidiary source of income. Milk as such is generally used for self-consumption. But they prepare ghee out of milk and sell it in the weekly markets which according to the prevalent rates fetches them a cash return of Rs. 30/-to 35/-per kilo. The butter-milk is kept for self-consumption. Cows, buffaloses or bullocks are also sold at the time of need due to marriage or some other socio-religious ceremonies.

Local varieties of fowl are reared by Bharias and are occasionally used for self-consumption, but when sold in the weekly markets, fetch cash money for purchase of their weekly requirements.

Rope-making in Patalkot is one of the important secondary sources of income. Bharias collect specific grasses and barks of trees and twine them into ropes. These ropes have a good demand amongst the villagers living in upland areas outside Patalkot. Baskets, fans, Khumris are prepared by them from bamboos. These items also have a ready demand in the weekly markets. Bharias of Patalkot are expert in preparing broom-sticks from Chhind leaves and deo-bahari is very much in demand. Businessmen from different areas come and purchase deo-baharis from Baharias in the weekly market and sometimes even from their villages. During field survey it was informed by the Bharias that these deo-baharis are purchased from them at a low price of 50 to 60 paise per broom, while they sell them in towns at rates ranging from Rs.1.50 to Rs.3.00 per broom. It is estimated that during season an average tribal household earns about Rs.15/-to Rs. 40/-per week from this source.

Poultry and cattle sale is also an important source of casual subsidiary income. Poultry is generally sold to meet out their weekly requirements while cattle are sold at the time of need for social obligations like marriage, death ceremonies or for acquisition of assets like land.

The benefits accruing to tribals of Patalkot from the forest are manifold, and include their requirements for food, shelter, fuel, agriculture and allied pursuits. There are some forest products which are collected only for sale while others are partly used as agricultural tools and implements. Rearing of cattle to a great extent depends on the availability of grass from the forest. Fuel-wood is yet another item, for which the local people depend to an appreciable degree on the forest. Fuel-wood is not only used for cooking but is also used for warmth during winter. The only method by which they keep themselves warm during winter is by keeping themselves near the fire. The forests of Patalkot are also rich in many kinds of medicinal herbs. At the time of distress the only medical care available to them is their knowledge of the medicinal herbs. They collect them from the forest and use them for their ailments. A tentative list of items collected from the forests by Bharias of Patalkot is given in Table 21.12.

TABLE-21.12

Forest Products collected in Patalkot Area

S.No.	*Items*	*Use*
1.	Edible, roots, shoots, tubers, leaves and fruits	Self-consumption as food items
2.	Honey	Self-consumption and sale
3.	Chhind leaves	Preparation of brooms and mats for use in householdfor sale
4.	Deobahari	Preparation of brooms for sale
5.	Harra, Achar, Aonla, Kosa Cocoons	Collected primarily for sale
6.	Timber, fuel-wood and grasses	Household use
7.	Medicinal herbs	Self-consumption
8.	Bamboo	House construction and preparation of baskets for sale
9.	Tendu fruits, mahua, mangoes, etc.	Primarily for self-consumption

Wage earning by employment as casual labour is the third important economic pursuit on which Bharias of Patalkot subsist. Presently, landless labourers or the 'Thaluas' are the main source of labour supply in this area. They form 24.88% of the total working force. This labour force is generally engaged by big cultivators (mostly Gonds) for agriculture work and are paid in the form of a small share in the agriculture produce. Sometimes, they are employed by Forest Department as casual labourer in some of the forestry operations, such as, plantation works, repair of forest roads or felling and logging of timber trees.

The first attempt to educate Bharias was made only after Independence by opening a primary school at villages. The decade 1951-61 saw an appreciable increase in the number of educated. In that year, literacy was 10.08% for males and 4.33% for females, the total literacy percentage being 7.31%. During the decade 1961-71, the literacy percentage among males went down to 10.04 whereas among females it went down from 4.33 in 1961 to 1.91 in 1971. The decade 1971-81, however, presented a different picture. During this decade, the absolute number of literates went up from 83 in 1971 to 105 in 1981.

7. OTHER DRAVIDIAN TRIBES

There are some more tribes in Madhya Pradesh which according to ethnologists are of uncertain origin. However, most of them are said to have some near or distant relationship with Gonds or Dravidian tribes.

The number of such tribes is around 12. All these may be briefly described as under.

There are some anomalies in the List of Scheduled Tribes of M.P.:

1. Tribes which have been twice entered in the List of Scheduled Tribes of M.P. (number in bracket shows serial number of the list):

   A. Pardhi (39) Pardhi (40)
   C. Manji (29) Manjhwar (30)

2. Tribes which have not been reported in Madhya Pradesh but still their names exist in the list:
   A. Andh
   B. Damor C. Kolam

Korku tribe (27) which has been described among Kolarian tribes also has been entered twice in the list. The name 'Korku' (19) also denotes the same tribe.

It will be proper to repeat that such anomalies in reporting was with good intentions. The Government intended that no tribal group, however, small or living in small area, should be ignored.

AGARIA/AGARIYA, ASUR

This is the name of one and the same tribe. However, the incongruity in the List of Scheduled Tribes is that at one place Agara is shown to be an independent tribe while, at another, it is shown as a sub-tribe of the Gonds. The Agaria (Agariya) are tribal blacksmiths found in central and eastern Madhya Pradesh, in Jabalpur, Mandla, Balaghat, Sidhi, Surgjua, Shahdol, Raigarh, Raipur, and Rajnandgaon districts.

The population of this tribe in 1981 in Madhya Pradesh was 55, 757. This was 0.53 per cent of the tribal population of M.P.

ANDH

Andh is, in fact, a tribe of Maharashtra where they are mostly found in Pardhani, Nanded, Yeotmal and Aurangabad districts, and in Adiliabad district of Andhra Pradesh. It is no use looking for this tribe in Madhya Pradesh.

DAMOR, DAMARIA

Damors are not a Madhya Pradesh tribe, and none of them were returned in the Census reports of 1961 and 1971. The Damors are a tribe belonging to Dungarpur and adjoining areas of Rajasthan.

In the year 1981, the population of the tribe was found to be 1,114 in Madhya Pradesh.

BIAR, BIYAR

This tribe is mostly confined to Sidhi district. Crooke has described them as a tribe of cultivators and labourers, the word Biar meaning a seed-bed.

In the year 1981, their population in the State was 7,371 which was 0.06 per cent of the tribal population of Madhya Pradesh.

KEER

There is area restriction in respect of this tribe and it is Scheduled only in Raisen, Sehore and Bhopal districts though they are also found in adjoining areas of Hoshangabad and Narsimhapur districts. The Keers cultivate river beds and river banks. There is hardly any tribal characteristic in this ethnic group. Between 1961 and 1971, the Keer population registered more than 40 per cent growth-rate which tends to suggest that people other than Keer proper are returning themselves in, as such.

The population of this tribe in 1981 in Madhya Pradesh was found to be 9,893 which was 0.08 per cent of the tribal population of the State.

KOLAM

The Kolams are not a Madhya Pradesh tribe and are, in fact, restricted to Wardha and Yeotmal districts of Maharashtra, in spite of the fact that 344 Kolams were returned from Bilaspur district. A survey of this tribe was conducted by Adimjati Anusandhan Parishad, Bhopal, which revealed that this tribe does not live in Bilaspur district. Kolam is a Dravidian tribe. They trace their history from Bhim and Hidimba of the *Mahabharata*. According to Russell and Hiralal, the tribe has many similarities with Todas of Nilgiri .

MAJHI AND MAJHWAR

The two names denote one and the same tribe.

Majhi

The correct name of this tribe is not Majhi but Manjhi. In fact, Manjhi is a synonym for Majhwar. The tribe is found in Surguja and Raigarh districts. Their population in Madhya Pradesh in 1981 was 1,1074.

Majhwar

This tribe is confined to Bilaspur, Surguja and Raigarh districts and broadly speaking their proportionate distribution in these districts was 40 per cent in Bilaspur, 35 per cent in Surguja and 25 per cent in Raigarh. Russell and Hiralal considered the Majhwars to be a mixed tribe having originated from Gond, Munda and Kanwar. As has already been stated, Majhwar and Majhi are one and the same tribe.

The population of the tribe in 1981 was 6,511 in Madhya Pradesh.

Panika

The Panika Tribe is scheduled with area restriction. In fact, this tribe is confined to Sidhi and Shadhol districts only. Census figures may sometimes appear to be confusing because there is a tendency among Pankas of Raipur, Bilaspur, Mandla districts, etc. to return themselves as Panika. Colonel Dalton considered them in all probability to be remnants of the Aryans. On the other hand, Risley considered them to be Dravidian in origin.

In 1981, their population in Madhya Pradesh was found to be 52,980 which was 0.44 per cent of the total tribal population of the State.

Pao

This tribe is also known as Pabia and they are mainly confined to Shahdol district where a little more than 90 per cent of them are found, the rest being found in Satna and Sidhi districts in almost equal proportion. The Paos are agricultural labourers and wage-earners.

The total population of this tribe in 1981 was 7,223 which was 0.97 per cent of the tribal population of Madhya Pradesh.

Pardhi

In the List of Scheduled Tribes, Pardhi occur at two serials—one at serial number 39 where they are shown as Scheduled in the three districts of the erstwhile Bhopal State and second at serial number 40 where, along with Bahelia and their sections of Pardhi, they are Scheduled in some specified areas of erstwhile Mahakoshal. This arrangement is not quite clear and is baffling to researchers.

Be that as it may, the Pardhis are a tribe of wandering fowlers and hunters, the word Pardhi having come from the Marathi word Paad meaning hunt. The Pardhis do not use fire-arms in hunting, as opposed to Shikaris who form a separate endogamous group. Chita Pardhi is now more or less an extinct group. They used to employ leopard in hunting. Langoli Pardhi is a wrong name, the correct being Langoti. Takankar and Takia are actually found in Maharashtra and their job is to roughen the grindstone. The Bahelia and Pardhi are indistinguishable now except that they are mostly bird-catchers as opposed to Pardhi who are hunters also. The Pardhis are nomadic people and their area of concentration is difficult to define.

The population of Pardhi tribe (serial no. 40) was 3,659 in 1981 or 0.06% of the total tribal population of the State.

NOTES AND REFERENCES

1. Dube, S.C. (1951): *The Kamar,* Universal Publishers, Lucknow.
2. Elwin, V. (1942): *The Agaria,* Oxford University Press.
3. Father Fuchs, Stephens (1960): *The Gond and Bhumia of Eastern Mandla,* Asia Publishing House, Bombay.
4. Greigson, W.V. (1946): The Aborigines in Future India, *Man in India.*
5. Hislop, Rev. Stephen (1866): *Papers relating to the Aboriginal Tribes of Central Provinces,* ed. with notes and preface by R. Temple, Nagpur.
6. Khurana, B.K. (1957): *Bharais of Patalkot and their Dahiya Cultivation,* 4th Conti. Scheduled Tribe and Tribal Areas.
7. Mehta, B.H. (1984): *Gonds of Central Indian Highlands,* Concept, India.

8. Nag, D.S. (1957): *The Agaria,* Vanyajati, Vol. 5, p. 58.
9. Nayak, T.B. (ed): *The Abujh-madias,* Chhindwara.
10. NCAER (1963): *Socio-Economic Survey of Primitive Tribes in Madhya Pradesh.*
11. Negi, R.S. (1963): The Bhatra, Muria and Mahra of Bastar, *Bull. of Anthropological Survey of India,* Vol. XI.
12. Ramsay, J. (1872): Gonds and Kurkus, *Indian Antiquity,* Vol. I.
13. Roy, S.C. (1928): *Oraon Religion and Customs,* Ranchi, Man in India Office.
14. Russell and Hiralal (1916): *Tribes and Castes of Central Provinces of India* (4 Vols.), Macmillan, London.

XXII

LATER GOND RULERS AND POLITICAL UNREST IN THE GOND REGIONS

The brightest period of Gond rule was over after the fall of the Garha-Mandla dynasty. During the later period, their existence was marked by the rule of the following weak dynasties and political unrest in the regions of their rule:

1. The Gond Dynasty of Deogarh
2. The Gond feudatory States of Chhattisgarh
3. The Gond Kingdom of Kherla
4. Tribal Rebellions in Bastar
5. Tragic Episode of Pravin Chandra Bhanj Deo.

Before we discuss these, it has to be remembered that the classical culture of the modern Gonds is reflected in their folk-literature. Youth dormitories are common and among the primitive Gond tribes of Gadchiroli and Bastar—the youth dormitories called Ghotul are still functioning. Young boys and girls assemble, sing, dance and choose their life partners. Transmission of culture and accumulated wisdom of the tribe through songs is also done in the hotuls.

Songs are composed extempore and are sung while dancing. Theirs is a community entertainment. Men and women of all ages participate. Beating of drums (*dhols*), musical bells (*ghunguru*) and other instruments are used. Dances and songs are specific for occasions and on festivals. Drinking of toddy or mahua precedes all such occasions. On the occasion of marriage and festivals like Dussehra, Holi, etc. dancing on community scale is common. The teen-aged boys and girls assemble near the Ghotul and dance daily in the evening. Songs replete with mythology and knowledge about their culture, forest environment, etc., are learnt at the Ghotul. Some songs contain folk-tales and Gond mythology. Others contain themes classified according to the occasion. The *Relaa* dance of the Madia-Gonds and of the Bison-Horn Madias is very popular. The more cultured Gonds do not have dancing as a regular feature. But on occasions like marriage they call the Patadis (singers from the Pardhan tribe) who sing the songs called dhemsa which contain the mythology of the Gonds. This has ceremonial as well as religious significance for the Gonds.

1. THE GOND DYNASTY OF DEOGARH

The Gond dynasty of Deogarh came into existence in the Satpura hills in the last quarter of 16th century A.D. and it continued to exist till the middle of the 18th century A.D. In its history running to about one hundred and seventy-five years, the kingdom of Deogarh initially formed the eastern part of the Gond kingdom of Garha-Mandla and consequent upon Akbar's defeat of the Garha rulers became a part of Mughal empire. The Deogarh kings always took advantage of the location of their region in an inaccessible area and neglected the supremacy of their overlord, and for this they had to pay dearly. For a short period towards the end of its existence, the Deogarh kingdom assumed such importance as to overthrow those of Mandla and Chanda and to take first place among the Gond states. They came in contact with the Marathas on the occasion of the downfall of the Mughal empire and they lost their power in the hands of the Bhonsalas of Nagpur.

Deogarh is a small village containing a hill fortress, situated in Chhindwara tehsil, about 38.4 km to the southwest of Chhindwara. The earliest headquarter of the Deogarh family of Gonds were at Harya or Haryagarh, a village in the present Chhindwara district, about 18 km from the borders of Betul district.

Of the earlier history of Deogarh dynasty, practically nothing is known, but here, as elsewhere, popular tradition tells of a Gaoli kingdom preceding the Gonds. The tradition says that Deogarh was originally a Gaoli kingdom and was conquered by Sharabh Shah (Sarbasha), a Gond king of Garha

Jatba, known as Ajanbahu Jatbasha, was eighth in descent from the founder of the dynasty, and was so-called because of the length of his arms, his fingers reaching to his knees. It is said that Jatba, who ruled during Akbar's reign, visited the Mughal court at Agra.

The family history of the dynasty is recorded in a Marathi document. In the words of C.U. Wills (1923), the document provides the following information:

> It indulges in the extravagances inseparable from records of the kind. The family tree is carried back to Vishnu, the supreme God. The 44th in descent from Vishnu was Raja Karna, one of the heroes of the *Mahabharat*. Raja Karna while wandering through the dense forests of Pachmarhi and Mansal reached the capital of the Nag Raja at Panhalgarh. He had connection with the king's daughter who in due course gave birth to a child named Bhurdeo or Bhuwarrao. The 35th in descent from Bhurdeo by name Sarba Shah invaded Deogarh and settled down there after killing the Gaoli kings of that place. But five generations later his descendant, Birbhan Shah, was deposed by Ransur and Ghansur, Gaoli kings of Hatyagarh. The Gaolis, it is said, ruled over Deogarh for 70 years, from A.D. 1472 to 1542, after which they were massacred by the famous Jatba, son of Birbhan Shah. Fourteen years later Akbar the Great became emperor of India and in A.D. 1590 he visited Deogarh and loaded Jatba with honours. Jatba died in A.D. 1602 after a prosperous reign of 60 years. He was buried at Deogarh where his tomb is still to be seen.

Wills has dismissed the genealogy provided by the Marathi document as worthless. As per him, the tradition of Gaoli chief's overthrow by Jataba is incorrect. The earliest contemporary allusion to Haryagarh or Deogarh is contained in Abul Fazl's account of the 28th year of Akbar's reign (A.D. 1584). Haryagarh had been a tributary of Mughal empire since Akbar's conquest of Garha-Mandla in A.D. 1564. However, Akbar found the management of this hilly tract difficult. Towards the end of the reign, therefore, the Mughal *mansabdars* of Garha-Katanga were withdrawn and the control of this outlying country was entrusted to local overlords, although Garha continued to be included in the list of Akbar's possessions. Jatba, who had won for Deogarh its dominating position and possessed wealth and strength, was accepted by the Emperor as a vassal chieftain to whom the control of the minor chiefs in his neighbourhood could be entrusted. The Deogarh chief, therefore, emerged as the 'Maharaja' of an extensive tract of country which, before Jatba's death, probably comprised at least half the territory which formerly owed allegiance to Durgavati.

Abul-Fazl writes that during the 28th year of Akbar's reign (A.D.1584), Jatba killed Muhammad Zaman (or zamin), the cousin of Muhammad Yusuf Khan. Muhammad Zaman, with thirst for wealth, had attacked Jatba with an army. Jatba, however, welcomed Zaman, presented him a *Nazar* and promised to obey his orders in future. But Zaman proved to be a greedy and headstrong man. He, therefore, concealed the news of agreement and attacked the town of Hariagarh with a force. He looted the town of Hariagarh and later Deogarh too. After looting the two towns, he retraced his steps through a dense forest. During his return journey, he lagged behind with a few of his soldiers. One day when he was overdrunk, Jatba sought the opportunity and attacked him with an army. Zaman was killed in the action. Earlier, Hariagarh had been a tributary of the empire since Akbar's conquest in A.D. 1564. Zaman had attacked Deogarh with selfish ends and without the orders of the Mughal Emperor. As a result, he met with a tragic end.

In the *Memoirs of Jahangir*, it has been described that Emperor Jahangir, in the eleventh year of this reign (A.D.1616), arrived in Malwa from Ajmer. While crossing the boundaries of Malwa, Jatba sent two elephants as a present to the Emperor. This indicates that Jatba was an influential zamindar of the region. He had a larger army than the other zamindars of Gondwana. That he was a ruler wielding considerable authority is evident from the fact that there was a mint in Jatba's dominion. He struck copper coins in his own name on which he styled himself 'Maharaja'.

Though Jatba had accepted the suzerainty of the Mughal emperors, yet he never agreed to the subordination of the Garha rulers. It is also certain that Jatba had a considerable territory under his control. He extended his territories far and wide. He had subdued a number of parganas in the Kherla *sarkar*. Prior to his death, his power had extended down to the Nagpur plain ('Deogarh below the ghats' as it was later called). The shifting of the capital from Hariagarh to Deogarh clearly indicated the direction of his territorial expansion. He may indeed have occupied Nagpur itself, for it was in A.D. 1637 regarded by the governor of *Subah* of Berar as an integral part of Deogarh kingdom. The Deogarh chiefs were tributary, first to Garha and then to the Mughals, and this inferiority in their political status is reflected in the limitation of their social advance.

The traditional dates given to Jatba in the family history are A.D.1542 to 1602. He is mentioned in the *Akbarnama* in A.D. 1584 and later in the *Ain-i-Akbari*. He also appears in the *'Memoirs of Jahangir'* in A.D. 1616. Therefore, he must have ruled for a long time to have attained the position which he did. It can, therefore, be conjectured that Jatba ruled his territories from A.D. 1580 to 1620.

Kok Shah succeeded Jatba as the ruler of Deogarh. When he occupied the throne, the Deogarh territory had already extended to occupy the country at least from Lanji in Balaghat district of M.P. to Berar, including Nagpur. The old "orientation" had also changed as the Mughals had included Deogarh under the *Subah* of Berar instead of Malwa. Thus its history in future was to involve, first, the Mohammedan viceroys of the Deccan and governors of Berar, and second, the Maratha chiefs who were gradually encroaching upon Mughal dominions. With these changes, Kok Shah had to face the reigns of three Mughal emperors viz. Jahangir (1605-27), Shahjahan and Aurangzeb.

While Jahangir was emperor, there was a great confusion South of the Narmada. There was no sign of stability in the region. Jahangir never succeeded in obtaining a firm control over any campaign in Deccan or elsewhere. As a result, the Deogarh rulers took advantage of the situation, stopped payment of tribute and extended their authority not only over Lanji and Karola to the East but also over some Mughal territories to the West.

With the accession of Shahjahan in A.D. 1627, the situation changed, as he revived Akbar's forward policy in the Deccan. The Ahmadnagar kingdom was overthrown in A.D. 1633, while Golkonda and Bijapur submitted in A.D. 1636. The young Aurangzeb was appointed Viceroy of the Deccan; and shortly after he had taken charge, Deogarh which had extended rapidly South of the Satpura hills, was invaded by one of Shahjahan's generals named Khan Duran. Abdul Hamid Lahauri, in his *Badshahnama,* has given an account of this expedition. He writes that in the 10th regnal year of Shahjahan (A.D. 1637), Khan-i-Dauran marched towards the frontiers of Deogarh and captured the forts of Kutaljhar (Keljhar) and Ashta (both on the borders of Wardha district) on his way. Khan-i-Dauran then sent Kanak Singh to Kok Shah, the ruler of Deogarh, with message that, if Kok Shah was desirous to defend his people and wealth, he should come and submit to Khan-i-Dauran with a suitable present or else he would have to bear the consequences. On arrival of the Mughal army within a distance of four and a half miles of Nagpur, Kanak Singh returned to Khan-i-Dauran with a representative from Kok Shah. After deliberations with the representative, it became evident that Kok Shah had paid no regard to what Khan-i-Dauran had proposed to him through Kanak Singh. Khan-i-Dauran, therefore, reached Nagpur and besieged the fortress. In the course of five days only, he broke the morale of the besieged. The garrison in the fort therefore sought shelter from the Mughal army. Thereupon Khan-i-Dauran asked them to evacuate the fort leaving all their property, weapons and cattle within the fort. But the garrison turned a deaf ear to his proposals and endeavoured to improve the defences of the fort.

Ultimately the fort was captured with the assistance of the zamindars of Chanda and Ganor (Kanor). Deoji, the governor of the fort, was made a prisoner. Then Kok Shah traversed a distance of about sixty miles from Deogarh and had an interview with Khan-i-Dauran. He offered Khan-i-Dauran one and a half lakh of rupees and 170 elephants in the form of presents. He also promised not to waver from his old path of obedience and loyalty and to subscribe 4 lakh of rupees to the imperial treasury every three years. Thereupon Khan-i-Dauran returned the fortress of Nagpur to him, and approaching the frontiers of Kali with his victorious army, accepted as a present two elephants from Bhimsen, the governor of the place. The account of this expedition leads us to conclude that Nagpur was held by the chiefs of Deogarh as early as A.D. 1637 and it had long been included in Deogarh dominions, probably from the time of Jatba. Moreover, this attack by Khan-i-Dauran was in no sense a conquest of new territory but it was merely the reassertion on the Emperor's part of a long established right to the receipt of tribute from the local chief. It was only refusal to pay tribute which led to the assault on Nagpur. The attack by Khan-i-Dauran also led to the fortunes of Deogarh chiefs at a low ebb.

The Mughal incursion into Deogarh occurred again in A.D.1648, the 22nd year of Shahjahan's reign. It was then conducted by Umdat-ul-Mulk Shah Nawaz Khan Safavi and was successful. Aurangzeb, however, writing in A.D. 1655 to the Emperor Shahjahan who had learnt that the ruler of Deogarh possessed 200 elephants, alludes to the poor results of Shah Nawaz Khan's expedition in support of his contention that Deogarh chief was not worth squeezing.

In the 28th year of Shahjahan's reign, Mirza Khan Manuchihr was appointed governor of Ellichpur (Achalpur). Kok Shah, the ruler of Deogarh, had paid tribute to Khan Dauran Nasrat Jang, after the 10th year of Shahjahan's reign. But his son and successor, Kirat Singh (Kesri Singh), did not remit a single *dirliam* to the treasury. Aurangzeb, *Subahdar* of the Deccan, therefore, in the 29th year of Shahjahan's reign (A.D.1655) in compliance with an imperial order, appointed Mirza Khan in conjunction with Hadidad Khan, the governor of Telingana, and a number of nobles of the Deccan, to lead an expedition against Deogarh. When Mirza Khan reached the borders of Deogarh, the ruler felt that his only chance of escape lay in the compliance with the Emperor's orders. He, therefore, behaved very humbly and submissively. He visited Mirza Khan and promised to pay the arrears of tribute up to the preceding year. Thereupon Mirza Khan brought him to Aurangzeb with all his elephants, 20 in a number.

In the 29th year of Shahjahan's reign (A.D.1665) also, when Aurangzeb directed Mirza Khan, *nazim* of Berar, to collect the arrears of tribute from the ruler of Deogarh, the prince sent Maloji to accompany the nobles of the Deccan. Later Maloji accompanied Aurangzeb and took part in the siege of Golkunda and received honours in return for his services.

During his viceroyalty in the Deccan, Aurangzeb wrote a number of letters to Shahjahan in A.D.1655 regarding the conditions prevailing in Deogarh. All these letters have been included in *Adab-i-Alamgiri* which give us details about the activities of the then ruler of Deogarh and the Mughal method of administration in dealing with these local chiefships. Shahjahan ordered Deogarh to be conquered and annexed. Aurangzeb wrote back to say", It can be easily conquered, but not so easily held or controlled. The annual cost of administration will be very high". Aurangzeb, just before marching North to claim succession to the Mughal throne in A.D. 1657, wrote friendly letters to the Gond Rajas of Deogarh and Chanda.

During the war of succession (A.D. 1657-58) amongst the sons of Shahjahan for the Mughal throne, the Mughal tyranny relaxed its hold upon outlying portions of the empire. Another expedition was, therefore, eventually sent to bring Deogarh into submission in A.D. 1667, the 9th year of Aurangzeb's reign. Diler Khan, one of his generals, by the orders of Aurangzeb, proceeded first to Chanda and then to Deogarh. Diler Khan compelled the ruler of Deogarh (probably Kok Shah II, grandson of Kok Shah I) to pay Rs 15 lakh on account of arrears of tribute and raised his annual contribution to Rs.3 lakh. Thereafter he left for the Deccan with his victorious troops. It is clear from the large amount collected from Deogarh by way of arrears in A.D. 1667 that the period of relaxed control of the Mughals had been considerable, while the enhancement of the annual tribute suggests that the estate had meanwhile been prospering.

In the 13th year of Aurangzeb's reign (A.D. 1670) Kok Shah II had been ousted by some rival faction, but securing Aurangzeb's support through Diler Khan, he was able to regain the *gaddi.*

The most famous ruler of Deogarh dynasty was Bakht Shah (Bakht Buland Shah) who succeeded to the *gaddi* of Deogarh, and was the third or fourth in descent from Jatba. Bakht Shah was an ambitious ruler and waited upon Aurangzeb with costly presents. According to the family chronicle of Deogarh, Bakht Shah's brothers turned against him in the 18th year of his reign and he had to go to Delhi in A.D. 1686 to invoke the aid of the emperor Aurangzeb, whose tributary chief he was. Aurangzeb promised to help him if he adopted the Muhammadan faith. Thereupon Bakht Shah found himself in a difficult position and reluctantly embraced Islam. Aurangzeb then acknowledged him as Raja of Deogarh giving him the name of Bakht Buland. The Emperor also sent his *wazir* with Bakht Buland to Deogarh with an army, and the *wazir* reinstated him in his father's possessions.

It is also believed that Bakht Shah performed some signal exploit and gained favour, and that the Emperor induced him to abandon the rites of Bhimsen and to adopt the Muhammadan faith. Having done so, he was acknowledged as Raja of Deogarh under the name of Bakht Buland.

Bakht Shah, after his return from Delhi, made attempts to extend his territories and reorganise the administration of his kingdom. It was at this time that the Nagpur country received a great infusion of Hindu cultivators and artificers who were tempted away by him from their homes with liberal grants of land.

Bakht Buland added to his kingdom the territories from those of the Rajas of Chanda and Mandla, acquiring from the latter, who then ruled at Chauragarh, possession of Seoni, Katangi, Chhapara and Dongartal, which were held for him by a relative, Raja Ram Singh. Partabgarh and Sangarhi in Bhandara were conquered for him by Raj Khan, a Pathan adventurer, whom Bakht Buland had selected as governor of Dongartal in Seoni; and his territories comprised the modern districts of Chhindwara and Betul, and portions of Nagpur, Seoni, Bhandara and Balaghat. The plateau and plain country were known respectively as Deogarh above and Deogarh below the Ghats. Bakht Buland usually resided in Deogarh except when out on military expeditions. He also founded the modern city of Nagpur on the site of some hamlets then known as Rajapur Barsa. He used to go to visit the town occasionally. At this time, the kingdoms of Chanda and Deogarh were attached to the Subah of Berar and an officer resided at one of the hamlets then existing on the site of the present city of Nagpur for the purpose of collecting the tributes on the part of the faujdar of Paunar.

In the 35th year of Aurangzeb's reign (A.D.1692), Bakht Buland had been ousted by his brother Dindar who was recognised as Raja by Aurangzeb. But Dindar's success was short-lived, for a sanad exists which was issued in Bakht Buland's name to the Fatehpur Rajas of Hoshangabad in V.S.1752 (A.D. 1695).

From A.D. 1670 onwards, the Subah of Berar, to which Deogarh belonged, began to come under the heavy hand of the Marathas. In December, A.D. 1670, occurred the first incursion of Shivaji's forces with the looting of Karanja and the imposition of *Chauth*. Henceforth the rivalry began between the Mughals and the Marathas for predominance in the Deccan. Down to A.D. 1689, the Mughal arms prospered, but thereafter their strength declined as Aurangzeb grew old and lost his hold upon the helm of affairs. Deogarh, therefore, threw off the Mughal yoke after A.D. 1700 and stood forth for a brief period as a semi-independent or practically independent kingdom. Bakht Buland even plundered the Mughal territory on both sides of the Wardha.

During Narind Shah's (the Raja of Garha-Mandla) reign interminable domestic disputes arose which led to the cession of the territory to the Mughals, the Bundelas and the Raja of Deogarh.

Taking advantage of the disorderly affairs of the region and of the weakness of Narind Shah, the two jagirdars (Azim Khan and Lunde Khan) made an attempt to establish an independent authority over all the territories South of the Narmada. Narind Shah, realising the situation, sought the help of Bakht Buland, the Raja of Deogarh. Their united force defeated both the Pathan rebels and they were killed in the actions. For this assistance, Narind Shah ceded to Bakht Buland the districts of Chaurai, Dongartal and Ghansor, which now constitute parts of Seoni district. Bakht Buland then entrusted the administration of his new dominions to Ram Singh, one of his relatives. Thus, the major parts of present Seoni district came under the control of Deogarh ruler in the beginning of the 18th century.

Bakht Buland, after entrusting the administration of Chaurai, Dongartal and Ghansor to Ram Singh, came to his new dominions and was engaged one day in a hunting expedition near Seoni, when he was attacked by a wounded bear. Suddenly Raj Khan, an unknown Pathan adventurer, appeared on the scene and killed the bear thus saving the life of Bakht Buland at a critical juncture. Bakht Buland was so much pleased with the courage of Raj Khan that he made him the Governor of Dongartal *taluka*, then in a very unsettled condition. Towards the end of Aurangzeb's reign when the empire was weakened by constant wars against the Marathas, Bakht Buland declared himself independent and plundered the Mughal territory on both sides of Wardha.

Bakht Buland's relations with Aurangzeb's have been summarised in *Muntakhab-ul-Lubab* dealing with the 43rd year of the Emperor's reign (A.D.1700). According to Khafi Khan, Bakht Buland had joined hands with Ram Raja, the son of Shivaji, in plundering and ravaging Berar. An order was, therefore, issued that he should be styled 'Nigun Bakht' (of low fortune) and prince Bidar Bakht was appointed to lead a suitable army to punish Ram Raja and Nigun Bakht. The expedition was successful, for we find it recorded in the same year (the 43rd of Aurangzeb's reign). According to *Maasir-i-Alamgiri,* an intimation was sent to the imperial court that Nigun Bakht had been reduced to poverty and that his capital had come into the possession of the Mughal officers. After an illustrious career, Bakht Buland died in A.D. 1731 and was succeeded by his son Chand Sultan.

Chand Sultan resided principally in the country below the hills. He fixed his capital at Nagpur and fortified it with a city wall three miles in length. He followed the policy of his predecessor and under him the wealth of the country increased considerably. The Marathas, therefore, after establishing their power in Berar, desired to acquire the wealth of Deogarh kingdom.

During the reign of Chand Sultan, there were inroads of Marathas and Muhammadans in his territory. Grand Duff speaks of partial conquests in Gondwana by Kanoji Bhonsla and the Sena Saheb Suba. We also learn that during Chand Sultan's reign the *Chauth* was levied by Kanoji Bhonsla and other Maratha officers.

After the death of Chand Sultan in A.D. 1739, quarrel broke out between his sons, Mir Bahadur, Akbar Shah and Burhan Shah (legitimate) on one side and Wali Shah (illegitimate) on the other. Wali Shah was successful in the usurpation of the *gaddi* after killing Mir Bahadur. Chand Sultan's widow Rani Ratan Kaur, thereupon invited the Maratha chieftain Raghuji Bhonsla to come from Berar to the assistance of her son Burhan Shah. Raghuji came readily enough, captured and put Wali Shah to death and placed Burhan Shah on the throne. Rani Ratan Kaur was grateful for Raghuji's timely assistance. She divided her possession into three equal parts. Raghuji received Rs. 11 lakh and several districts on the Wainganga as the price of his assistance, and he became the intermediary for communication between the Gonds and the Maratha Government of Satara. Raghuji returned for time being to Berar.

About the year 1742-43, a perfidious Diwan having excited dissensions between the two brothers Burhan Shah and Akbar Shah, Raghuji was summoned again to the aid of the former, whilst the latter was forced to fly to Hyderabad, where Raghuji managed to get him poisoned. The Gonds who sided with Akbar Shah were hunted down and massacred without mercy. This pleased the surviving brother Burhan Shah and he handed over his deceased brother's share of the kingdom to Raghuji. Thereafter Raghuji became protector of the Deogarh Chhindwara kingdom. He established himself at Nagpur making it as his capital and gradually, subdued the whole of Deogarh. He kept up the forms of Burhan Shah's authority, and gave him a fixed share of the collections.

From the year A.D. 1743 the history of Deogarh coincides with that of Nagpur under the Bhonslas. Raghuji, after establishing himself in Nagpur, reigned nominally as the representative of the Gond prince from A.D. 1743 to 1755. The Gond Raja, by concession of a nominal authority used to apply Tika to the Bhonslas on their accession and had right of putting his seal to certain revenue papers.

Raghuji died in 1755 and was succeeded by his son Janoji and the latter by Raghuji II and during his reign there was considerable expansion of Maratha territory towards the north. However, with the beginning to the 19th century, the conditions worsened and in 1803, Raghuji had to sign the treaty of Deogarh with the British which deprived him of Berar which included Deogarh. During the raids of the Pindaries from 1803 to 1818, the Gond hill chiefs had nothing to do excepting plundering and harassing the country without restrictions. Raghuji was succeeded by Parsoji and the latter by Appa Saheb. In 1817 Appa Saheb was defeated by the British in the battle of Sitabuldi. He was deposed and sent as a prisoner to Allahabad on May 3, 1818. On way, at Lakhnadon (Jabalpur district), he escaped in the garb of a British sepoy. He was joined by the Gond chief Diwan Chain Shah of Harrai along with 500 followers. The British Govt. directed Major O'Brien to take action. He marched on Harrai on Feb.3, 1819, defeated Chain Shah and arrested him. His followers fled away. Appa Saheb escaped towards Betul, crossed over the Narmada and fled towards Rajputana and Punjab.

The contemporary Gond ruler Burhan Shah died in 1814 and was succeeded by his son Rahman Shah. A sanad dated 1841 issued by him indicates that the authority of putting seal on certain revenue papers was maintained by him even now. Possibly this tradition continued till the end of Bhonsla rule in 1856. Rahman Shah died in 1852 and was succeeded by Suleman Shah who died in 1855. Azam Shah was his successor but his right of succession was not recognised by the British Govt. and his entire property was confiscated and put under Court of Wards. In 1951 Azam Shah adopted Hinduism along with his entire family.

2. THE GOND FEUDATORY STATES OF CHHATTISGARH

Some of the feudatory States of Chhattisgarh which came into existence after the British occupation of the region and which finally merged into Indian Union after Independence, claim descent from the Gonds. The concerned states were Kawardha, Raigarh, Sakti and Sarangarh.

The rulers of Kawardha state claim their descent from the Gond rulers of Mandla. Kawardha was a junior branch of the Pandaria zamindari of Bilaspur district which originally belonged to the zamindars of Bhonda. The zamindars of Bhonda had a treaty with the Gond rulers of Mandla. Later, the ruler of Mandla offered Kawardha to Mahabali Singh, the brother of contemporary Pandaria zamindar Prithvisingh. Mahabali Singh who ruled for 50 years was followed by Ujiyar Singh (47 yrs. rule), Toksingh, Bahadur Singh, Rajpal Singh, Jadu Nath Singh and a series of his successors with no significance, till the State was merged in the Indian Union in 1948.

The rulers of the feudatory State of Raigarh were descendants of the Gond dynasty ruling at Chanda (modern Chandrapur) in Maharashtra. The founder was Madan Singh who was succeeded by Takht Singh, Baith Singh, Deep Singh and Jujhar Singh. In 1804, being afraid of Maratha invasion, Jujhar Singh accepted suzerainty of the British. He was succeeded by Deonath Singh who helped the British in 1833 in the suppression of rebellion of Ajit Singh, the ruler of Bargarh (Orissa). In the revolt of 1857 also, he helped the British in the arrest of sundar Sai of Sambalpur and Shivraj Singh of Udaipur. He died in 1862 and was succeeded by Ghanshyam Singh who was declared as a feudatory ruler by the British. He died in 1890 and was succeeded by Bhup Deo Singh and his weak successors till the State was merged in the Indian Union.

The rulers of Sakti State were Rajgonds. The founder Hari and his brother Gujar were, as per tradition, twins employed as soldiers in the army of Sambalpur king Kalyan Shah. With the weak rule of a series of successors, the State became a feudatory State under the British and was merged in the Indian Union in 1948.

The feudatory State of Sarangarh was founded by Kalyan Sai who ruled between 1736 and 1777. Names of seven of his predecessors viz. Narendra Sai, Dharhamir, Barbar Sai, Dhangji, Udai Bhan, Vir Bhan and Udho Sai are available without any details. Vishvanath Sai succeeded Kalyan Sai in 1777 and in 1781 he was offered the Sanad of Saria pargana by the British on account of help offered by him. He was succeeded respectively by Subhadra Sai, Bhikam Sai, Tikam Sai and Gajraj Singh. During the reign of Subhadra Sai, Sarangarh accepted suzeranity of the British. Sangram Singh who succeeded to throne in 1830 ruled for a long period. He helped the British in suppression of the Revolt of 1857 and was offered the feudatory status by the latter. His death in 1872 was followed by a series of weak rulers till the merger of the State in the Indian Union in 1948.

In addition to the above-mentioned four feudatory States of Chhattisgarh which claim to be Gond in origin, Markai in Harda district of M.P. was an important centre of Gond activities. In the list of 52 garhs of Sangram Shah, the famous ruler of Garha-Mandla, supplied by Col. Sleeman, Markai was one. In A.D. 1564 after the defeat of Rani Durgavati, among the ten forts which were surrendered to the Mughals, Markai was one.

The history of Markai State has been narrated in a small booklet entitled *Markai Mahatmya* written by Syed Kasim Ali and, published in 1928. Though the account is not very authentic and the source of information is not quoted, it is the only source of the history of the Gond State of Markai. The founder of the State is stated to be Karkatrai or Maharaj

Singh who was originally an inhabitant of Chandrapur. To him the ruler of Garha-Mandla gifted the State on account of services rendered by him during the invasion of the Bundelas. In the 25th position of the genealogical table has been mentioned Bhim Singh who is stated to have been born in A.D. 1541. His rule is stated to have lasted from A.D. 1569 to 1579. A long list of succession with narration of incidents appears in the booklet. The State is stated to have been taken over by the British in A.D. 1844. The last ruler was Todar Shah and during his regime, the Gond State of Markai was merged in the Indian Union in 1948.

3. THE GOND KINGDOM OF KHERLA

The hill fort of Kherla is of medieval fame. It stands in the village of the same name in the tehsil of Betul. It was the headquarter of the Gond kingdom of Kherla during the 14th-15th centuries A.D. It is the assumption of several writers that Narsingh Rai and his successors who "reigned at Kherla during the 14th-15th centuries, were, if not pure Gonds, at any rate of mixed Gond and Rajput stock, and that the Kherla kingdom, was, therefore, a Raj Gond kingdom on a par with Garha and Deogarh". But some other writers are not certain about the Gond origin of the Kherla dynasty and describe it as a Hindu dynasty. Kherla became a bone of contention between Malwa and Bahmani kingdoms. During the 17th-18th centuries, Kherla was the headquarter of Sarkar under the Subah of Berar, and was governed by the Gond kings of Deogarh under sovereign Mughal kings.

4. TRIBAL REBELLIONS IN BASTAR

Bastar district which lies between 17° N to 20°34′ N Latitudes and 80° 15 ′E to 82° 15′ E longitudes, has an area of 15,124 sq. miles or 39,191 sq. kilometres. It represents two former feudatory states of Kanker and Bastar. Tribal communities lived peacefully in Bastar since ancient times. However, from the 18th century onwards, there was a series of tribal rebellions in the area on account of interference in the life style of the tribals by the ruling power.

Hiralal Shukla (1988) in his book "The Tribal Revolutions in Colonial India" and "History of the People of Bastar" (1992) has enumerated as many as 12 tribal revolts. He has propagated the principle of tribal revolution in many of his books. In his book entitled "Bastar Ka Mukti Sangram (1774-1910)", Hiralal Shukla (1995) has narrated the following uprisings in Bastar during the last 200 years:

1. Halba Revolution (1774-79)
2. Patalkot Agitation (1825)
3. Tarapur Rising (1842-54)
4. Meria Insurgency (1842-63)
5. Great Rising (1856-57)
6. Koi Revolution (1859)
7. Muria Insurrection (1876)
8. Women's Rebellion (1876-86)
9. Great Bhumkal (1910)
10. Lady's Movement (1924)

Of these revolts, Shukla (1991) considers the revolt of 'Bhumkal' (1910) as most serious as the tribals of Bastar took up arms to expel the British.

The causes of Bhumkal rebellion were many but the main cause was harassment in general due to promulgation of the new British laws which went against the traditional life style of the tribals. The ownership of forest area and produce was snatched.

The first victims of the 1910 rebellion were the Parja tribals. They were mishandled and unduly opposed by police officers. The Parjas were better known a Dhurwas. The rebellion gradually attracted all other ethnic population. Hiralal (1991) writes: "In addition to Dhurwa-region, other ethnic regions of Bastar suffered with the same oppressive mentality of British Government. These were the Gadba, Bhatra, Rajmuria, Muria, Dandami, Maria, Abujhmaria, Dorla and Halba. All other ethnic minorities such as Mahra, Dhakar, Panara, sundi, Kolar, Banjara, Kshatriya, Brahman and

Kayastha groups participated in the rebellion. Thus the whole Bastar become rebellious; only zamindars, Jagirdars and Mukasdars kept out themselves from the rebellion".

Hiralal (1991) explains that a large part of Bastar was involved in the revolt. "Out of 84 parganas of Bastar at that time, 46 parganas actively participated in the rebellion, the rest of them also supported the cause of unrest".

According to British authorities, Lal Kalindra Singh, a member of Royal family had incited and organised the rebellion because he had once lost the chance of being the ruler, and consequently was not prepared to lose it again which was likely to be his last chance. Lal Kalindra Singh was supported by some members of the royal family and other nobility. He was also very much dear and near to the aboriginals, as he was once the Diwan of the State.

A rumour of the illegitimacy of existing ruler Rudra Pratap Deo was successfully spread. This shook the traditional faith of tribals in the Raja who was also chief priest of Goddess Dandeshwari. Lal Kalindra Singh managed to make Gunda Dhur as the chief leader of the rebellion. Gunda Dhur was the hero of Bhumkal, who refused to make submission to the Britishers, because they were treacherous. His mission failed because his own trusted persons cheated him. He faught gallantly for his country and he remains still in the memory of the Bastar tribes. Songs of his great deeds are still sung. Nobody knows what happened to him after the rebellion was crushed. Bhumkal poetry narrates him fighting with British for three days without food and water. After the defeat, Gunda Dhur his associate Dibri Dhur, retreated to dense forests. British Government announced a cash prize of Rs. 10,000/- and Rs. 5000/- to capture both of them but they could never be traced.

Whereas Gunda Dhur of Netnar was selected as the chief leader of the rebellion and 46 parganas were given in charge of different leaders of difficult ethnic groups, Hiralal Shukla (1991) gives the names of rebel leaders as shown in Table 22.1.

TABLE-22.1

Rebel Leaders of Bhumkal

S.No.	*Region*	*Names of the Rebel Leaders*
1.	Antagarh	Aytu Mahra
2.	Kondagaon	Bhagi
3.	Dantewara	Dinda and Kurati Masa
4.	Bijapur	Ramnath Singh
5.	Sukma Zamidari	Bodki Bori and Daniya
6.	Konta	Dhaniram Halba
7.	Indrawati valley	Roda Peda
8.	Jagdalpur	Sitadhar Mahra and Kodra Gadba (Kalhora) Jagdera Mara and Milap Dhakar (Kesarpal), Muchiya (Marpal), Kondariya (Kaikagarh), Hari Chalki and Buddu Maja (Agarwara) Hunnam (Padmera) Narsingh and Markami Masa (Chakrakote), Suka (Raykera) Jaysingh (Jaitgiri)
9.	Bastar	Jogi
10.	Barsur	Koriya Majhi and Jakra Pedda.

The Jagdalpur trial did follow on 13th March 1910 and up to 28th April 1910 and 78 persons representing all sections of society were sentenced on various charges. The punishments were as follows:

1.	Life imprisonment	5 persons
2.	11 years' Rigorous punishment	1 persons
3.	8 years' Rigorous punishment	2 persons
4.	7 years' Rigorous punishment	8 persons
5.	6 years' and six months' Rigorous punishment	1 persons
6.	5 years' Rigorous punishment	1 persons
7.	4 years' Rigorous punishment	2 persons
8.	3 years' Rigorous punishment	5 persons
9.	2 years' Rigorous punishment	9 persons
10.	1 years' Rigorous punishment	17 persons

As many as 27 prisoners died in the jail. A rebellion by unorganised tribals was destined to fail. There were many shortcomings in the attitude, planning strategy and in the unity, but all these shortcomings are integral parts of any tribal movement. Standen (1910) noted: 'The men behind the movement could not in the presence of British officers venture to lead them openly and they thus became collection of mobs, each with its own minor leader, but with no common chief to the whole'.

Raghvaihah (1971) in 'Tribal Revolts' narrates only a few incidents of political importance, which includes the 1910 revolt. "In 1886 owing to tribal uprisings the Raja Bhairam Deo was deposed in 1891. The British India Police Rules, the Criminal and Civil Procedure Codes did not suit the culture of the tribal people which were resented by them then as is done even now. Forest villages were destroyed and the residents driven out. Obnoxous forest laws came to be introduced to infringe the freedom of the tribal and cattle. All this paved way for the 1910 rebellion. All except the zamindars and Abujhmarias joined the revolt. The rebellion was suppressed and could have been easily anticipated".

5. TRAGIC EPISODE OF PRAVIN CHANDRA BHANJ DEO

Raghvaihah (1971) again gives a detailed description of a tribal revolt led by Pravin Chandra Bhanj Deo in March 1966, who was the ex-king of Bastar. In this incidence, the ex-king was killed by police bullets. This was an unfortunate incident of Independent India. Ragavaihah (1971) has given a graphic description of this incident. "Taking the disturbances of 25th March 1966 as a whole it has been established, that while some of the Adivasis assembled in the palace premises shot arrows at the members of police party, killed one of them (Head constable Avtar Singh)., inflicted arrow shot injuries on 7 of them and caused simple abrasions to 3 others, the police party, its part, fired more rounds of 303 bullets, both modified or unmodified, caused the death of Pravin Chandra Bhar Deo and 11 Adivasis and inflicted gunshot and other injuries on more than 20 persons". No doubt this was an unfortunate incident of Independent India.

NOTES AND REFERENCES

1. Abdul Hamid Lahauri: *Badshahnama.*
2. Beveridge, H. (tr.): *Akbarnama of Abu-l-Fazl.*
3. Bhalla, A. and S. Chandra (1993): *Indian Responses to Colonialism in 19th Century,* Sterling, India.
4. Duff, Grant: *A History of the Marathas.*
5. Jenkins, R.: *A Report on the Territories of the Raja of Nagpur.*
6. Mehta, B.H. (1984): *Gonds of Central Indian Highlands,* Concept, India.
7. Mishra, Suresh, (2000): *Madhya Pradesh Ke Gond Rajya,* Madhya Pradesh Hindi Granth Academy, Bhopal.
8. Pathak, Ganesh Dutta (1905): *Garha-Mandla Kal Puratan Itihas.*
9. Raghvaiah, V. (1971): *Tribal Revolts,* Andhra Rastra Adimjati Sevak Sangh, Nellore.
10. Rogers and Beveridge (tr.): *Tuzuk-i-Jahangiri.*
11. Russell and Hiralal (1916): *Tribes and Castes of Central Provinces of India* (4 Vols.), MacMillan, London.
12. Sammantary, D.K. (1971): *The Khonds Rebellion,* Man in India, Vol.12.
13. Sarkar, J.N.: *History of Aurangzeb.*
14. Shukla, H.L. (1991): *Bhumkal: The Tribal Revolt in Bastar,* Sharda Prakashan, Delhi.
15. Shukla, B.P.: *Chhindwara Chhabi.*
16. Sinha, H.N.: *Selections from Nagpur Residency Records,* Nagpur.
17. Smith, E.C. (1945): The Bastar Rebellion, *Man in India,* Vol. XXV-4.
18. Tiwari, S.K. and K. Mishra (1992): *The Raj Gonds,* Agam, Delhi.
19. Will, C.U. (1923): *The Rajgond Maharajas of Satpura Hills,* Nagpur.

XXIII

TRIBAL COMMUNITIES IN INDEPENDENT INDIA

After Independence, the Indian Constitution adopted by the Constituent Assembly on January 26, 1950, visualised a policy of progressive acculturation of the tribal communities in India. Thus, the former policy of their isolation and segregation was, finally, abandoned.

Independent India has inherited from the British colonial system a complex tribal problem in view of our commitment to the objectives of justice—social, economic and political; equality of status and opportunity as enshrined in the Preamble to the Constitution of India.

To promote the desired integration of the tribals into the national life of India, the Constitution provided special safeguards for the tribal population (along with the Scheduled Castes and other underprivileged communities).

The situation of tribal communities in independent India may be studied under the following heads:

1. Meaning of 'Tribe' in Independent India.
2. Constitutional Tribal situation.
3. International Concern for Indian Tribes.

1. MEANING OF 'TRIBE' IN INDEPENDENT INDIA

Before independence Indian tribes were variously termed as aboriginals, adivasis, forest tribes, hill tribes, primitive tribes, etc. Up to 1919, the tribes were included under the head of 'Depressed Classes'. The Indian Franchise Committee in 1919, accorded a separate nomenclature for the Census Reports-1931: Primitive Tribes; 1941: Tribes. In free India, 'Scheduled Tribes', became the legal and accepted term for the tribes with effect from 1950.

2. CONSTITUTIONAL TRIBAL SITUATION

The term 'tribe' has not been defined in the Constitution of India. The term 'Scheduled Tribes' was inserted in the Constitution vide Article 342 (i), which empowered the President of India to specify the tribes or tribal communities by public notification.

Article 342 (i) lays down that, 'The President may, by public notification, specify the tribes or tribal communities or part of or groups within the tribes or tribal communities or parts which shall, for the purposes of this Constitution, be deemed to be Scheduled Tribes...'.

Part (XIX) of the Constitution deals with miscellaneous matters. Article 366 under this part specifies the meaning of Scheduled Castes and Scheduled Tribes. According to clause 25 of this Article, 'Scheduled Tribe' means such tribes or tribal communities or parts of or groups within, as are deemed to be Scheduled Tribes for the purpose of this Constitution.

In pursuance of the powers conferred on the President of India, as mentioned above, the following Presidential Orders have been issued under Article 342 (i) of the Constitution with a view to specify some tribal communities as 'Scheduled Tribes'.

1. The Constitution (Scheduled Tribes) Order, 1950.
2. The Scheduled Areas (Part A States) Order, 1950.
3. The Scheduled Areas (Part B States) Order 1950.
4. The Constitution (Scheduled Tribes) Part C States Order, 1951.
5. The Madras Scheduled Area (Cessar) Order, 1951.
6. The Andhra Scheduled Areas (Cessar) Order, 1955.
7. The Scheduled Tribes List (Modification) Order, 1956.
8. The Constitution (Andaman and Nicobar Islands) Scheduled Tribes Order, 1959.
9. The Constitution (Dadra and Nagar Haveli) Scheduled Tribes Order, 1962.
10. The Constitution (Scheduled Tribes) U.P. Order, 1967.

11. The Constitution (Goa, Daman and Diu) Scheduled Tribes Order, 1968.
12. The Constitution (Nagaland) Scheduled Tribes Order, 1970.
13. The Scheduled Areas (Himachal Pradesh) Order, 1975.
14. The Scheduled Areas (States of Bihar, Gujarat, Madhya Pradesh and Orissa) Order, 1977.
15. The Constitution (Jammu & Kashmir) Scheduled Tribes Order, 1989.

Constitutional Safeguards Conferred on the Scheduled Tribes

The tribal population in India can be classified into four discernible divisions:

(i) Tribals who confine themselves to original forest habitats and are still distinctive in their pattern of life. They may be termed as tribal communities.

(ii) Tribals who have more or less settled down in rural areas, taking to agriculture and other allied occupations. This category of people may be termed as semi-tribal communities.

(iii) Tribals who have migrated to urban or semi-urban and rural areas and are engaged in 'civilised occupations' in industries and other vocations and who have, with discrimination, adopted traits and culture of other population of the country. These may be classed as 'semi-assimilated' tribal communities; and

(iv) Totally assimilated tribals.

The first two categories have been specially provided for in the Indian Constitution and the policies related to Scheduled Areas. A number of special provisions have been made in the Constitution for safeguarding the rights and interests of Scheduled Castes and Scheduled Tribes who constitute 16.48% and 8.08% respectively of total population of this country (Census, 1991), as well as for their accelerated rate of development so as to bring them up to the level of the general population of the society at large, as early as possible.

All these safeguards have apparently been provided to facilitate the implementation of the Directive Principles contained in the Article 46 in Part IV of the Constitution, which reads as follows:

The state shall promote, with special care, the educational and economic interests of the weaker sections of the people, and in particular, of the Scheduled Castes and Scheduled Tribes, and shall protect them from social injustice and all forms of exploitation.

The Directive Principles of State Policy as enshrined in Part IV of the Constitution, have a bearing on the welfare of backward classes. These enjoin the state to ensure that while the health and strength of the workers, men and women, and the tender age of children are not forced by economic necessity to enter a vocation unsuited to their age and strength, and that, childhood and youth are protected against exploitation and against moral and material abandonment.

The constitutional perspective relating to Scheduled Tribes is to be gathered from the following Articles:

(i) Fundamental Rights to Equality-Articles 14, 15 and 16.
(ii) Rights Against Exploitation-Articles 23 and 24.
(iii) Directive Principle of State Policy-Article 38, 39, 39A 41, 43, 46, 47, 48 and 48A.
(iv) A Minister-in-Charge of Tribal Welfare in States-Article 164 (i), Provision.
(v) Administration of the Scheduled Area and Tribal Area-Article 244 and 244A.
(vi) Grants from the Union to certain States-Article 275.
(vii) Special Provisions-Articles 330, 332, 335, 338, 339 and 342.
(viii) Provisions as to the Administration and Control of Scheduled Areas and Scheduled Tribes-5th Schedule, by virtue of Article 244 (i) of the Constitution.
(ix) Provisions as to the Administration of Tribal Areas in the States of Assam, Meghalaya and Mizoram-6th Schedule, by virtue of Articles 224 (2) and 275(i) of the Constitution.

The safeguards provided in the Constitution make

provision for their representation in Parliament and the State Legislatures, appointment of Ministers-in-Charge of tribal welfare, particularly, in Bihar, Madhya Pradesh and Orissa, appointment of a Minister, specially in-charge of the welfare of the autonomous districts and autonomous regions in Assam, representation in the Central and State services, abolition of the practice of untouchability, throwing open of the Hindu religious institutions, admission into educational institutions, special provisions for social, educational and economic advancement, banning of traffic in human beings, appointment of special officer to investigate all matters relating to safeguards provided for the Scheduled Castes and Scheduled Tribes and the development and administration of Scheduled Tribal Areas, etc.

Article 338 of the Indian Constitution provides for the appointment of a special officer by the President to investigate all matters relating to the safeguards provided for the SCs and STs under the Constitution. By virtue of the Constitution (Sixty-fifth Amendment) Act, 1990, the provision of special officer under this Article has been substituted by the appointment of a National Commission for Scheduled Castes and Scheduled Tribes. Such commission would consist of one President, one Vice President, and five other members. It would have wider powers and duties. To execute the new provisions, a National Commission for Scheduled Castes and Scheduled Tribes was constituted with effect from March 12, 1992.

In addition to the above, special provisions for the Scheduled Tribes were also made through certain Acts and Orders which are protective, ameliorative and concessional in nature. Special provisions have been made for family and land rights, exempting the Scheduled Tribes from the Hindu Succession Act, 1956, Hindu Adoption Act, 1956 and Hindu Marriage Act, 1956. Thus, the customary marriage and succession rules of the Scheduled Tribes have been saved.

Tribal Welfare in Free India

The Government of India's foremost concern which moulded

its policy was securing the welfare and socio-economic upliftment of the tribal people. The policy, imbued with a high sense of respect for the tribal cultures and traditions, is stoutly opposed to any kind of interference by outside agencies which are likely to contribute to the destruction of tribal art, culture and so on. This has amply been demonstrated in five fundamental principles of tribal development evolved by Pandit Nehru. In the Constitution of India various articles have been provided with the object of promoting and safeguarding the interests of the Scheduled Tribes.

There are three special provisions common to all the Scheduled Tribes living within or outside the Scheduled Areas. *Firstly,* for political representation they are provided for together as one group, their representation both in the Lok Sabha and in the State Vidhan Sabhas, being proportional to their number in their State. *Secondly,* similar provision is made for reservation of services, posts in the State. *Thirdly,* in States where tribals live both in the Scheduled Areas and outside such areas, the compulsory Tribes Advisory Council is formed to advise on such matters pertaining to the welfare and advancement of the Scheduled Tribes in the state as may be referred to them by the Governor.

Thus, the Constitution has provided numerous statutory measures to uplift these groups who are at a less advanced stage than the one reached by other sections of the national community. In Part IV of the Constitution, in Article 46 under the Directive Principles of State Policy, it has been declared that 'the State shall promote, with special care the educational and economic interests of the weaker sections of the people, and in particular, of the Scheduled Castes and the Scheduled Tribes, and shall protect them from social injustice and all forms of exploitation'.

At a general level, we may divide these safeguards as being of two kinds: (i) Protective; and (ii) Ameliorative and concessional. Of these two, the first impresses upon the Government's concrete show of respect for the customary laws of the tribes. Provisions are there to ensure non-intervention in their customary marriage and succession rules.

The protection of tribal land by stopping its transfer to the non-tribals, has also been a generally adopted policy, in order to put an effective check on land alienation.

As regards the second ameliorative and concessional type of measures, under Articles 330 and 332 of the Constitution, provision has been made for the reservation of seats for the Scheduled Castes and Scheduled Tribes in Parliament as also in the State Assemblies. Similar provisions have also been made for their representation in local bodies, e.g., Municipalities, district Boards, Panchayats, etc.

Apart from all these, they have the privilege of getting certain reserved quota in services, educational institutions of higher and specialised studies and so on, including some concession in age, qualifications, etc. as granted to them by the Central and State Governments.

After the adoption of the Constitution of India on January 26, 1950, the country moved forward to counter the challenges of mass poverty, backwardness and illiteracy through a planned change and progress. The Five Year Plans, started on April 1, 1951, were considered to be the basic tool of overall advancement and prosperity. The Plans provided great impetus to tribal welfare activities by making ample funds available for their implementation. The First Five Year Plan provided Rs. 39.00 crore for tribal welfare, the Second Five Year Plan allocated a total of Rs. 47.00 crore; and with these allocations programmes were drawn up and implemented to improve the educational and economic status of the tribals on the basis of area development approach.

Tribal Development

From the very beginning of the First Five Year Plan (1951-56), the 'Scheduled Areas' (areas having more than 50% tribal population) were given more emphasis for their all-round development. To overcome the traditional constraints on the economy and social life of these people, while trying to accelerate their growth through the implementation of a series of specially evolved development programmes within plan, other specific schemes had been undertaken so that within the shortest time and at the fastest pace, the existing social and economic inequalities could be wiped out.

During the First Plan period, more emphasis was placed on categories and areas to bring overall changes through the instrumentality of outside agencies, i.e. Community Development Programmes which tried to induce the visualised process of change. Here people's participation and favourable motivation were two most important factors. It allowed the people to adapt themselves to a change through the process of diffusion of innovations for improving their life, while preserving their own cultural norms. Later, this was succeeded by the National Extension Service which meant to prepare people to receive the accrued benefits. Considering the nature of problems of the tribals, related with their life styles, ecology and geographical diversity, multifaceted development efforts (through multipurpose projects) were made for their all-round development.

During the Second Five Year Plan, 'Tribal Development Blocks' were created for speeding up the welfare activities for the tribals. During this period, massive programme based on 'Integrated Approach' was initiated by organising 43 special Multipurpose Tribal Blocks in areas with tribal concentration. Such programmes incurred an expenditure of Rs. 6.42 crore, which formed part of Rs. 43.93 crore spent on tribal welfare during the Second Plan. Top priority was assigned to the educational development followed by communications, agriculture, animal husbandry and medical facilities.

During the Third Five Year Plan (1961-66), greater emphasis was placed on higher food production and individual Farm Crop Production Plan (FCPP) was initiated. The expenditure went up to Rs. 53.40 crore during this period and the integrated development benefits had been made available to all the tribal areas through the 489 Tribal Development Blocks opened by the end of 1966-67 on the basis of the recommendations made by the Elvin Committee and Dhebar Commission. Economic uplift was given top priority during the period, followed by education, health and housing schemes and communications.

The expenditure figures show that although the amount spent on tribal welfare during the Third Plan increased by 21.56% over the amount spent during the Second Plan, the per capita expenditure decreased from Rs. 3.90 to Rs. 3.58 (this was mainly because of the increase in tribal population during the period). Further, the percentage of expenditure on tribal welfare to the total plan expenditure also decreased from 0.81% during the Second Five Year Plan (1956-61) to 0.61% during the Third Plan.

During the Fourth Plan, funds were frequently allotted for individual schemes at different times in the course of the same year and were not often fully utilised. Finally, efforts were made to draw resources provided under the general development programmes into the Tribal Development Blocks to a much greater extent than had been done in the past.

The entire issue of tribal development was critically reviewed on the eve of the Fifth Five Year Plan (1974-79) and the whole issue was broadly classified into two categories: (a) in areas of tribal concentration, and (b) for dispersed tribals. In the cases of 17 states of Arunachal Pradesh, Assam, Bihar, Gujarat, Himachal Pradesh, Karnataka, Kerala, Madhya Pradesh, Maharashtra, Manipur, Orissa, Rajasthan, Sikkim, Tamil Nadu, Tripura, Uttar Pradesh and West Bengal and two Union Territories of Andaman Nicobar Islands and Goa, Daman and Diu (now Daman and Diu), it was decided to adopt the strategy of having a Tribal Sub-Plan within the state plan for the welfare and development of the area with focus on development of the Scheduled Tribes population.

The plan adopted an 'Integrated Area Development Approach' after reviewing the defects in earlier plans. This was more or less well-defined. Details of tribal groups, their life styler, ecology and other resources were considered together, for finalising the project. A few centres were chosen for correct investment and to generate uniform growth impulses throughout entire hinterland. These centres are generally known as 'Growth Centres'. There are some other factors on the basis of which 'Growth Centres' are determined. These are, the size of population, level of services already available, etc. 'Growth Centres' in tribal areas have close relationship between the core and periphery, in respect of economic activities. The development inputs in these points strengthen the parasite elements. The presumption that there will be speed-effect and the advantage will filter to the peripheral areas does not hold good, the parasite begins to grow faster. The local community is either ignored or a completely dependent relationship develops.

The table 23.1 shows plan expenditure for the Scheduled Tribes up to Fifth Five Year Plan.

TABLE-23.1

Plan Expenditure for Scheduled Tribes

Plan Period	*Total Expenditure (Crore Rs.)*	*Expenditure for ST (Crore Rs.)*	*% of Total Expenditure*	*ST Population (Crore)*	*Per Capita Expenditure (Rs.)*
1st Plan 1951-56	1.960	17.47	0.83	2.25	7.76
IInd Plan1956-61	4.672	48.86	0.87	2.62	18.65
IIIrd Plan 1961-66	8.577	52.55	0.61	2.99	17.57
Annual Plans1966-69	96.756	34.64	0.51	3.36*	10.31
IVth Plan1969-74	15.902	75.00	0.47	3.80	19.74
Vth Plan 1974-79	54.411	105.00	0.22	4.11*	25.57
		500.00**	0.92	4.11*	121.65

* The increase being 32.73% in five years for 1956, 32.73% in five years for 1966 and 27.09% in three years for 1974.

** This amount of Rs. 500.00 crore had been allotted as an additional fund for the development of hilly and tribal areas in the country.

The Tribal Sub-Plan approach, being implemented from the Fifth Five Year Plan onwards, gives importance, on the one hand, to elimination of exploitation of Scheduled Tribes, especially in the fields of land alienation, money-lending, forestry operations, etc., and, on the other hand, to development of the population and the area through plan schemes. Under the plan schemes, allocations are earmarked from out of the State Plan. Other sources of funding for the Tribal Sub-Plan are flow of funds from Central Sector and Centrally Sponsored Schemes, flow from Institutional Finance and the Special Central Assistance (SCA) given by the Ministry of Welfare, mainly to act as a gap filler in schemes having direct bearing on the generation of income for ST families below the poverty line. In order to ensure effective implementation of the Tribal Sub-Plan, 184 Integrated Tribal Development Projects (ITDPs), 277 Pockets of Tribal Concentration known as Modified Area Development Approach (MADA) Pockets, 73 Micro Projects for primitive groups and 32 clusters have been established or identified in the country.

Table 23.2 shows sector-wise share of percentage in the outlays of the Fifth Plan (1974-78).

TABLE-23.2

Sector-wise Percentage Share in the Total Outlay of the Fifth Plan

Sector	*Percentage Share in the Total Outlay*
Agriculture and Allied Sectors	29
Cooperation	5
Irrigation and Power Development	27
Transport and Communications	10
Industries	4
Social and Community Services	22
Economic and General Services	3
Total	**100**

Sub-Plans for Tribal Areas

In the Sixth Plan some further areas of tribal concentration were proposed to be brought within the ambit of Tribal Sub-Plans, by identifying tribal pockets of 50% concentration in a population of 10,000 in contiguous areas. The coverage of the tribal population was thus supposed to go up from 63%

as at the end of the Fifth Plan to 75%.

The Tribal Sub-Plan (TSPs) envisaged development efforts in the identified areas with the resources pooled from (i) outlays from state plans; (ii) investment from Central Ministries; (iii) Special Central Assistance (SCA); and (iv) institutional finance. An analysis of the investments made in the Fifth Plan shows that out of states' share of funds, larger outlays had gone into infrastructural schemes and only 5% of investment was done for family-oriented schemes. Though allocation for infrastructural programmes might help create employment and build facilities, there would be a long time lag between the infrastructural facilities being created and utilisation by the tribal people. To expedite this, the planning process was re-oriented in favour of family-oriented schemes with a sharper focus on the target group. In the family-oriented planning, institutional finance becomes crucial. During the Fifth Plan period, the contribution of financial institutions in tribal areas had been inadequate. The same is true for the flow of funds from Central and Centrally Sponsored Schemes. In the Sixth Plan, both these sources were proposed to be tapped fully to promote tribal development.

So far administrative machinery in tribal areas is concerned, there had been adverse criticism about the complex pattern of administration. A multiplicity of Government Departments are advising beneficiaries for development activities, and separation of revenue, judicial and development administration had caused confusion and resulted in lack of confidence in administration. It was necessary to integrate administrative functions in the ITDP areas. The chain of command could be from the state level through the Commissioner of a Division, Collector of a district, Project Administration of ITDP, BDO to block level extension officer, and to the village level worker. In the Sixth Plan, therefore, an attempt was proposed to be made to have such unified administration.

The training of personnel for tribal areas and provisions of necessary facilities like housing, health and education for the tribals was accorded high priority. Often suitable personnel are not available at the field level in remote tribal areas. In such condition the local youths with minimum educational qualification would be selected and given required training for assisting in developmental activities.

The programme content of the TSPs would require to increase the productivity levels of agriculture and horticulture, animal husbandry, forestry, small and village industries and marketing. These would need to be linked with improved post-harvest technology. The Large Area Multi-Purpose Societies (LAMPS) were to be improved to enhance credit and marketing facilities. Transfer of technology was to be attempted; it was also to be endeavoured not to destroy economic base of the tribals but gradually introduce improved techniques of agriculture, horticulture and animal husbandry, etc.

Resettlement of shifting cultivators amongst tribals in 233 blocks over 62 districts across the country was to be improved by provisions of package of services required.

During 1961 Census, five Presidential Orders (1951, 1956 [i], 1956 [ii] 1959 and 1960) were taken into consideration which automatically resulted in an increase in the number of tribal communities, thereby increasing the tribal population which stood at being 2,98,79,249 (6.87% of the total population). Later, five more Presidential Orders (1962, 1966, 1967, 1968 and 1970) were issued which again resulted in an increase in the number of tribal communities. Consequently their number rose to 3,80,15,162 during 1971 Census. It was 6.94% of the total population.

In 1981 (Census 1981), the population of Scheduled Tribes rose to 5.38 crore which was 7.85% of the total population. As per Census 1991, it increased to 67.76 million or 8.08% of the total population of the country, excluding Jammu and Kashmir where the Census was not held.

Strategy for the Eighth Plan (1992-97)

Tribal development during the Eighth Plan paid special attention to vulnerable groups, especially tribal women. It included the following major points:

1. Intensification of efforts to bridge developmental gap between the Scheduled Tribes and the rest of the population by the turn of the century.
2. High priority to elimination of exploitation and removal of all forms of oppression.
3. Removal of usurious money-lending, land alienation, non-payment of minimum wages, and restrictions on right to collect minor forest produce to enable these people avail the benefits of development efforts.
4. Reviewing of the strategy of TSP to make it an effective instrument of planning to ensure tangible flow of benefits to the target groups, both individuals and families.
5. Reorientation of administrative structure at all levels for functional co-ordination, integration and effective delivery of services.
6. Full cognizance to inter-tribe variations in the levels of socio-economic development and responding to their specific problems and needs through decentralised participatory planning.
7. Alleviation of poverty through sustained employment and generation of incomes, skill development, diversification of their trades and occupations, assistance to tribals in the choice of projects, marketing, procurement of raw materials and introduction of new technologies.
8. Evolving a national policy on rehabilitation of people displaced by large developmental projects.
9. Codification of rights and concessions of the tribals in forests; and implementation of the Forest Policy in letter and spirit to maintain the symbiotic relationship between the tribals and the forests.
10. Inclusion of a major thrust for the benefit of tribal womenfolk, as their situation is far worse by all development indicators.
11. Promoting and assisting voluntary organisations so

as to make them play a partnership role in the designing and implementation of programmes. Their help can also be received in the training of grass-roots level workers and in mobilising community resources.

12. Development of facilities like schools, hostels and institutional structures for health care, nutrition, drinking water supply, road linkages and housing, etc. in such a way that they promote integration of these communities with the rest of the society.
13. Appropriate incentives to agencies and institutions excelling in promotion of their integration and removal of discrimination.

Approved Outlays

Apart from the inflow of funds for TSP from the State Plans, a provision of Rs. 1,250 crore had been made for Special Central Assistance to Tribal Sub-Plan. Also, Rs. 3,086,06 crore for the State Plans under Backward Classes Sector had been provided which has a share for STs as well.

Inter-Decennial Trends in Occupation

The inter-decennial trends in occupational categories among the working population of Scheduled Tribes are brought out in Table 23.3.

TABLE-23.3

Inter-Decennial Trends in Occupation* Percentage Distribution

Occupational Categories	*Share of Total Population*			*Share of Scheduled Tribes Population*		
	1971	1981	1991**	1971	1981	1991***
Cultivators	43.4	41.5	38.4	57.60	54.43	54.50
Agricultural Labourers	28.7	25.2	26.4	33.00	32.67	32.69

Occupational Categories	*Share of Total Population*			*Share of Scheduled Tribes Population*		
	1971	*1981*	*1991***	*1971*	*1981*	*1991****
Non-Agri cultural Activities	27.9	33.3	35.2	9.40	12.90	12.81

* Source: Government of India, Draft Seventh Five Year Plan, 1985-90. Vol. II p. 329

** Census 1991, Series I, Paper 2 of 1992, p. 18.

*** Census 1991, Series1, Paper 1 of 1993, pp. 44-49.

It is evident from the above Table that there is a decline for the Scheduled Tribes in the share of cultivators. It also shows a slight decline in the share of agricultural labourers. Thus, an increasing trend of non-agricultural activities is clearly discernible among the total population and the Scheduled Tribes, when we compare census data for 1971 and 1981. However, when we compare it with 1991 data we find that this trend, though, further continues for total population, it is not so in case of Scheduled Tribes. In 1991, share of STs in non-agricultural activities has declined while there is slight increase in their share among the cultivators and agricultural labourers. This indicates towards the negligible and non-serious efforts made towards diversification of their occupation.

TRIBAL LITERACY

Literacy rate is also one of the major indicators of social advancement. It is also a prerequisite for socio-economic and overall growth and advancement of any community. As regards tribal literacy, the position is evident from the fact that while the literacy percentage for the total population of India showed an increase from 27.86% in 1961 to 33.8% in 1971; 41.22% in 1981 and to 52.21% in 1991, the corresponding increases for Scheduled Tribes have been much less.

Tribal Development in Madhya Pradesh

The concept of Tribal sub-Plan as formulated by the Central Government was implemented in the Tribal Development Schemes in Madhya Pradesh. Accordingly, 30,034 villages, i.e. 40.5 per cent of the geographical area of the State was brought in the sub-Plan area. The tribal development zones consisted of full and parts of the Development Blocks as given in Table 23.4.

TABLE-23.4

Development Blocks and Population Covered Under Various Development Schemes

Tribal Zones	*No. of Blocks*		*Population*	
	Full	*Part*	*Total*	*Tribal*
Southeastern	40	06	32,41,835	20,54,798
Eastern	45	06	41,18,528	24,29,817
Northeastern	12	07	19,70,775	9,82,669
South-central	37	23	40,31,860	21,01,050
Western	43	07	47,35,524	29,63,288
Total	177	49	1,80,98,522	1,05,31,622

Government of India has recognised seven tribal communities of Madhya Pradesh as PTG or Primitive Tribal Group. These are Abujhmarias of Bastar, Baigas of Baigachak, Bharias of Patalkot, Saharias of Gird and Hill Korwas, Kamars and Birhors of Chhattisgarh. For the development of these primitive tribes, six development agencies have been constituted. These are Saharia Development Agency (HQ at Gwalior, Morena, Shivpuri and Guna), Baiga Development Agency (HQ at Mandla, Shadol, Balaghat, Bilaspur and Rajnandgaon), Hill Korwa and Birhor Development Agency (HQ at Raigarh and Sarguja), Kamar Development Agency (HQ at Gariband, Raipur), Abujhmaria Development Agnecy (HQ at Narainpur, Bastar), and Bharia Development Agency (HQ at Tamia, Chhindwara).

The concept of Tribal sub-Plan was accepted in the Fifth Plan period. Since then there had been steady increase in the development funds as shown in Table 23.5.

TABLE-23.5

Budgetary Provisions of Tribal Sub-Plans in M.P. from Fifth Plan to Ninth Plan

Period	*Provision in Rs. Lakh*	*Actual Expenditure in Rs. Lakh*
Fifth Plan (1974-79)	26,000	30,808
Sixth Plan (1980-85)	83,916	81,454
ySeventh Plan (1985-90)	1,62,207	1,58,525
Annaul (1990-91)	55, 379	45, 447
Annual (1991-92)	59,517	51,277
Eighth Plan (1992-97)	3,33,497	2,90,345
Ninth Plan (1997-2002)	3,66,105	Continued

The Budgetary Provisions of Tribal Sub-Plans were for 10 major Expenditure Heads as indicated in Table 23.6.

TABLE-23.6

Budget Provisions (in Crores of Rupees)

S.No.	*Heads*	*Budget Provisions*
1.	Agriculture-related Services	429.47
2.	Village Development	271.30
3.	Irrigation and Flood Control	991.77
4.	Power	245.10
5.	Industry and Minerals	123.65
6.	Transport	198.59
7.	Scientific Services	9.55
8.	Social Services	997.28
9.	Economic Services	112.69
10.	General Services	0.60
	Total	3,334.97

It is clear that the Government aimed at the total development of the tribals. Literacy, health and agriculture were given priority. In Madhya Pradesh some employment-oriented schemes were also launced. These are:

1.	Navjivan	:	To provide nearly free cost of housing
2.	Vasundhara	:	Interest free loan to tribal farmers
3.	Jaljivan	:	Collective irrigation
4.	Swawalamban	:	Loan for personal business
5.	Pavanputra	:	Scheme to provide auto-rickshaws to tribal youths
6.	Madhuvan	:	Collective dairy farming schemes
7.	Nirmit	:	Scheme for small constructions
8.	Sahkar	:	Brick-making and minerals related schemes
9.	Raftar	:	Schemes for Trucks and Buses
10.	Vanaja	:	Schemes related to minor forest products
11.	Dhanwantari	:	Schemes to help tribal doctors to establish clinics
12.	Nyaya Niketan	:	Schemes to help tribal lawyers
13.	Sahara	:	Financial help to tribal lepers, widows and others

Criticism of Development Schemes

If Governments, Central and State, have produced volumes full of statistics, proving that they have done everything to help and raise the standard of living of the tribals, there is a section of intellectuals which feels that money spent on tribal development has either not reached the tribals or it has little impact on the general improvement and the socio-economic conditions of the tribals at large.

We should certainly not side with any one of such extreme views, particularly when we find amongst us tribal intellectuals, well-placed bureaucrats and even rich farmers; but then we may not overlook the Naxalite movements in the tribal areas and relatively slow rate of progress amongst tribal population in all spheres.

3. INTERNATIONAL CONCERN FOR INDIAN TRIBES

The fact emerging from the UNESCO Committee of Experts on Race Problems in 1950 declared that scientists have reached on general agreement in recognising that mankind is one; that all men belong to the same species of Homo sapiens. 'Beyond the difference of race, climate, economic structure and system of idea, the History of Mankind shows the fundamental identify of the various human groups'.

The conditions of life of the tribals have been moulded by the geographical terrain (forests, hills) resulting in inaccessibility and remoteness. 'There is no denying of the fact that the tribal population is living below the poverty line and hence the problems of shelter, food and health, education and communication are crying for solution... the tribal problem is not purely an economic one but multidimensional, sociological, cultural and so on'.

The year 1993, was declared by the United Nations as the year of the indigenous peoples against the backdrop of many European countries celebrating 1992 as Columbus Year, which was considered by the indigenous of America as the beginning of colonialism, invasion and genocide.

In India, this may be considered in the context of another fact. In 1957, the International Labour Organisation (ILO) had adopted a Convention relating to Indigenous and Tribal population. India had ratified this Convention. It implies that India had agreed to treat the indigenous peoples of the American and Oceania countries as analogous to the tribal peoples of India. This does not mean that India and other countries of Asia which had ratified the Convention had agreed to treat only the tribal population of their respective countries as indigenous. In 1989, ILO had adopted another Convention which also considered the indigenous of America and Oceania at the one end and the tribal of other parts of the world at the other as two distinct, though analogous social categories.

B.K. Roy Burman (1993) commented on the whole situation: "In this matter some confusion has arisen because while the U.N. has failed to define the indigenous, agencies close to the U.N. have been identifying the indigenous social entities in a questionable manner".

Officially, the U.N. has not adopted any definition as to

who are the indigenous; but according to the General Secretary of the U.N. Working Group on the Indigenous, the Group follows a working definition. In fact, Special Rapporteur appointed by the U.N. gave one definition in 1972 and another in 1983. According to the definition of 1972, "Indigenous population are composed of the existing descendants of the people who inhabited the present territory of a country wholly or partially, at the time when persons of a different culture or ethnic origin arrived there from other parts of the world, overcame them and, by conquest, settlement or the means reduced them to a non-dominant or colonial situation". There was general understanding that this working definition applied to the descendants of the pre-invasion people of American continent, Australia and New Zealand.

Eleven years after this, the same Special Rapporteur proposed another definition expanding the scope of the concept 'indigenous' to cover the isolated and marginalised peoples in other parts of the world. But according to sources close to the U.N., except for the circumpolar region, the social category of 'indigenous' does not exist in Europe, as Europe was never under colonial rule. In that case, no ethnic group in Asian countries like China or Thailand also should be treated as 'indigenous'. But the same sources are treating ethnic minorities in China and the tribal peoples in Thailand as 'indigenous'. Obviously, they are applying double standards with hardly concealed Eurocentric bias.

However, without being bogged down with the question as to who are the 'Indigenous', India should observe one Year of 'indigenous' to display the solidarity of the people of India with the indigenous peoples of America and Pacific regions, who had been and still are (in some areas) subjected to the processes of ethnocide and genocide. Besides, all sections of the people of India should avail of the occasion to reaffirm their concern for analogous, though not necessarily of identical social category of peoples, who still suffer from many disabilities, notwithstanding the inclusion in the Constitution of India several provisions protecting their rights and ensuring their welfare.

NOTES AND REFERENCES

1. Bhandari, J.S. *et al.* (ed. 1997): *Tribes and Government Policies*, Cosmos, New Delhi.
2. Brochure (1987): *Reservation for Scheduled Castes and Scheduled Tribes in Services* (Brochure, Seventh edition), Department of Personnel and Training, Government of India, New Delhi.
3. Danda, A. K. (1989): *Policies of Tribal Welfare in India*, in M.K Raha (ed.), *Tribal India: Problem Development Prospect*, Vol. I, Gian Pub., New Delhi.
4. Dhebar, U.N. (1962): *Report of the Scheduled Areas and Scheduled Tribe Commission*, 1960-61, Vol.1, Manager of Publications, Delhi.
5. Mann, R. S. (edited,1996): *Tribes of India, On going Challenges*, M.D. Publication, New Delhi.
6. National Policy of Education (1992): *Programme of Action 1992*, Ministry of Human Resources Development, Department of Education, New Delhi.
7. Ramaiah, P. (1988): *Issues in Tribal Development*, Chugh Pub., Allahabad.
8. Sharma, O.P. (1991):*Scheduled Tribes: Population and Literates*, Kar Kripa Publishers, New Delhi.
9. Tiwari, D.N. (1984): *Primitive Tribes of India*, Govt. of India, Ministry of Home Affairs, Tribal Development Division, New Delhi.
10. Tiwari, S.K. (1994):*Encyclopaedia of Indian Tribals*, Rahul, New Delhi.
11. Tiwari, S.K. (edited, 1995):*Tribal Situation and Development in Central India*, M.D. Publication, New Delhi.

EPILOGUE

Central India, comprising modern Madhya Pradesh, Chhattisgarh and adjoining regions strategically forming the heartland of our country has played a key-role in the development of historical and cultural traditions of the nation. It has been the playground of interacting political and cultural forces passing from North to South, East to West and *vice versa* in all ages of Indian history. Interaction led to experimentation in diverse spheres of cultural life and in this process, the tribal population migrating to this part of the country in different phases of its history as well as those inhabiting the region had an invaluable contribution. It may be admitted that the study of the history and culture of a nation is never complete without having a thorough knowledge of the history and cultural growth of its tribes, and with whom they come in contact in natural process, giving rise to the process of mutual give-and-take, resulting in cultural transformation. Keeping this in view, a careful and exhaustive study of Tribal Communities of Central India from the earliest times to the present-day has been presented in historical perspective leading to findings which may be summarised under three heads viz.:

(1) Tribal Communities of Prehistoric and proto-historic times,
(2) Tribal Communities of Ancient and Medieval periods and
(3) Tribal Communities of Modern Age.

1. TRIBAL COMMUNITIES OF PREHISTORIC AND PROTO-HISTORIC TIMES

The original inhabitants of Central India were the primitive hunter-gatherers of Stone Ages who in the process of development passed through several stages viz. Lower Palaeolithic, Upper Palaeolithic, Mesolithic and Neolithic. They were nomads with no settled life. valleys of major and minor rivers of Central India and their tributaries along with caverns and isolated spots were the chief places of their changing habitats. Evidence of the existence of various Stone Age tribal cultures in Central India has been roughly dated from the earliest times to 4th millennium B.C. Since then tribal migrations to Central India during the proto-historic period took place in five different phases.

The first phase of tribal migration to Central India took place in the beginning of second millennium B.C., when the Kayathans migrated to western part of Madhya Pradesh. Kayatha was the earliest known village farming culture of Central India. A comparative study of the Kayatha pottery and other antiquities has unmistakably revealed that their culture though possessing a distinct identity of its own had some pre-Harappan and Matured Harappan inspiration behind it. On account of these cultural affinities, scholars have termed Kayatha culture as junior contemporary of the Harappans. As is well-known, the close of the third millennium was the heyday of the Harappans but the decline also starts from the pinnacle of glory. The beginning of the second millennium marks the emergence of Chalcolithic cultures. The authors of these cultures obviously had to locate their settlement outside the pale of the Harappans. The earliest among them, the Kayatha culture, selected the western parts of Malwa, forming the western districts of the present Madhya Pradesh. With excellent climatic condition throughout the year and having black cotton soil well-drained by the Chambal and its tributaries, this area had, all the times, attracted the evil eyes of the invaders throughout its chequered history. The Kayathans were the first among them. By the time they reached Malwa through Rajasthan, they had already a matured tribal culture as is noticed in the excavated remains of the Kayatha culture. Having settled in Madhya Pradesh, this culture had far reaching effects on the proto-history of Central

India till its decline in about 1800 B.C.

Emergence of the tribal culture of Ahar in around 2000 B.C. was the second phase of culture migration. That this culture migrated to Central India from outside is a settled point as no roots of it have been found in M.P. Excavations reveal that the migration seems to have been through the western part of it. But whether the source was Rajasthan or Gujarat is still a debatable point. Different views expressed in this regard reveal that scholars are not yet unanimous on this issue. Much work remains to be done about the relations between the proto-historic tribal cultures of Rajasthan and Malwa. Close association of these two regions during the proto-historic times is an undoubted fact. But its exact nature shall be determined only after suitable evidences come.

The third and the most important phase of tribal migration in Central India was the emergence of Malwa culture. Much controversy exists regarding the date of its arrival based on diverse evidences provided by different sites. The question of the origin and authorship of this culture is also full of controversy. That it had wide ranging contacts with the contemporary Chalcolithic tribal cultures of the Deccan, the Gangetic Doab, Saurashtra and Eastern India proves it to be the most important phase of the proto-history of Central India. The decline and fall of the culture is yet shrouded in obscurity.

The picture of post-Chalcolithic tribal cultures of Central India, representing its fourth phase, is covered by the period between c.1300 B.C. and 600 B.C. The scenario is vague on account of paucity of material. Archaeological excavations and explorations reveal that many of the Chalcolithic sites were deserted, others continued with some break, the rest totally abandoned.

Emergence of Megalithic tribal culture is the last phase of cultural migration in Central India during the proto-historic times. During the post-Chalcolithic period when the western and northern parts of M.P. were inhabited by cultures discussed above, in the eastern and southeastern regions were living communities who practised Megalithism. The origin, authorship, decline and possible connections of the Megalithic communities of Central India with similar communities living in other parts of the country is a matter of research. No doubt, the rise of material culture during the period of history led to gradual disappearance of Megalithic culture, but its tradition continues to survive even today among the tribal people of inaccessible regions like Bastar.

Primitive man learnt the art of painting and painted the walls and roofs of the rock-shelters in which he lived in joyous profusion. These paintings represent his sophisticated mind, his life, its pleasures, pain and environment. India has the proud privilege of possessing a rich stock of such paintings. Its richest concentration has been located in M.P. and Chhattisgarh where more than two-thirds of the rock-paintings in the entire country have been found. These are folk-art traditions of the early man which were borrowed in later ages by the painters of the Gonds of Bastar, the Santhals of Chotanagpur and the Bhils of M.P. and Rajasthan. In the wall-paintings of villagers all over the country and even in our own houses, there are certain art traditions which compel us to believe that these are remnants of the rock-art traditions of the primitive tribal cultures. Central India abounds in such traditions and many more the roots of which are traceable to tribal cultures of Pre-and proto-historic times.

2. TRIBAL COMMUNITIES OF ANCIENT AND MEDIEVAL PERIODS

The Vedic literature, the Epics and the Puranas are the sources of traditional history of ancient India. They provide legendary and traditional accounts of tribal migrations to Central India in different phases of history before 6th century B.C. The Aryan tribes who are mentioned in these literary works to have some connection with Central India in the context of the expansion of their territories are: the Chedis, the Kosalas, the Satvatns and the Haihayas. During the Yayati period, the Mandhatri period, the Parasurama period, the Ramachandra period, and Krishna period, the Aryan tribes, under their respective leaders, made best efforts to penetrate Central India with a view to expand their territorial jurisdiction. The traditional history mentions the Raksasas, the Vanaras, the Asuras, the Daityas, the Danavas, the Nagas, the Nishadas, the Dasyus, tribes outside the Aryan fold. Some of these were inhabitants of Central India.

The Aryans extended their stay and colonised fresh lands not by conquests alone with the aid of big armies. The colonisation was also effected by small bands of adventurous Brahmins and Ksatriyas who went to the newly conquered territories and set-up hermitages and residences there. The Brahmana missionaries who accompanied the Ksatriya conquerors introduced the essentials of Aryan culture and tradition to the masses, converted the principal figures and paved the way for social and cultural contact by allowing high-born Aryans to marry the non-Aryans. Thus was started the process of racial synthesis of the Aryans and the non-Aryans which continued throughout the long cultural history of India and it is in existence even today. In the tribal history of Central India, a number of examples of this nature may be sited.

In the succeeding centuries, the Buddhist literature, the Jaina literature, other literary sources, foreign accounts and archaeological sources point to the existence of a number of major and minor tribes. The major tribes who played role in shaping the history and culture of Central India during the ancient period were: the Chedis, the Kosalas, the Avantis, the Malavas, the Gardabhillas, the Dasarnas and the Nagas. Minor tribes who were active simultaneously during the period were: the Abhiras, the Ambasthas, the Anupas, the Asuras, the Aulikaras, the Bodhis, the Dandakas, the Kauravas, the Mahisakas, the Mekalas, the Nalas, the Nishaadas, the Nisadhas, the Paurikas, the Prarjunas, the Sanakanikas, the Kakas, the Kharaparikas, the Pulindas, the Pusyamitras, the Sabaras, the Traipuras, the Tundikeras, the Vaidisas and the Valhikas. Some of these were migrants, the others original inhabitants of Central India.

Ancient India also witnessed invasions of the foreign tribes. Some of them reached up to Central India and occupying parts of it, stayed in the region for a long period, initially as rulers and later as ordinary citizen till they were finally hinduised and absorbed in the mainstream of Indian culture, no doubt leaving a mark of their cultural contributions. The tribes were the Sakas, the Kusanas and the Hunas.

The early medieval history of Central India was highlighted by the rule of major Rajput dynasties, like the Paramaras, the Kalachuris, the Chandellas, and the Kachchhapaghatas. Attempts have been made by the some Indian and foreign scholars to prove that these along with other Rajput families of medieval India descended from the Gujaras, the Hunas or some other foreign tribal elements who entered the body politic of India from time to time. The basis of their argument was the Agnikul theory which has now been totally rejected. That the Rajputs are not descendants of any foreign tribe has now been firmly established.

After the decline of power of the Rajput dynasties of Central India, the people of the tribe which controlled the fate of a major part of Central India were the Gonds. Not only did the Gonds dominate the entire history, Gondawana, the region named after them, their impact is being felt even now. Today the Gonds are the largest tribal group of Central India consisting of about three-fourths of its total tribal population. They are found in almost all the districts of M.P. and Chhattisgarh though their major concentration is in the southern and eastern parts. The Gonds are one of the most well-known tribes of India.

Latest archaeological evidences have proved that Chhattisgarh is the original homeland of the Gonds from where they gradually migrated to reach up to Godavari in the South through Bastar and Vidarbha; Uttar Pradesh in the North through Surguja; Orissa in the East through adjoining Chhattisgarh; and further East to Assam. Thus the process of migration of the Gonds was from Central India to the South and other directions and not *vice versa* as was believed by most of he scholars till date.

The Gonds of Central India had, for the first time, a taste of political power when a dynasty was founded by them in the second half of the 14th century A.D. at Garha, now a part of the modern city of Jabalpur. Passing through the various vicissitudes of history, the Gonds established several seats of ower viz. at Mandla, Deogarh, Kherla, Chandrapur, etc. and crossed swords with the Mughals, the Marathas and the British with varying results. They continued to enjoy power and prestige till their downfall in the hands of the British and subsequent merger of their feudatory states in the Indian Union in 1948.

In the history and cultural growth of Central India, the Gonds have left a mark on the sands of time. An interesting feature of their monarchial system was that it was based on Hindu political ideas, and in this they had risen above the tribal custom. The real account of the Gonds were their religion and social history. The strength and the power of the Gonds was their contacts with the upper class Hindus, resulting in the elevation of their status in the society, and their contacts with Rajputs resulted in far reaching effect of the rise of the Raj Gonds. The Raj Gonds alone were responsible for the upliftment of the tribal Gonds to choose that career of conquest and rule from which they never turned to look back.

3. TRIBAL COMMUNITIES OF MODERN AGE

With the advent of British rule in India, a new concept of tribal identity was formulated. The authors were the British administrators and the Christian missionaries and the aim was to highlight the difference between the forest-dwelling communities and the surrounding population with a view to exploit the sentiments of the so-called Depressed Classes so that the path of conversion to Christianity could be smoothened. For political reasons, the Hindu population was divided on the so-called basis of race, culture and religion as Tribals and non-Tribals. The colonial writers conceived number of hypothesis to separate the forest-dwelling Hindus from the rest, irrespective of the fact that no such distinction ever existed in Indian tradition which recognised the entire population of the country as one. It was advocated that the forest-dwelling population was not only different from the surrounding Hindu population, but such a population were the original inhabitants of India. The later population of the Hindus were their exploiters right from the beginning of history. Thus the seed of dissention was sown. To prove their contention, unsuccessful attempts were made to harness evidences provided by different sciences.

Though the contentions advocated by the colonial authority and English writers had not much ground, the British government being in power moved ahead to implement the policies based on their hypothesis. In the Census Reports published by the Government every decade, the Hindu population was shown separate from the tribal population. The theory of alienation encouraged writers like Verrier Elwyn to suggest "National Park theory" for the tribals. Authors like Haimendrof went a step further to appreciate tribal terrorism or the Naxalite movement of Andhra Pradesh. Conversion to Christianity was not only justified but looked upon a synonym of "progressiveness" of the tribals. This resulted in far-reaching consequences and one may unhesitatingly remark that the root of much of modern India's problem of tribal unrest may be traced to this policy of the colonists.

The colonial rule had an immediate taste of the negative aspect of their new theory in the form of tribal revolts which took place in different parts of the country. Pursuing the policy of mercantile colonialism, the British authorities attempted to penetrate into the tribal areas and impose new rules upon them. The tribals could not tolerate any encroachment on their traditional habits and this resulted in armed revolts in several parts of the country including Central India. In M.P. the regions affected were occupied by the Gonds. The British government had to use force, but realising their folly, made reconciliatory efforts by declaring the tribal areas non-regulatory areas and according recognition to their traditional system of administration. However, the Christian missionaries were encouraged to intensify their activities and in the name of helping hands and message of love and humanity they succeeded to a great extent in converting a good part of tribal population of the country to Christianity.

The British Government tried to collect and classify the information about the tribals in various Census Reports published from time to time. How confusing are this informations may be gauged by the fact that the Government itself was not clear as to who should be counted as a tribal. Their definition about the tribe differed from Report to Report. In the Census Report of 1891, they were entitled as "Forest Tribes". This was changed to "Animists" in the Census Report of 1911; to "Hill and Forest Tribes" in the Report of 1921; to "Primitive Tribe" in the Report of 1931; to "Backward Tribe" in the Government of India Act of 1935; to "Tribes" only in the Report of 1941. Later, the term "Tribe" meant for the western writers, "an ethnic group, geographically isolated or semi-isolated, identified with one particular territory and having distinct social, economic and cultural traditions and practices". The term has undergone further change in the post-Independence era when the emphasis is more on poverty and backwardness.

Under the Constitution of India, certain tribes have been recognised as "Scheduled Tribes". These tribes are entitled to be given special treatment envisaged under the Constitution. In Central India which is the largest tribal belt of the country with about one-fourth of India's total tribal population, the List of Scheduled tribes includes 46 tribes. But for Santhals, all the six largest tribal communities of India having more than 10 lakh population are represented in this rion.

SELECT BIBLIOGRAPHY

ORIGINAL SOURCES

1. Archaeological Sources

A. Prehistoric and Proto-historic Explorations and Excavations

Ahmad, N., *The Stone Age Cultures of the Upper Son Valley*, Delhi, 1977.

Ansari, Z.D. and Dhavalikar, M.K., *Excavation at Kayatha*, Poona, 1975.

Bajpai, K.D. and Pandey, S.K., *Excavation at Tumain*, Bhopal, 1985.

——, *Malhar 1975-78*, Sagar, 1978.

Banerji, N.R., *Nagda: 1955-57*, New Delhi, 1986.

Chakravarty, K.K. *et al.*, *Dangwada Excavations*, Bhopal, 1989.

de Terra, H. and Paterson, T.T., *Studies in the Ice Age in India and Associated Human Cultures*, Washington, 1939.

Dikshit. M.G., *Tripuri-1952*, Nagpur, 1959.

Jorge Armand, *Excavations at Durkadi Nullah*, Delhi, 1984.

Khare, M.D., *Painted Rock-Shelters*, Bhopal, 1981.

Khatri, A.P., Stone Age Cultures of Malwa, Unpublished Thesis, Poona.

Masih, P., *Madhya Pradesh Ki Pragaithiasik Chitrakala*, Bhopal, 1966.

Mathpal, Y., *Prehistoric Rock Paintings of Bhimbetka*, Delhi, 1984.

Mishra, V.N., Mathpal Y., and Nagar, M., *Bhimbetka: Prehistoric Man and His Art in Central India*, Poona, 1977.

Neumayer, E., *Prehistoric Indian Rock-Paintings*, Delhi, 1983.

Pandey, R.P., *Prehistoric Archaeology of M.P.*, Delhi, 1987.

Pandey, S.K., *Indian Rock Art*, Delhi, 1993.

Sankalia, H.D., Subbarao, B. and Deo, S.B., *Excavations at Maheshwar and Navdatoli*,1952-53, Poona -Baroda, 1959.

Sankalia, H.D., Deo, S.B. and Ansari Z.D., *Chalcolithic Navdatoli The Excavation at Navdatoli*, 1957-59, Poona-Baroda, 1971.

Sharma, R.K. and Mishra, S.N., *Excavátion at Kakrehta*, Delhi, 1993.

Singh, R., "Palaeolithic Industries of northern Bundelkhand", Unpublished Thesis, Poona, 1965.

Supekar, S.G., Pleistocene Stratigraphy and Prehistoric Archaeology of the Central Narmada Basin, Unpublished Thesis, Poona, 1968.

Wainright, G.V., *Pleistocene Deposits of the Lower Narmada valley and Early Stone Age Industry from the River Chambal*, Baroda, 1964.

Wakankar, V.S., *Kasrawad Utkhananan*, Ujjain.

——, *Kayatha Excavation Report*, Ujjain.

B. Inscriptions

Barua, B.M. and Sinha, G. (Eds.), *Barhut Inscriptions*, Calcutta, 1926.

Bhandarkar, D.R.(Ed.), List of Inscriptions of northern India, Appdx, *EI*. XIX-XXIII.

Dwivedi, H.N. (Ed.), *Gwalior Rajya Ke Abhilekh*, Gwalior, 1947.

Fleet, J.F. (Ed.), Inscriptions of Early Gupta kings and their Successors, *CI* ,I, III, Calcutta, 1988.

Hiralal, R.B. (Ed.), *Inscriptions of the Central Provinces and Berar*, Nagpur, 1932.

Lele, C.B. (Ed.), *Paramara Inscriptions in the Dhar State*, Dhar State Historical Series.

Luders (Ed.), List of Brahmi Inscriptions up to 400 A.D., *EI*, X.

Mirashi, V.V. (Ed.), Inscriptions of the Kalachuri Chedi Era, *CI* I, IV, I-II, Ootacumund, 1965.

Shastri, A.M. (Ed.), *Inscriptions of the Sarabhapuriyas, Panduvamsis and Somavamsis*, pt. I-II, Delhi, 1995.

Trivedi, H.V. (Ed.), *Inscriptions of the Paramaras, Chandellas, Kachchhapaghatas, etc.* Pt. I-III, Delhi.

C. Coins

Allan, J., *Catalogue of Coins of Ancient India in the British Museum*, London, 1936.

Altekar, A.S., *Coinage of the Gupta empire.*

Chakravarty, S.K., *A Study of Ancient Indian Numismatics*, Calcutta, 1931.

Gupta, P.L., *A Survey of Indian Numismatography*, Varanasi, 1964.

——, *Bibliography of Indian Numismatics.*

Gupta, P.L., *Ancient Indian Silver Punch Marked Coins,* Nasik, 1985.
Herzfeld, E., Kushno-Sassanian Coins, *MASI,* Calcutta, 1930.
Jain, B.C., *Inventory of the Hoards and Finds of Coins and Seals from M.P., NNM.,* No.5, Varanasi, 1957.
Maity, S.K., *Early Indian Coins and Currency System,* New Delhi, 1971.
Narain, A.K., *Coin Types of Indo-Greek kings.*
Rapson, E.J., *Indian Coins,* Strassburg, 1897.
Roy, P.C., *The Coinage of northern India,* Delhi, 1980.
Sarma, I.K., *Coinage of Satavahana empire,* Delhi, 1980.
Satya Sharva, *The Kusana Numismatics,* Delhi, 1985.
Singhal, C.R., *Bibliography of Indian Coins,* Bombay, 1950.
Trivedi, H.V., *Catalogue of Coins of the Naga Dynasty of Padmavati,* Gwalior, 1957.

D. Art and Architectural Remains

Agrawal, Urmila, *Khajuraho Sculptures and their Significance,* New Delhi, 1964.
Ali, R., *Art and Architecture of the Kalachuris,* Delhi, 1980.
——, *Pratihara Art in India,* Delhi, 1987.
Banerji, R.D., *The Haihayas of Tripuri and Their Monuments,* Calcutta, 1931.
Barenes, E., *Dhar and Mandu,* Bombay, 1907.
Barua, B.M., *Barhut,* pt. I-III, Calcutta, 1934.
Chakravarty, K.K. and Sharma, R.K. (Eds.), *Art of the Kalachuris,* Bhopal, 1991.
Cunningham, A., *Bhilsa Topes,* London, 1854.
Dhavalikar, M.K., *Sanchi-A Cultural Study,* Pune, 1965.
Ganguli, O.C., Goswami, A. and Tarafdar, A., *The Art of the Chandellas,* Calcutta, 1957.
Haldar, A.K., *Buddhist Caves of Bagh,* 1910-11.
Krishna Deva, *Temples of Khajuraho,* Delhi, 1965.
Maisey, F.C., *Sanchi and its Remains,* London, 1892.
Manwani, S.N., *Evolution of Art and Architecture in Central India,* Delhi, 1988.
Marshall and Foucher, *Monuments of Sanchi,* 3 vols., Delhi, 1940.
Mishra, R.N., *Sculptures of Dahala and Dakshina Kosala,* Delhi, 1987.
Trivedi, R.D., *Temples of Pratihara Period of Central India,* Delhi, 1990.

Vidya Prakash, *Khajuraho,* Delhi, 1967.
Zennas, E. and Auboyer, J., *Khajuraho,* The Hague, 1960.

TEXTS AND TRANSLATIONS

A. The Vedas

Rg. Veda, Vedic Research Institute, Pune, 1993.

B. The Epics

Ramayana, Eng. Tr. M.N. Dutt, Calcutta, 1895-1905.
Mahabharata, Eng. Tr. M.N. Dutt, Calcutta, 1895-1905.

C. The Puranas

Bhagavata Purana, Ed.B.C. Bandopadhyaya, Calcutta, 1830.
Brahma Purana, Ed. V.N. Mandalika, Poona.
Kurma Purana, Ed. N. Mukhopadhyaya, Calcutta, 1890.
Linga Purana, Ed. Vidyasagar, Calcutta, 1876.
Matsya Purana, Ed. Vidyasagar, Calcutta, 1876.
Markandeya Purana, Eng.Tr. Pargiter, Calcutta, 1888-1905.
Padma Purana, Ed. Mandalik, Poona, 1893-94.
Shiva Purana, Ed. Raverkar, Bombay, 1909-11.
Vayu Purana, Ed. R. Mitra, Calcutta, 1880-88.
Varaha Purana, Ed. H. Sastri, Calcutta, 1893.
Vishnu Purana, Tr. H.H. Wilson, 5 vols., London, 1864-70.

D. Buddhist Literature

Dighanikaya, Ed. T.W. Rhys Davids, London, 1890.
Dhammapada, Ed. S.S. Thera, Oxford, 1898.
Mahavamsa, Ed. W. Geiger, P.T.S., London, 1908, Eng.
——, Tr., W. Geiger, London, 1912.
Mahavastu, Ed. Senart.
Majjhima Nikaya, Ed. V. Trenckner and R. Chalmer, P.T.S., London. 1888-1902.
Milinda Panho, Tr. Rhys Davids, Cambridge, 1905.
Jatakas, Ed. Fousball, 7 vols., London, 1877-97.
——, Eng. Tr. E.B. Cowell, 7 vols. Cambridge, 1895-1913.
Anguttaranikaya, Pali Text Society, Ed. R. Morris, London, 1885-1900.

E. Jaina Literature

Pauma Chariyam, Ed. H.Jacobi, Bhavnagar, 1914.
Grantha-traya, Ed. M.K. Shastri, Ahmedabad, 1939.
Avasyakacurni, Ed. Jinadasa Jain, Rutlam, 1928.
Vividhatirthakalpa, Ed. Jinaprabha Suri.

F. Sanskrit Literature

Arthasastra of Kautilya, Ed. R. Sama Sastry, Mysore, 1919.
Astadyayi of Panini, Ed. S.C. Vasu, Allahabad, 1891.
Amarakosa by Amarasimha, Ed. T. Ganapati Sastri, 4 parts, 1914-17.
Abhijnanasakuntalam of Kalidasa, Ed. S. Roy.
Brhatsamhita of Varahamihira, Ed. Kern, BI, Calcutta, 1865.
Brhatkathamanjari, (Kavyamala Series) by Ksemendra, Bombay, 1931.
Dasakumaracharita of Dandin, Ed. G. Bulhar, Eng. Tr. M.R. Kala, Bombay, 1928.
Harasacharita of Bana, Ed. K.P. Parab, Bombay, 1925.
Jayamangala, Commentary of Vatsyayana's Kamasutra: by Yasodhara.
Kathasaritsagara by Somadeva, Eng. Tr. C.H. Tawney Ed., Penzer.
Kavyamimamsa of Rajasekhara, G.O.S. No.1, Baroda, 1924.
Kumarasambhava of Kalidasa, Eng. Tr. Griffith, London, 1879.
Malvikagnimitra of Kalidasa, Eng. Tr. Tawney.
Meghaduta of Kalidasa, Ed. E. Hultzsch, London, 1911.
Mrcchakatika by Sudraka, Eng. Tr. Ryder, Cambridge, 1905.
Namamalika of Bhoja, Ed. R. Kulkarni, Poona, 1955.
Navasahasankacharita of Padmagupta, Ed. Islampurkar, Bombay, 1895.
Prithviraja Raso of Chand Bardai, Pandia and Das, Banaras, 1913.
Prabodhachandrodaya of Krsnamisra, Eng., Tr. J. Taylor, London, 1962.
Prabandhachintamani by Merutunga, Tr. C.H. Tawney, Calcutta, 1894-1901.
Raghuvamsa of Kalidasa, Tr. G. Naudargikar, Bombay, 1897.
Rajamartanda of Bhoja, Tr. R.Mitra, Calcutta, 1883.
Salihotra of Bhoja, Ed. E.D. Kulkarni, Poona, 1953.
Samarangana Sutradhara of Bhoja, Ed. T.G. Sastri, G.O.S. 2 vols., Baroda, 1924-25.
Srngara-Prakasa of Bhoja, Ed. G.R.Josyer, Mysore, 1955.

Saraswati Kanthabharana of Bhoja, Ed. R. Barooha, Calcutta, 1883-84.

Tilakamanjari of Dhanapala, NSS, Bombay, 1903.

Yuktikalpataru of Bhoja, Ed. S.S. astri, Calcutta.

G. Greek and Chinese Sources

Hiuen Tsang, Tr. S. Beal (Buddhist Records of the western World), London, 1884.

——, *Indica: Fragments of Megasthenes*: Ed. E.A. Schwanbeck, Bonn, 1846.

Yuan Chwang, Tr. T. Watters, London, 1904-5

Periplus Maris Erythaci, Eng. Tr. Schoff, London, 1912.

H. Muslim Literature

Ain-i-Akbari of Abul Fazl, Eng. Tr. Blochmann, Vol. I-III, Calcutta, 1868-94.

Kitab-ul-Hind and Atharal-Baquia of al-Biruni, Eng. Tr. (Alberuni's India) by Sachau, London, 1914.

Tabaquat-i-Akbari of Nizamuddin, Eng. Tr. B. Dey, Calcutta, 1931.

Tabaquat-i-Nasiri of Minhaj-ud-din, Eng. Tr. by H.G.Raverty, London, 1881.

Taj-ul-Masir of Hasan-un-Nizami, Extr. Tr. HIED, II,204-43

Tarikh-i-Alai, of Amir Khusrav, Eng. Tr. M. Habib, Bombay, 1931.

Tarikh-i-Firishta, Eng. Tr. J. Briggs. Vol. I-IV, London, 1829.

Tarikh-i-Firuz-Shahi of Zia-ud-din Barni, Ed. W.N. Leesele, Calcutta, 1860-62.

Tarikh-i-Yamini of Al-utbi, Ed. Eng. Tr by J. Raynolds, London, 1858.

Taziyat-l-Amsar of Abd-u-lah Wassaf, Extr. Tr. HIED, III, 24.

MODERN WORKS

Agrawal, K.L., *Vindhya Kshetra Ka Aitihasik Bhugol*, Satna, 1987.

Ali, S.M., *Geography of the Puranas*, New Delhi, 1983.

Agrawal, V.S., *India as Known to Panini*, Allahabad, 1983.

Apter, David, *The Policies of Modernisation*, Chicago, 1983.

Agrawal, R., *Garah Mandal Ke Gond Raja*, Mandla, Sam. 2042.

Bailey, F.G., Tribe and Castes of India, *Contribution to Indian Sociology*, No. V,7-19, 1961.

Bhattacharya, P.K., *Historical Geography of M.P.*, Delhi, 1976.

Bhardwaj, A.N., *The Problems of Scheduled Castes and Schedule Tribes in India*, New Delhi, 1979.

Bhowmick K.L., *Tribal India*, Calcutta, 1971.

Banga, K., *An Historical Geography of the Homeland of the Gonds-1550-1605*, Delhi.

Census of India, *District Census Handbook and Series, No. 10, Mandla District*, 1971-74.

Chandra, R.P., *Indo-Aryan Races.*

Caunningham, A., *Archaeological Survey of India Reports*, Vol. I-XXIII.

Chaudhuri, B., *Tribal Development in India*, New Delhi,1982.

Datt, J.M., "Population of India about 320 B.C.,"*Man in India*, 42 (4) 1962.

Davids, T.W.R., *Buddhist India*

Day, N.L., *Geographical Dictionary of Ancient and Medieval India*, London, 1927.

Deo, J.P.S., *Cultural Profile of South Kosala*, Delhi, 1987.

Dwivedi, H.N., *Madhya Bharat ka Itihas*, Gwalior, 1950.

Day, U.N., *Medieval Malwa*, Delhi, 1965.

Desai, A.R., "Tribes in Transition', in Romesh Thapar (Ed.), *Tribe, Caste and Religion in India*, Delhi, 1977.

Desai, *History of Rural Development in Modern India*, New Delhi, 1977.

Deogaonkar, S.G., *Problems of Developments of Tribal Areas*, New Delhi, 1977.

Dubey, S.C., "Approches to the Tribal Problem in India", *Journal of Social Research*, III (2), 1960.

Dubey, S.C., *Tribal Heritage of India*, New Delhi, 1977.

Eaton, J., *Political Economy*, New York, 1973.

Elwin, V., *A New Deal for Tribal India*, New Delhi, 1963.

——, *The Muria and their Ghotul*, 1947.

Elliot, *History of India as Told by Her Own Historians.*

Ghosh, A. (Ed.), *Encyclopaedia of Indian Archaeology*, Delhi, 1989.

Gupta, P.L., *Prachin Chhattisgarh*, Raipur, 1973.

Govt. of India, *Report of Commissioner for Scheduled Castes and Scheduled Tribes*, 1971-72., 1978-79.

Greigson, W.V., *The Maria Gonds of Bastar*, London, 1938.

——, *The Aboriginal Problem in C.P. & Berar*, 1944.

Habib, Irfan, *The Agrarian System of Mogul India*, London, 1963.

Hopkins, *The Great Epics of India*

Haimendorf, C.Von Furer, *Tribes of India*, London, 1982.

Hiralal, R.B., *'Baiga', Man in India*, 4, 273-76, 1924.

Hislop, S., *Papers Relating to the Aboriginal Tribes of Central Provinces left in mss.* ed. R. Temple, Nagpur, 1866.

Jain, J.C., *Life in Ancient India as depicted in Jain Canons*, Bombay, 1947.

Jain, K.C., *Malwa through the Ages*, Delhi, 1972.

Jain, C.K. and Sharma, S.K., "Tribes of Madhya Pradesh: Habitat and Economy" in G.P. Gupta (Ed.), *Socio-Cultural Environment of Tribal Landscapes*, Jaipur, 1991.

Jha, V.D., *Bastar ka Muritishilpa*, Bhopal, 1989.

Law, B.C., *Tribes in Ancient India*, Poona, 1943.

——, *Kshatriya Tribes in Ancient India*, Calcutta, 1923.

——, *Ancient Mid-Indian Kshatriya Tribes*, Calcutta, 1924.

——, *Historical Geography of Ancient India*, Paris, 1954.

Majumdar, R.C. (Ed.), *The History and Culture of the Indian People*, Vol. 1-X, Bombay.

——, *Classical Accounts of India*, Calcutta, 1960.

M.P. Govt., *The Report of the Study Team on Tribal Development Programmes*, M.P.

——, *Committee on Plan Project, Planning Commission.*

——, *Tribal Economic organisation and Market*, 1963.

Majumdar, D.N., *The Matrix of Indian Culture*, Lucknow, 1950.

——, *Races and Cultures of India*, Bombay, 1958.

Malcolm, Sir John, *A Memoir of Central India*, vol. I, Calcutta, 1880.

Mishra, S., *Garha ke Gond Rajya ka Utthan Aur Patan*, Jabalpur, 1986.

Naik, T.B., *Impact of Education on the Bhils*, Delhi, 1969.

N.C.A.E.R., New Delhi, *The Socio-Economic Conditions of the Primitive Tribes of M.P.*, 1963.

Ossowki, S., "Old Notions and New Problems: Interpretation of Social Structure in Modern Society" in *Social Inequality*, London, 1969.

O. Malley, I.S.S., *India's Social Heritage*, New Delhi, 1976.

Patel, M.L., *Tribal Development*, Delhi, 1984.

Patil, D.R., *The Cultural Heritage of Madhya Bharat*, Gwalior, 1952.

Paliwal, C.M., *Advasi-Harijan Arthik Vikas: Bastar Jile Ke Sandharhb Mein*, Delhi, 1982.

Puri, B.N., *India in the Time of Patanjali*, Bombay, 1957.

Raghavaiah, V., *Tribals of India*, New Delhi, 1972.

Roy Burman, B.K., "Some Dimensions of Transformation of Tribal Society in India", in *Jour. of Social Research,* II (I), 29-24, 1969.

Roy, S.C., "The Effect on the Aborigines of Chotanagpur of the contact with Western Civilization", *Man in India,* 62 (I), 65-102, Reprint, 1962.

Russell, R.V. and Hiralal, R.B., *Tribes and Castes of Central Provinces of India,* 4 vols., Reprint, Delhi, 1975.

Raza, M. and Ahmad, A., *An Atlas of Tribal India,* Delhi, 1990.

Raizada, A., *Tribal Development in Madhya Pradesh,* Delhi, 1984.

Ramakrishna Mission, *The Cultural Heritage of India,* 6 Vols., Calcutta.

Saran, P., *Descriptive Catalogue of Non-Persian Sources of Medieval Indian History,* Bombay, 1965.

Sastri, K.A.N., *A Comprehensive History of India,* Vol. II, Calcutta, 1957.

Shastri, A.M., *India as seen in the Brhatsamhita of Varahamihira,* Delhi, 1969.

Singh, M.R., *Geographical Data in the Early Puranas,* 1972.

Sircar, D.C., *Cosmography and Geography in Early Indian Literature,* Calcutta, 1967.

Sorensen, S., *Index to Mahabharata,* London, 1904.

Sharma, R.K., *Madhya Pradesh Ke Puratattva Ka Sandharbha Granth,* Bhopal, 1976.

Sankalia, H.D., *The Prehistory and Proto-history of India and Pakistan,* Poona, 1974.

Shah, K.K., *Ancient Bundelkhand,* Delhi, 1974.

Sherring, M.A., *Hindu Tribes and Castes,* Delhi, 1974.

Sharma, S.K., *Resource Development in Tribal India,* Delhi, 1989.

——, "Use of yield raising Technology in Tribal Blocks of M.P", pp. 71-81, Ed. Tiwari and Sharma, *Tribal Eco System and Malnutrition in India,* Delhi, 1990.

Shukla, H.L., *Bhumkal: The Tribal Revolt in Bastar,* Delhi, 1991.

Tiwari, D.N., *Prmitive Tribes of India,* Delhi, 1986.

Tiwari, S.K., *Madhya Pradesh Ke Adivasi,* Bhopal, 1982.

——, *Bharat Ki Janajatiyan,* Delhi, 1992.

——, *Encyclopaedia of Indian Tribes,* Delhi, 1994.

——, *Baigas,* Anmol, Delhi, 1997.

——, *Antiquity of Indian Tribes,* Swarup and Sons, Delhi, 1997.

Upadhyaya, B.S., *India in Kalidasa,* Delhi, 1967-68.

Vaidya, C.V., *Epic India,* Bombay, 1907.

REPORT, GAZETTEERS AND JOURNALS

Ancient India
American Anthropology
Artha Vijnana
Archaeological Survey of India Reports by Cunningham
Bulletin of the Tribal Research Institute, Chhindwara
Bulletin of the Deccan College Post-Graduate and Research Institute, Pune
Current Anthropology
Critique of Anthropology
Economic and Political Weekly
Epigraphia Indica
Gazetteers of M.P.
Human Organization
Indian Archaeology-A Review
Indian Antiquary
Indian Historical Quarterly
Indian Economic and Social History Review
Indian Historical Review
Journal of Indian Anthropology
Journal of Social Research
Journal of Indian History
Journal of Royal Asiatic Society
Journal of Contemporary Asia
Journal of Peasant Studies
Memoirs of the Archaeological Suvery of India
Man in India
Man and Environment
Politics and Society
Puratattva
Review of African Political Economy
Science and Culture
Science and Society
Sociological Bulletin
Social Scientist
South western Journal of Anthropology
The Indian Geographical Journal

INDEX

NOTES

NOTES

NOTES

NOTES